Transforming Disability Welfare Policies

Public Policy and Social Welfare
A Series Edited by the European Centre

 European Centre Vienna

Volume 29

Bernd Marin, Christopher Prinz, Monika Queisser (Eds.)

Transforming Disability Welfare Policies

Towards Work and Equal Opportunities

ASHGATE

Published by

Ashgate Publishing Limited
Gower House
Croft Road
Aldershot
Hants GU11 3HR
England

Ashgate Publishing Company
Suite 420
101 Cherry Street
Burlington, VT 05401-4405
USA

This publication was sponsored by
the Austrian Federal Ministry for Social Security,
Generations and Consumer Protection

Copy-editing and DTP: Willem Stamatiou
European Centre for Social Welfare Policy and Research
Berggasse 17, 1090 Vienna, Austria

British Library Cataloguing-in-Publication Data. A catalogue record for this book
is available from the British Library.

ISBN 0-7546-4284-4

Printed by Facultas Verlags- und Buchhandels AG, Vienna, Austria

Contents

5

6

8

Preface

On the occasion of "The European Year of People with Disabilities 2003", the OECD and the European Centre for Social Welfare Policy and Research organised an international conference at the United Nations Office in Vienna on "Transforming Disability into Ability". The conference addressed key challenges in disability policy for the working-age population, and discussed policy recommendations as outlined in the recent OECD report on disability policies (OECD, 2003). Particular emphasis was laid on the implementation and practical aspects of the report's conclusions. Participants represented various social science disciplines, such as economics, law, public health and (rehabilitation) medicine, and a wide variety of institutions. Policy-makers, administrators, legislators, and representatives from the disabled people's movement exchanged views with the common goal of improving disability policies in their countries.

The discussions were broadly structured along the report's main policy conclusions with panels and discussions focusing on the following six questions:

- What do we mean by "being disabled"?
- What rights and responsibilities for society and for persons with disabilities?
- Who needs activation, how, and when?
- How should disability benefits be structured?
- What should and what can employers do?
- Which barriers to participation exist?

This book follows the structure of the conference. The *preface* gives a brief overview of the conference debates by presenting summaries of the panel discussions. The volume continues with an *introduction* summarising the main policy conclusions of the 2003 OECD report "Transforming Disability into Ability", followed by the opening statements of the conference. The proceedings of each panel are introduced with a short presentation of the respective theme outlining the OECD's policy conclusions in this particular area. The conference speakers and contributors are presented with short biographies at the end of this volume.

The first session focussed on *disability definitions*. The definition and use of the term "disability", both in the context of the OECD report and in more general terms, is crucial for the discussion of disability policies. As policies evolve, definitions change to reflect changes in community attitudes towards disability. In recent years, the medical model of disability, which sees disability as a characteristic of the individual, has been replaced by a socio-environmental model, which regards disability as an attribute resulting from the interaction between the individual and the social and physical environment. This interpretation is reflected in the WHO's new International Classification of Functioning and Disability (ICF).

This definition of disability, however, is neither universal nor are there common measurement instruments. Consequently, comparative statistics on the prevalence of disability are not readily available. The OECD report that formed the basis for this conference (OECD, 2003) mainly uses measures of self-reported disability.[1] People are classified as *disabled* if they have a long-term or chronic physical or mental health problem, illness or disability *and* if they are moderately or severely hampered in their daily activities by this problem. This corresponds to "functional limitation or disability caused by a chronic or long-term impairment" (in the ICF this constitutes the second layer). These subjective measures of disability are derived from national population surveys providing information on disability status, but also on respondents' employment and income status.

The aim of the OECD project was to measure the impact of income replacement and employment policies (some of the "environmental factors" used in ICF) on the extent to which disabilities translate into disadvantage in terms of employment and economic well-being ("activities and participation" in ICF). To measure the impact of policy, a second type of data is used: Administrative statistics on beneficiaries of disability benefits[2] and participants of disability-related employment programmes. When comparing findings across micro data and administrative data, one has to keep in mind that the definition of disability used for benefit eligibility may be quite different from the subjective self-assessment of disability applied in the national surveys. Nevertheless, contrasting the two data sources can be revealing, since a large divergence between self-assessed and administrative disability prevalence points to major challenges for policy-makers.

The urgent need for more and better data on disability and much more comparative analysis was indeed one of the main conclusions of the panel debating the definitions of disability in order to move on from the somewhat disappointing conclusion in the OECD report that best practices in disability policy were very hard to identify using the existing evidence.

The second panel was devoted to the issue of *rights and responsibilities for society and disabled persons.* The OECD report proposes an approach of mutual obligations, according to which society must propose an individually tailored participation package to the disabled person who, in turn, is expected to co-operate and participate in activation measures. Failure to do so would eventually result in sanctions, provided that society had fulfilled its part of this contract. Several panellists argued that societies today were so far away from achieving this goal that the mutual obligations approach was not of practical relevance for policy-making. There was a shared consensus among the discussants that no discourse on sanctions for disabled people should even be initiated, until the balance of constraints and resources has changed.

Activation measures, and their targeting and timing were discussed in the third panel. There was a lively debate on the pros and cons of wage subsidies, early interventions and the effectiveness of anti-discrimination legislation. The discussions showed that there are still a number of issues that need to be addressed urgently both in research and policy design. A major shortcoming of national and international studies is the lack of cost-benefit analysis in this area; tailored intervention is likely to raise administrative costs, at least in the short term. These increased costs are likely compensated through long-term gains in labour market reintegration of disabled persons. More precise information on this complex relationship, however, is essential. Discussants also noted that more attention should be given to the health dimension and the impact of the business cycle on the effectiveness of activation policies.

The panel on the *structure of disability benefits* showed that the way benefits are delivered, in particular benefit administration, was judged to be at least as important as the level of assistance itself. In order to adequately address the wide range of disabilities and their impact on an individual's capacity to work, a multitude of different cash benefit types would be necessary. Discussants agreed that reforms on the benefit side needed to be accompanied by incentives for recipients to return to work. Country examples, in particular those of Sweden and Luxembourg, served to underline this argument. Further, there was consensus that activation of disability policies alone would be insufficient. Instead, the entire welfare system needed an overhaul towards activation if this approach were to be effective.

The session on *what employers should and can do* looked at the experience in various OECD countries. The Americans with Disabilities Act of 1990 was discussed in detail and interesting evidence was presented showing that this policy had been rather unsuccessful compared to the welfare-to-work policies targeting single mothers. The panellists' views regarding the involvement of employers differed: while there was agreement that such involvement was crucial, opinions were divided on how this could best be achieved. While some discussants favoured obligatory quotas, others preferred subsidies to those employers who cooperate in rehabilitation efforts and make necessary accommodations to reintegrate disabled persons in their workforce. Much attention was given to the trade-off between job retention and new hires with the conclusion that more research of the determinants of employment rates of disabled persons was necessary.

The panel on *barriers to participation* was organised by the European Disability Forum, an umbrella organisation of disabled persons' associations in Europe. The panellists represented a French employer, a UK local authority and a Swedish disability organisation, and provided impressive evidence of the barriers that disabled persons face in everyday life. The discussion showed that barriers to participation of disabled persons exist at all levels and policy-makers need to take a wide perspective for integration policies to be effective. To promote employment, anti-discrimination measures are not sufficient; they need to be complemented by positive action measures.

Given the widely shared diagnosis and the remedies recommended, disability policies will remain under review in any future social policy. But whether a systematic review of disability policies based on empirical evidence will actually lead to transforming it; and whether transforming disability policies towards work and equal opportunities will actually improve the situation of disabled people is still to be seen.

*

*   *

We finally wish to thank the Austrian Federal Ministry for Social Security, Generations and Consumer Protection, headed by Mr. Herbert Haupt. A special grant supported the dissemination conference in Vienna as well as this publication.

Paris and Vienna, December 2003
                                                     Bernd Marin,
Christopher Prinz,
Monika Queisser

Notes

1   Estimates of the prevalence of disability based on self-assessment are sometimes criticised for being biased and endogenous; in other words, there may be a tendency to exaggerate the severity of health problems and the incidence of disability in order to rationalise labour force non-participation and the receipt of disability benefits. But there is also ample evidence that self-reported disability indicators are a reasonable predictor of a person's objective health status (e.g. Benítez-Silva et al., 2000) – especially for self-assessed disability relating to general (rather than work) limitations.

2   The term "disability benefit" is used to denote public transfer programmes designed to pay income replacement benefits to persons with reduced work capacity caused by a health problem.

Introduction:

1. Main Findings and Conclusions from the OECD Report – and Critical Queries

Disability Programmes in Need of Reform

OECD

Summary

OECD countries spend at least twice as much on disability-related programmes as they spend on unemployment. Disability benefits on average account for more than 10% of total social spending. In the Netherlands, Norway and Poland they reach as much as 20%.

In spite of such high spending, disability rates remain stubbornly high. In most countries, people who enter disability-related programmes remain there until retirement. This is expensive, inefficient and encourages segregation. Persons with disabilities often wish to participate actively in society and are capable of doing so, given the opportunity, the necessary training, and support.

The low employment rate of people with disabilities reflects a failure of government social policies. Societies hide away some disabled individuals on generous benefits. Others isolate them in sheltered work programmes. Efforts to help them find work in the open labour market are often lacking. The shortcomings affect moderately disabled individuals, as well as those with severe handicaps, but are particularly true for people over age 50.

Recent research in 20 countries found none to have a successful policy for disabled people. But many employ innovative measures which, taken together, point toward a comprehensive policy that emphasises economic and social integration. We propose reforms to move disability policy closer to the philosophy of successful unemployment programmes, based on five key features:

- recognise the status of disability independent of the work and income situation,
- emphasises putting people to work,
- restructure benefit systems,
- introduce a culture of mutual obligations,
- require individuals to make a concerted effort to find a job, if they are capable of working,
- give a more important role to employers.

Why Is Disability on the Rise?

In the general public, disability is often equated with severe handicaps, such as visual, hearing and mobility problems that require substantial aids and workplace adjustments. Severe disabilities, however, affect only about one third of the working-age disabled, and congenital disabilities account for only a small minority of cases. The majority of the working-age disabled suffer from diseases and problems that have arisen while at work. Many diseases are stress-related, muscular, and cardiovascular. Mental and psychological problems are on the rise: they are at the origin of up to a third of disability benefit cases in OECD countries.

Disability rates have been increasing in almost all OECD countries and policy efforts to help persons with disabilities return to work have hardly been successful in any of the countries. But there are still large differences in the nature and incidence of disability across countries. Some examples illustrate the range of problems encountered in member countries:

- In the Netherlands, the proportion of young women between the ages of 20 and 35 who receive disability benefits is three times higher than for their male counterparts.
- In Austria persons over 55 years are more frequently on disability benefits than in any other country, while rates for Austrians under age 50 are much lower than elsewhere.
- In Norway, disability benefit rates are much higher but unemployment benefit rates are much lower than elsewhere. Norway spends more than 5.5% of GDP on disability-related programmes – more than 12 times the amount spent on unemployment.

Figure 1:   Average Disability Prevalence of 14%, of Which One Third Are Severely Disabled

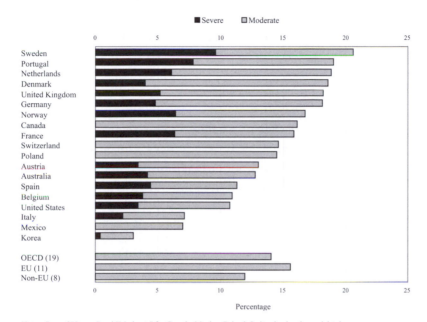

Disability prevalence, by severity of disability, as a percentage of 20-64 population, late 1990s

Note: Sum of "Severe" and "Moderate" for Canada, Mexico, Poland, Switzerland and unweighted averages.

Source: See Annex 1, Table A1.1.

Why Do Disability Rates Vary so Much from Country to Country?

Why is there such a large difference in disability rates across countries that enjoy similar levels of economic and social development? It is difficult to imagine why young Dutch women would be in so much poorer health than young women in other countries, or why older persons in Austria or Norway are so much more likely to become disabled than people in other countries.

The country-by-country comparisons in the study suggest that the ways in which disability is defined and assessed, and the ways in which benefits are awarded, have a strong impact on the numbers of people on benefit rolls. Countries with generous benefits, and where many people had access to them, tend to have higher disability rates, the study found.

Disability rates also depend on the ease of access to other out-of-work programmes. In the United States and the United Kingdom, for example, disability benefits became more heavily used when entry to other programmes,
such as unemployment or early retirement benefits, became more restricted.

In many countries, disability awards are highly concentrated among
people over age 50. This reflects the fact that disability becomes more frequent as people age. It also shows a tendency in some countries to park
unemployed workers in disability programmes until they reach retirement
age. Paradoxically, in countries such as Switzerland and the Netherlands a
surprisingly large proportion of those receiving benefits are young people.

A key reason government disability outlays remain so high is that very
few people actually leave benefit programmes. The numbers are virtually
nil in all countries studied, despite big efforts by some governments to rehabilitate and reintegrate persons with disabilities. Even in the United States
and Australia, where substantial monetary incentives are offered to those
who leave benefit rolls for work, few individuals do so.

22

Figure 2:   Successful Economic Integration in Many but Not in All Countries

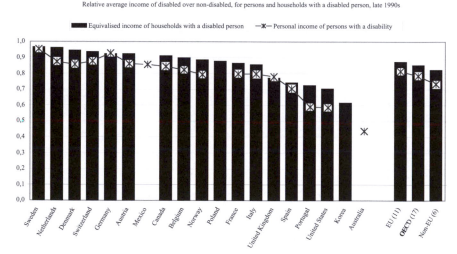

Relative average income of disabled over non-disabled, for persons and households with a disabled person, late 1990s

■ Equivalised income of households with a disabled person   —✻— Personal income of persons with a disability

Notes: Countries are ranked in decreasing order of the ratio of equivalised incomes of households with a disabled person over those without.
No personal income data for Korea and Poland, and no household income data for Australia and Mexico.

How to Get Persons with Disabilities into Employment?

Employment rates for persons with disabilities are low. Severely disabled people, disabled persons over the age of 50 and disabled people with low levels of educational attainment are least likely to be employed. Most countries offer special employment programmes for people with disabilities. These programmes are important for some groups, especially the severely disabled. However, they do not have a large-scale impact on overall employment rates of persons with disabilities.

In addition, integration programmes strongly discriminate against older disabled persons. Vocational rehabilitation and training are offered almost exclusively to people below the age of 45, which partly explains why so many older people are found in disability benefit programmes. But even special employment programmes, such as sheltered workshops or subsidised forms of employment, are also geared to mostly young and severely disabled persons.

Figure 3: **Disability Benefit Recipiency Rate Concentrated at 5 to 7%**

Disability benefit recipiency rates in 1999 by benefit programme, percentage of 20-64 population, late 1990s

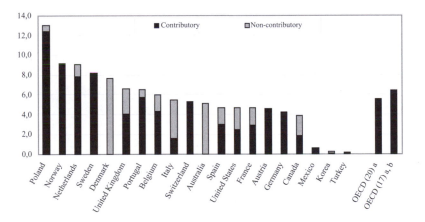

Note: The rate is corrected for persons receiving both contributory and non-contributory benefits, except for Canada (unknown).
a) Contributory and non-contributory benefits.
b) Excluding Mexico, Korea and Turkey.

Source: OECD database on programmes for disabled persons, see Annex 1, Table A1.2.

Overall, vocational rehabilitation and training is offered too seldom, and often initiated too late. More should be done to involve employers in this process. The average per capita cost for vocational rehabilitation and training is low compared to the average cost of disability benefits. Given that such programmes help secure permanent employment, the investment should quickly pay for itself.

Different employment policy approaches seem to have similar effects. While legislated approaches to employment promotion differ – some are rights-based, while others are obligations-based, or rely on incentives – all approaches tend to benefit people already in employment much more than those who are out of work. Some countries oblige employers to hire a certain percentage of disabled persons, however such rules work only if tough sanctions are imposed on companies that fail to comply.

Finally, there is a close relation between employment rates of disabled people and those of non-disabled people. This suggests, first, that general labour market forces have a strong impact on the employment of people with disabilities and, second, that general employment-promoting policies also foster the employment of special groups in the labour force, such as people with reduced work capacity.

What Are the Policy Conclusions?

Although no single country in this review has a successful overall policy for disabled individuals, researchers drew on the experience from specific programmes in some countries to make the following recommendations.

Recognise the status of disability independent of the work and income situation.

Societies need to change the way they think about disability and those affected by it. The term "disabled" should no longer be equated with "unable to work". Disability should be recognised as a condition, but it should be distinct from eligibility for, and receipt of, benefits. Likewise, it should not automatically be treated as an obstacle to work. The disability status, i.e. the medical condition and the resulting work capacity, should be re-assessed at regular intervals. The recognised disability status should remain unaffected by the type and success of intervention, unless a medical review certifies changes.

Some countries have recently moved in the direction of uncoupling an individual's disability status from his or her ability to receive benefits. Countries use different terminology, such as "linking rules" (United Kingdom), "let the pension rest" (Denmark) or "freezing a disability pension" (Sweden) to refer to the possibility of keeping the disability status while trying to work. Individuals also retain the option to go back on benefits should they lose their job, or should work not be acceptable.

Introduce a culture of mutual obligations. Most societies readily accept their obligation to make efforts to support and integrate disabled persons. However, it is less common to expect disabled persons themselves, or employers, to contribute to the process. This change of paradigm will require many countries to fundamentally rethink and restructure the legal and institutional framework of disability policy. Moreover, it will only be effective if it is accompanied by a change in the attitude of all those involved in disability issues.

Participation in vocational rehabilitation, for instance, is compulsory in a number of countries (Austria, Denmark, Spain, Sweden, Switzerland, and in a mitigated form also in Germany and Norway), and disability benefit settlement is conditional upon completion of the vocational rehabilitation process. In most cases, however, this obligation is administered with great flexibility and subjectivity, e.g. as to the age or the employment experience of the disabled person.

Figure 4: **Low Outflow Rates from Disability Benefits**

Annual rates of outflow from disability benefits, 1995 and 1999, percentages

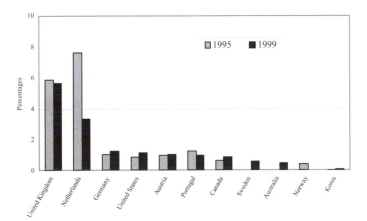

Note: Countries are ranked in decreasing order of the 1999 rate.

Source: OECD database on programmes for disabled persons, see Annex 1, Table A1.2.

Design individual work/benefit packages.

Merely looking after the financial needs of disabled people through cash benefits is insufficient. That approach would exclude many individuals from the labour market, and sometimes from society more generally. Therefore, each disabled person should be entitled to a "participation package" adapted to individual needs and capacities. This package could offer rehabilitation and vocational training, job search support, benefits, and the possibility of different forms of employment (regular, part-time, subsidised, or sheltered). It could also in some circumstances contain activities that are not strictly considered as work, but contribute to the social integration of the disabled person.

Some countries, for example Germany and Sweden, have tried to ensure access to a wider range of disability-related services through legislation that entitles disabled persons to certain services. More permanent on-the-job support is necessary for many disabled persons participating in the regular labour market. Support measures, such as individual job coaches and personal help for work-related and social activities, appear to have strong potential. In Denmark, for example, a personal assistant can be hired to assist in occupational tasks.

Introduce new obligations for disabled people.

Benefit receipt should in principle be conditional on participation in employment, vocational rehabilitation and other integration measures. Active participation should be the counterpart to benefit receipt. Just as the assisting caseworker has a responsibility to help disabled persons find an occupation that corresponds to their capacity, the disabled person is expected to make an effort to participate in the labour market. Failure to do so should result in benefit sanctions. Any such sanctions would need to be administered with due regard to the basic needs of the disabled person and those of dependent family members. Furthermore, sanctions would not be justified in any case where an appropriate integration strategy had not been devised, or proves impossible to formulate, e.g. because of the severity of the disability.

Figure 5: Remarkable Age Differences in Benefit Recipiency

Age-specific disability benefit recipiency rates, 1999,
per 1 000 in each age group

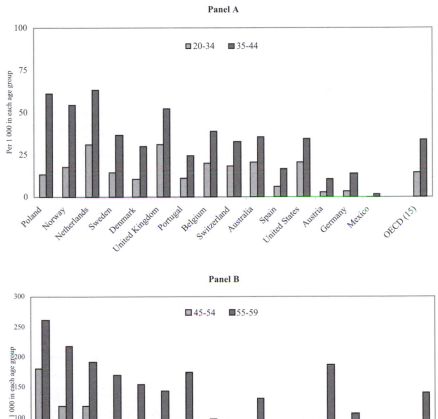

Note: Countries are ranked in decreasing order of the 1999 recipiency rate for 20-64 years old.
Different scales in panels A and B to make cross-country differences visible.

Source: OECD database on programmes for disabled persons, see Annex 1, Table A1.2.

Involve employers in the process.

Involving employers is crucial to the successful re-integration of disabled persons. Different approaches exist, ranging from moral suasion and anti-discrimination legislation to compulsory employment quotas. In Italy, employers were recently made responsible for assigning the disabled person equivalent tasks. Swedish employers must provide reasonable accommodation of the workplace or, if possible, a different job in the company. In Germany, employers have a general obligation to promote the permanent employment of disabled employees, and in France, employers with at least 5,000 employees are obliged to offer training to make sure that persons hit by a disease or an accident can keep a job in the same company. The effectiveness of these measures depends on the willingness of employers to help disabled persons enter the workforce, or stay there.

Promote early intervention.

28

Early intervention can in many cases be the most effective measure against long-term dependence on benefits. As soon as a person becomes disabled, a process of tailored vocational intervention should be initiated, including job search assistance, rehabilitation, and further training. Where possible, such measures should be launched while the person is in an early stage of a disease or a chronic health problem. Early "in-work" intervention is most common in Germany and Sweden, where rehabilitation schemes are designed to kick in early. In Norway, "active sick leave" is designed to prevent long-term disability by combining sickness absence with either of two types of intervention: adjustment of tasks at the regular workplace, or vocational rehabilitation. Several countries (Denmark, France, Portugal, Sweden and Switzerland) have even introduced a specific benefit that is paid during the rehabilitation period.

Make cash benefits a flexible policy element.

The cash part of the work/benefit package needs to reflect the disabled person's capacity to work, but also needs to take into account whether the person has actually been able to find a job. Cash benefits would have to be available with sufficient flexibility to take into account different job capabilities, as well as changes in an individual's disability status over time. In addition, benefit entitlements should be designed so that a disabled person is not penalised for taking up work.

Reform programme administration.

Such an individual approach will place new demands on the people who administer benefits for disabled individuals. Caseworkers will need an extensive knowledge of the range of available benefits and services. More time will be required to assist individuals and follow each case. Implementation of a one-stop approach will help gatekeepers to manage the full menu of available interventions, and promote equal access to all programmes for all people.

Design disability programmes as active programmes.

Often, disability benefit systems function as early retirement programmes, providing a route for quasi-permanent exit from the labour market. Emphasising activation and the mutual obligations of both society and the disabled person moves disability policy closer to the underlying logic of unemployment programmes, which expect an active contribution and effort from beneficiaries. Unreformed disability programmes are likely to attract applicants who may find it difficult to comply with the stricter obligations of unemployment schemes. There is a need for a consistent strategy in disability and unemployment policy that extends the culture of mutual obligations to all labour market programmes.

For more information

More information about this *Policy Brief* can be obtained from Christopher Prinz at the Social Policy Division (email: christopher.prinz@oecd.org, tel: +33-1-45.24.94.83).

For further reading

Transforming Disability into Ability: Policies to Promote Work and Income Security for Disabled People (2003) ISBN 92-64-19887-3, 33 Euro, 220 p.

Beyond Rhetoric: Adult Learning Policies and Practices (2003) ISBN 92-64-19943-8, 42 Euro, 256 p.

Society at a Glance: OECD Social Indicators 2002 ISBN 92-64-17590-3, 16 Euro, 84p.

OECD Economic Outlook No. 72. Increasing Employment: The Role of Later Retirement (2002) Electronic publication, 7,50 Euro. Available from the OECD Online bookshop: www.oecd.org/publications/

More information is also available on our Internet site at: www.oecd.org/els/social

Transforming Disability into Ability
A Commentary Based on Recent European Research

Deborah Mabbett[*]

The OECD report makes a major contribution to the cross-national policy
debate on promoting employment among people with disabilities. The report provides a comprehensive overview of data on receipt of income maintenance disability benefits, including analyses of inflow and outflow rates
and the incidence of recipiency by age and gender. These data are accompanied by concise and insightful explanations of the great variety of institutional and administrative factors that can influence income maintenance
disability benefit receipt, including availability of other benefits, linkages
between sickness and disability benefits, partial awards, rules on severity
of disablement and the impact of contribution requirements and means tests.

The report also contains a number of policy recommendations, particularly about measures that might be adopted to promote employment among
people receiving disability income maintenance benefits. In section 2.1, the
report defines what it sees as a consensus around the desirability of promoting paid employment among people with disabilities, invoking developments in OECD countries (p.17) as well as supra-national agreements
(p.18) in support of this position.

[*]   Brunel University recently hosted a research project on Definitions of Disability, funded
      by the European Commission and involving national reporters from all the EU member
      states except Luxembourg, along with Norway. The project report will shortly be pub-
      lished by the European Commission. Information about the project is available from its
      website: http://www.brunel.ac.uk/depts/govn/research/disability.htm.

Policy and Evidence

When there is broad agreement on policy goals, the task of the social scientist is straightforward: it is to explore the empirical evidence in order to map out the relationships between different policies and the outcomes or goals that have been agreed. Of course it is always difficult to come up with firm results in social science. The difficulty that the OECD study faces, and to its credit acknowledges, is that the data do not permit any strong conclusions to be drawn about the effectiveness of particular policies to promote employment among disabled people. Some of the policies favoured in some countries are evidently felt to be successful by national policy-makers, but comparative data on employment rates do not provide evidence for the success of these policies. The basic reason is that the contextual factors are extremely varied and complex. A particular problem is that disability is defined and assessed differently in different contexts, making comparative statistical analysis very difficult.

The absence of empirical evidence for the effectiveness of particular policies does not diminish the value of the report. On the contrary, the report helps us to understand why the evidence cannot be found, by explaining the multitude of factors that impinge on benefit recipiency and employment rates. However, the lack of empirical evidence means that the policy recommendations, of which there are a number, must be based on something else, and it is quite difficult to identify their basis. For a start, it is easy to be misled by the abundance of data into thinking that the recommendations are based on the data, even though the text of the report makes it clear that this is not so.

The Independence Axiom

The policy recommendations are derived deductively, on the basis of axioms that are not clearly stated, but can be inferred. A key axiom is as follows:

> There exists a group of truly disabled people. True disability is a state of affairs that is independent of a person's employment, income, insurance and benefit status (p.156).

This "independence axiom" provides a basis for the proposition that disability categorisation and income maintenance benefit receipt could be "unbundled". In other words, a truly disabled person could be recognised as such independently of the process of seeking access to particular benefits and services. Furthermore, given the agreed policy goal of promoting paid employment, it is possible to argue that unbundling not only could but should be done. Unbundling is advocated in order to provide a basis for wider access to employment measures for disabled people and to allow benefits to be structured more flexibly for those moving into and out of employment.

The report recognises that unbundling would involve a substantial change in the way disability is currently assessed. There is no single common idea of what disability is, or what it entails, embodied in the legislation of developed welfare states. Understandings of what constitutes disability, and methods of assessment, vary according to a person's employment, insurance (and work history) and benefit status, as well as being affected by other factors such as age. Different assessments are done for different social policy purposes. Furthermore, some commentators have argued that this diversity is desirable if social policy categories are to be relevant to their purposes (see e.g. Mashaw/Reno, 1996). In our research for the European Commission, we made relevance a central criterion for evaluating definitions of disability, and argued that relevant definitions would be different for different purposes. This argument was based on a detailed study of how disability was assessed for various purposes in the EU states, but the general reasons for our conclusion can be briefly stated. The fundamental problem is that the environment affects a person's degree of disability. Impairment may be seen as an inherent or person-level attribute, but the extent to which people are disabled by their impairments depends on the environments in which they endeavour to participate. Different social policy provisions pertain to different environments, and their assessment practices reflect these differences.

True Disability

The OECD report acknowledges the difficulty of identifying who is disabled and who is not, and the heterogeneity of the group (section 8.2). However, this does not lead to reconsideration of the independence axiom, even though two rather different views are taken about the nature of the true group. First, in chapter 3, survey measures of disability are reviewed. The definition of disability is of those reporting a health problem that limits general activities of daily life (ADLs). This is used because it is available from surveys in a number of countries. The report acknowledges that survey data have limitations: particularly, that they report a person's subjective self-assessment rather than an objective assessment. "[T]he reasonably objective definition of disability used for disability benefit eligibility is not necessarily [...] a subset of the subjective self-assessment of disability used in the national surveys" (p. 43). However, the problems of comparing surveyed disability with disability benefit receipt are not just problems of objectivity and subjectivity. The criteria used for disability benefits are frequently simply different. Only a few "extra costs" benefits (discussed further below) use criteria similar to surveys in being explicitly based on limitations in ADLs. The criteria for most income maintenance benefits refer only to limitations in ability to work, and this is sometimes evaluated in very specific contexts (e.g. previous work). It is possible to criticise these criteria: for example, it might be argued that a previous work-based assessment does not recognise the potential for a person to adjust (with appropriate rehabilitation and training) to a new job. However, criticisms such as these should be developed by engaging in a debate about the purposes of particular disability policies. The OECD report evades this debate, asserting instead that there is "inclusion error" when schemes pay benefits to people who are not surveyed disabled.

These comments are not intended to dismiss the real possibility that surveys may enable policy-makers to identify social problems, detect the flaws in existing social policies, and devise better policies. The point is a narrower one: the discussion in the report often assumes that survey data is an (admittedly flawed) indicator of true disability, and that social policy should be addressed to true disability. I would argue that social policy should be concerned with meeting needs, enhancing welfare and combating exclusion, and that categories should be constructed in the course of designing policies to achieve these aims. The characteristics of the group of people reporting a health problem that limits general ADLs are of interest, but we cannot assume that this group should be treated as a special category of people for social policy purposes.

The second main set of ideas about true disability are most clearly stated in chapter 8, where it is argued that disability assessment should be done in two steps which clearly differentiate biological difference (impairment and functional limitations) from limitations in activities and participation (p. 160).

The first step, assessing biological difference, should be done by medical specialists and based on medical grounds. The second step should determine the extent to which the disabling condition affects a person's ability to work. Disability status determined in this way would be unaffected by the person's employment status, unless the medical condition changes. In this sense, the medical step is seen as the fundamental and stable component of the disability assessment.

The OECD report notes that there are some examples of disability assessments that are independent of employment status and income maintenance benefit receipt. For example, a number of countries use impairment rubrics for administering their employment quota systems. As the report notes, these systems generally create a registered disability status that is kept irrespective of work status (p. 161). However, registered disability status does not bring with it entitlement to income maintenance benefits: it does not provide a unified disability category that is referred to both for employment service provision and for benefit administration.

The EC study shows that there are some important reasons why the use of impairment-based assessments is restricted, and why states impose further and/or different disability tests in their income maintenance systems. The oldest-established impairment rubrics assess the degree of disability directly from the description of a person's medical condition in terms of impairment. For example, degrees of loss of sight or hearing, measured using accepted technical equipment, may be translated directly into a degree of disability. This "direct measurement" approach is appealingly simple, but it is hard to sustain because of the difficulty of explaining why a particular impairment is more severe than another without referring to its disabling effects. As a result, the ratings in these impairment rubrics can seem rather arbitrary. The ratings are not widely used for benefit administration because they are not seen as relevant to the purposes of benefit provision.

This example suggests that the OECD's proposed approach to disability assessment may also fail the test of relevance. Social policy categories that are not sufficiently relevant are unsustainable. Irrelevant exclusions may mean that there will be a group of people whose needs and circumstances are suitable for the policy (e.g. the income maintenance benefit) who are denied access. Irrelevant inclusions may mean that people are offered employment-related services (for example) that they do not want and cannot utilise.

These criticisms do not mean that the OECD is wrong to advocate some form of unbundling of disability status from benefit receipt. To the extent

that existing rules and benefit structures make transitions into work difficult for disabled people, it would be desirable to reform them. Few would
dissent from the idea that "disability should not be equated with inability
to work", although they might question whether this designation is, in itself, an explanation for low outflows from disability benefits (p. 64). However, the report does not explain why a medically-based assessment of work
capacity should be determinative, or why a single definition is necessary.
(One might argue for a single definition to reduce administrative costs and
intrusion, but this argument is not made by the OECD, which advocates more
frequent reassessment than is currently done.)

Employment Neutrality and Employment Promotion

The report notes that benefits to compensate for extra costs of care or mobility may be paid independently of employment status and income maintenance benefit receipt (p. 161). However, it is puzzlingly dismissive of the
potential role of extra costs benefits in providing a structure for the types of
reforms it envisages, asserting that these benefits are "often not adequately
integrated with any other policy component". While the discussion is rather
brief, I think that the point is that extra costs assessments do not involve
any work capacity assessment or evaluation of the potential for vocational
rehabilitation or other employment measures. In other words, extra costs
benefits are (broadly) neutral with respect to a person's employment status,
but they are not employment-promoting in the way that vocational assessments might be.

Benefits to compensate for extra costs may be paid to disabled people
without designating them as unable to work. There are two different implications that might follow from this. One implication is that non-working
disabled people might be able or unable to work but the social security
administration would not endeavour to determine this question. The other
is that a person who is not unable to work would be seen as able to work.
The former implication is employment-neutral; the latter is employment-
promoting. The OECD report chooses the latter.

The report argues against the use of a disability category to exempt
certain people from labour market participation requirements (such as requirements to seek and be available for work) which are applied to unemployed people. However, it recognises that it would be pernicious to impose
participation requirements on all disabled people, and therefore advocates

a discretionary approach to these requirements rather than the use of a categorical criterion. Administrators should have flexibility in assembling benefit packages and developing return-to-work plans for disabled people (pp. 161-2).

The rejection of a categorical approach to participation could be explained logically as follows. From the independence axiom, we can deduce that a group of truly disabled people exists, and the true meaning of disability does not equate with inability to work. If it is further assumed that the disability categories used in social policy should correspond to the true meaning of disability, it follows that there is no valid disability category that could be used to exempt a group of people from labour market participation requirements. Therefore a discretionary rather than a categorical approach to these requirements should be adopted.

Clearly it is possible to avoid this conclusion by rejecting the postulate that the disability categories used in social policy should correspond to the true meaning of disability, in favour of the relevance criterion. This suggests instead that social policy categories are constructed for particular purposes: in particular, to facilitate the efficient allocation of resources while avoiding intrusive and burdensome administrative enquiries. We can note that one of the purposes for which disability categories have been constructed in social policy is to exempt certain people from labour market participation requirements. It is arguable that the notion of disability has, in the past, given legitimacy to this exemption. However, the use of the exemption has, in practice, raised a lot of issues about the meaning of disability: in particular, the extent to which age, labour market conditions and other social factors should be taken into account in exempting people from participation. It is clear that governments have manipulated the disability category for political and financial reasons, seeking sometimes to allow more exemptions and, at other times, wanting to extend participation.

It would be possible to detach disability from its problematic connection with participation exemptions in several ways, of which the OECD proposal (expectation of participation with discretion) is one. Another approach would be to base participation exemptions on other grounds. An obvious candidate is age: people over the old-age pension age are already exempt from participation, and many states do not impose participation requirements on older unemployed workers long before they reach pension age.

One objection to this is that states are generally trying to raise retirement ages, not lower them. The OECD report notes that contestation over disability classifications in social security is liable to increase rather than diminish as early retirement provisions are eliminated and access to old age pensions is delayed (pp. 168-9). The report argues that the appropriate policy response is to adopt employment-promoting policies and participation requirements, backed by the clear delineation of the disability category on medical grounds. Clearly, it is possible to draw the opposite implication: that disability classification will become even more of a minefield in the future than it is today, and that other approaches which do not rely on contentious distinctions need to be found.

One approach is to try to promote employment through choice rather than through administrative intervention. The report points out that benefit structures often deter employment, whether because of the difficulty of earning more than the out-of-work benefit entitlement, or because of high in-work costs, or because of the risk of losing future entitlement by giving up a hard-won disability classification. These deterrents could be removed by changing benefit structures: in particular, by allowing the income maintenance component of benefits for older workers to operate like a basic income. For people with disabilities that impose extra costs, additional benefits to meet these costs could be paid regardless of employment status (as noted above).

A number of states have old-age pensions that, with the easing of retirement (labour force exit) conditions, provide something very like a basic income to people over pension age. It would be possible to de-link policies on the pension age and the retirement age, allowing the age of access to a basic income to be lowered while also promoting extension of working lives by allowing work and benefit receipt to be combined.

One possible objection to paying unconditional income maintenance to older people is that it is desirable to establish an expectation of participation in order to motivate the search for effective employment-promoting policies and to encourage governments to provide adequate resources for them. The problem with this argument is that there is a risk that the expectation of participation could have adverse consequences for the fair and consistent treatment of social policy clients. In particular, hard-pressed administrators may develop their own low-level categories of disability based on clients' employment prospects, without these categories being subject to explicit definition and public and political scrutiny.

Conclusion

Implicit in the OECD policy recommendations is a view that there is a "true" cohort of disabled people who should rightly be the target of social security and employment policy, while current measures have constructed a partially "false" cohort whose presence on the benefit rolls is due to the adverse labour market conditions facing older workers and to policy decisions to promote exit among those workers. This discussion has shown that there are considerable problems in characterising the "true" disabled. The OECD proposes a medical and work capacity-oriented approach to disability. The findings of research done for the European Commission raise questions about whether this approach is consistent with the criterion of relevance that, in our view, should guide the construction of social policy categories.

The analysis advanced here has some wider implications. The criterion of relevance implies that a person may see him-/herself as disabled, and be seen as such by others, without this necessarily entailing recognition and separate treatment by social policy institutions. The effective conduct of social policy is facilitated by focusing on what is relevant to the benefits and services which these institutions provide. To justify the use of disability categories and determine the criteria for their construction, it is necessary to examine how disability might be identified administratively in ways that correlate to the purposes of the social policies in question.

Zola (1989) famously put forward the case for a "necessary universalising" of disability policy. He argued that the different disabling effects of different environments resulted in contingent and ever-changing experiences of disability. While his analysis did not rule out using disability categories in social policy to identify particular groups with relevant needs, it highlighted a number of possible problems. Many disabling conditions have complex patterns of progression and remission, implying frequent reassessment and adjustment of provision. Zola advocated more flexible universal policies. These might include not only changes to building and transport design, but also workplace policies allowing flexibility in hours and productivity, provision of benefits which would function as a non-categorical basic income, and so on. The OECD has advocated an approach which is flexible in the sense of being favourable to employment, but the policies it proposes leave little to individual choice and envisage a high level of administrative engagement which could be both costly and intrusive.

References

Mashaw, J./Reno, V. (eds.) (1996) *Balancing Security and Opportunity: The Challenge of Disability Income Policy*, Final Report of the Disability Policy Panel. Washington D.C.: National Academy of Social Insurance.

Zola, I.F. (1989) 'Towards the Necessary Universalizing of a Disability Policy', *The Milbank Quarterly* 67.

Introduction:

2. Opening Statements

Transforming Disability into Ability –
Results and Conclusions from the OECD Study of
Disability Policies for the Working-Age Population
in 20 Member Countries

Berglind Ásgeirsdóttir

Introduction

The paper presents the main results and conclusions of the first comprehensive analysis of disability policies for the working-age populations in the OECD. The first part includes some interesting facts and numbers about disability in OECD countries. The second part includes the policy conclusions and proposes a radically new approach to disability, which places employment, rather than income support, at the heart of disability policy.

Surprising Facts about Disability

- Did you know that Norway spends 5.5% of GDP on disability-related programmes? This is *more than 12 times* the amount Norway spends on unemployment. More generally, on average OECD countries spend at least twice as much on disability-related programmes as they spend on unemployment programmes. Yet compare how much press attention is devoted to unemployment as compared with disability!
- Did you know that in the Netherlands rates of disability benefit inflow among women under the age of 35 have *doubled* in the last 15 years, while the same rates have remained unchanged for women over age 55 and have even declined for men at all ages? Disability benefit recipients in many countries are now younger and are more likely to be female than previously.

- Did you know that in Austria every second man retires on grounds of disability? As in many other countries, disability benefits are used as support for early retirement.
- And did you know that in OECD countries about half of those with severe disabilities do not receive disability benefits? At the same time, about one third of those who get disability benefits say that they are not disabled!

Furthermore, why do we find such large differences in disability across countries that enjoy similar levels of economic and social development?

Disability benefit rates have been increasing in almost all OECD countries over the past decades. Disability programmes account for more than 10% of total social spending on average, reaching 20% in the Netherlands, Norway and Poland. In spite of such high expenditures disability benefit rates are not declining. And, in many cases, disability policies do not seem to reach those who need support the most.

The results of the OECD study suggest that disability benefits systems and their rules strongly influence the number of people on disability benefits. In other words, policy matters – there is no "natural" rate of disability. It matters how countries define and assess disability, how they define entitlement to benefits, how they award benefits and, especially, how generous disability benefits are. The availability of other social benefits also has an impact on disability benefit rates. The less accessible other out-of-work programmes are, the more heavily disability programmes are used. In the United States and the United Kingdom, for example, disability benefit rates increased as entry to unemployment and early retirement programmes became more restricted.

The OECD study also yielded a disheartening message for policy-makers: different policy approaches by different countries had little or no effect on outcomes. The most striking – and devastating – commonality was that the outflow from disability programmes to a job is virtually nil in all countries. Starting to receive disability benefit generally means that you will never work again. We found this to be the case even in those countries that make big efforts to reintegrate persons with disabilities. The United States and Australia, for instance, offer substantial monetary incentives to get people off disability benefit and back into work. Nevertheless, the result is depressing: very few people who receive disability benefit ever manage to find work.

Severely disabled people have particularly slim chances of finding employment; only one in four manages to find work. Disabled persons over the age of 50 and disabled people with low education levels are also very vulnerable. Most countries do offer special employment programmes for people with disabilities. These programmes are important for some groups, especially the severely disabled, but they do not have a large-scale impact on the overall employment rates of persons with disabilities.

Labour market integration programmes everywhere strongly discriminate against older disabled persons – this was another surprising result. Vocational rehabilitation and training are offered almost exclusively to people below the age of 45. Persons above this age are not even considered for such programmes, reinforcing the general labour market bias against older workers in most countries. Even special employment programmes, such as sheltered workshops or subsidised forms of employment, seek to help only young and severely disabled persons. Overall, vocational rehabilitation and training is offered too seldom, and often initiated too late. In most cases, employers are not sufficiently involved in the process.

It is not unrealistic to expect persons with disabilities to take up work rather than remain outside the labour market. Most persons with disabilities wish to participate actively in society and are perfectly capable of doing so. What is lacking is the opportunity as well as the necessary training and support to do so. Furthermore, the OECD study has shown that disabled persons in employment are doing much better economically than persons forced to rely on benefits.

In the general public, disability is often equated with severe handicaps, such as visual, hearing and mobility problems – impairments, which may require substantial aids and workplace adjustments and may make it very difficult for the affected person to stay in employment. In reality, severe disabilities affect only about one third of the working-age disabled. The majority suffer from stress-related, muscular, and cardiovascular diseases. In particular, mental and psychological problems are also on the rise: they are at the origin of up to a third of disability benefit cases in OECD countries.

More persons with disabilities should be able to re-enter the labour market after having been given proper rehabilitation and training. That many people with disabilities do not work is more down to policy failure and policy choice than personal preferences. Societies have dealt with some groups of disabled people by hiding them out of the way on often generous benefits but making no real effort to help them achieve their potential. Other groups were isolated on sheltered employment programmes, while programmes enabling them to work in the open labour market were often lacking or insufficient.

This segregating approach is not good enough for people with disabilities. Nowhere in social policy should we settle for income security only. This approach is also very expensive – the average per capita cost for vocational rehabilitation and training is low compared to the average cost of a disability benefit. This approach is, ultimately, not good enough for the taxpayers either. Finally, this policy is not good enough for the economy. Faced with population ageing, we simply cannot afford to tolerate a growing part of the working-age population being trapped in inactivity because they receive disability benefits.

Policy Conclusions

Let me now turn to the second part of my presentation, the OECD policy conclusions and our advocacy of a more ambitious approach towards disability policy. Usually, at the end of a big comparative OECD study, we come up with best practices and recommendations based on what we identified as particularly successful country experiences. That did not happen this time. In the 20 cases studied, we found plenty of examples of policy pitfalls to avoid, but no country has a particularly successful policy for working-age people with disabilities.

There is no need to despair, however. Many countries do have interesting approaches and measures in place that show a way forward. These add up to a new policy approach that emphasises the economic and social integration of persons with disabilities.

This new approach has *five* key features:
- it recognises the status of disability independent of the work and income situation;
- it emphasises activation;
- it proposes a new structure for benefit systems;
- it introduces a culture of mutual obligations; and
- it gives a more important role to employers.

Recognising Disability

The *first* key feature refers to the way that disability is understood. For policy to be effective, societies need to change the way they think about disability. For many people, the term "disabled" means "unable to work". This must change. Disability should be recognised as a condition but it should not automatically mean that a person goes on benefits, just as it should not automatically be treated as an obstacle to work.

We believe that access to disability-related services must be granted on the basis of disability, and not restricted only to those in receipt of a disability benefit. Too often, policy tries to put individuals into categories – those who need income support get help; those who do not are made to sink or swim on their own. This is not good enough. It can and does result in people becoming trapped on benefit, because moving into work means that they must give up other help that they need.

This change will also allow persons with disabilities to try out whether they are ready to take up work. They will keep the option to go back on benefits should they lose their job or should work turn out to be too hard. That way one can ensure that a person with disabilities is not penalised for taking the "risk" of re-entering employment.

Emphasising Activation

The *second* key feature is a strong emphasis on activation. Each disabled person should be entitled to an "individual participation package". This package would contain various rehabilitation and work elements, as well as benefits in cash and kind. This individualised approach will place a wide range of new demands on disability gatekeepers. Caseworkers will need extensive knowledge of the range of available programmes, benefits and services. More time will be required to assist individuals and follow each case.

The timing of activation measures is crucial. The longer a disabled person stays out of work, the more difficult it becomes for him/her to take up work again. In many countries, rehabilitation is only offered to people who already receive disability benefits and nothing is done during the whole previous period of sickness. Ideally, vocational training and rehabilitation should start at a very early stage of a health problem.

This new approach will not be cheap. Individually tailored assistance requires more resources than are currently spent on integration programmes. But in the long run, successful labour market integration of persons with disabilities will not only enable people to lead more fulfilled lives but will also generate substantial savings in benefit systems.

Restructuring Benefit Systems

The *third* key feature of the new approach is a restructuring of existing disability benefit systems. Most disability schemes are centred on income-replacing benefits and tie other services to the receipt of cash transfers. This discourages persons with disabilities from returning to work. We therefore propose to dismantle such systems so that all benefits and services can be awarded independently. In addition, cash benefits will have to be available with sufficient flexibility to adapt to different cases of remaining work capacity and to changes in the individual's disability status over time.

48

Take-up of work may need further encouraging. In-work benefits that top up the earnings from work are likely to be an effective policy instrument. Such payments should be strictly work-related and compensate lower earnings or reduced working hours that come about as a result of disability. In any case, *after-tax* income, including all transfers, needs to be higher for people in work than for those out of work. Otherwise, reintegration efforts are bound to fail.

Introducing Mutual Obligations

The *fourth* key feature – introducing mutual obligations – is a novelty in disability policy. Most societies readily accept their obligation to make efforts to support and integrate disabled persons, but it is less common to expect disabled persons to contribute to the process as well. As the focus of policy changes from primarily granting income replacement to providing individually tailored assistance for labour market integration, the relationship between society and persons with disabilities also changes. Disabled persons should receive income support, but if society makes a sincere and appropriate effort to help them to participate more fully in society in general, and in employment in particular, it is only right and proper that individuals make a genuine attempt to take advantage of such opportunities.

Involving the Employers

The *fifth* key feature is a more important role for employers. Involving employers is crucial for the successful re-integration of disabled persons. Existing employer-employee relationships should be utilised as much as possible. There are different ways to do this, ranging from moral suasion and anti-discrimination legislation to compulsory employment quotas. The effectiveness of the measures clearly depends on the willingness of employers to help disabled persons stay in or enter work. But there is also an important role for policy-makers who must minimise the possibilities for employers to circumvent legislation or simply pay the fines imposed for non-compliance.

Imposing undue hardship on employers would be counterproductive: employers would then be even more likely to discriminate against persons with disabilities seeking work. So policy should recognise that employers need help to behave in the way that we would want them to in a decent society. Workplace and job adjustments generally require only small financial investments, but even so, employers who make an effort to employ persons with disabilities should not be penalised financially *vis-à-vis* others who do not make this effort.

These, then, are the main policy principles that seem most likely to make for better disability policies. But we are not so naïve to think that there are no political problems to them being adopted. To name just two:

- Ministries of Finance worry about the short-term costs of provided more and better individualised help in overcoming barriers to work;
- talk of "mutual obligations" makes some people think of pointless "make work" programmes, designed only to punish only the most disadvantaged groups of our societies.

Politicians are well aware that for these reasons and others there are no votes to be won in reforming disability policies. We nevertheless believe that they must be persuaded to take action. The disability policies of many countries are a dismal failure: expensive; ill-targeted; used for purposes other than helping those with health problems; and, worst of all, excluding people from playing a full role in society rather than helping them to do so.

In conclusion, disability policies must be seen primarily as activation programmes rather than passive income support programmes. Many countries are already moving in this direction but much remains to be done. As we all know, the devil is in the details, and it will be a major challenge to translate the new approach into practical policy. The OECD would like to support this process by conducting in-depth country reviews of disability policy from this perspective.

The U.S. Department of Labor Perspective

W. Roy Grizzard

Thank you for the kind invitation to present at this event sponsored by the OECD and the European Centre for Social Welfare Policy and Research. The U.S. Department of Labor appreciates the important role of both organizations, the diversity of OECD membership, and the role of research to advance policy options across various important areas of activity.

I especially commend the leadership of both organizations for recognizing the importance of new knowledge informing the development of new disability policy.

I will look forward to learning from all of you as the conference unfolds. The diverse states of Europe harbour valuable lessons, as do the 50 states and 4 territories of the United States of America. Our countries will share valuable information that will hopefully lead to the most effective employment policies for people with disabilities.

The sovereign states on both sides of the Atlantic face a jobs and skills gap in the coming years of the 21st century. Our collective challenge is to match employer demand in the various labour market sectors with skilled supply. Working-age people with disabilities can help greatly to fill the gap.

We in America and in the United States Department of Labor place the highest value on the premise that people with disabilities are able to work. We agree with you, as stated in the OECD policy conclusions, that the term "disabled" should no longer be automatically equated with "unable to work".

We applaud the policy conclusion that disability and benefit receipt should be unbundled. I will later provide examples of work programmes meeting individual needs in different work situations.

We further believe that the individual worker with a disability should be afforded the right to choose what type of work to do, have technical assistance to perform essential functions of a job, and have the chance to advance and progress in work of choice. As such, individual worker needs must be embedded in policies and comprehensively addressed in practical implementations.

I want to speak about the opportunity we all have to create meaningful policy regarding people with disabilities. The word "opportunity" has an especially important meaning to me, for I have retinitis pigmentosa, and have been declared legally blind.

But that did not stop me from earning three degrees, or from serving in the field of education for over 25 years. It did not keep me from running a large state agency, or from being appointed as the first Assistant Secretary on disability employment issues in the history of the United States.

A large part of my success continues because I have come in contact with people who focus on my abilities – not on my disability. They give me opportunities to succeed, and I rise to the challenges.

Public policy, and the structures and systems that emanate from such policy, are in many ways a reflection of societal beliefs and values.

The key value on which the United States of America was founded is that of freedom. And one of the key definitions of freedom is: "the right of enjoying all of the privileges of membership or citizenship." The best form of economic security, the best pathway to full participation in citizenship, is employment.

The history of U.S. policy impacting people with disabilities is a long and winding road – moving from isolation and segregation to inclusion, empowerment and disability rights. History tells us that, as a group, people with disabilities were hidden from society, and viewed as a class of dependent people who would always require segregation, protection, charity and care.

But American policies have helped change this view. They have shaped the movement of people with disabilities from segregation to integration – from being hidden away to becoming full participants of an inclusive community, including the employment community. United States policy now clearly recognizes that people with disabilities can work and should be afforded the services and supports they choose to make that happen.

The Americans with Disabilities Act (ADA), signed into law July 26, 1990, is the "lens" for disability policy in the United States. Enactment of this landmark civil rights legislation struck a statutory and regulatory blow to discrimination against individuals with disabilities in employment, state and local government services, public accommodation, and telecommunications.

The ADA serves as the framework for government-wide actions to end discrimination against people with disabilities in the United States.

As with any significant civil rights legislation, later questions raised as to the scope and intent of this Act are further defined through implementation. An American freedom is the opportunity to raise questions. We have an environment of checks and balances established by our founding fathers to ensure refinement of policy and practices.

We are fortunate to have a President who is fully committed to extending the opportunity to succeed to people with disabilities. He believes that the ADA has been an integral component of the movement toward full integration of people with disabilities into every aspect of American life. But he also recognizes that there is far more to be done to integrate people with disabilities into the workforce.

Two weeks after taking office, President George W. Bush launched the New Freedom Initiative, or NFI, as we call it. This Presidential Administration understands well the integration and synergies across government.

The President charged federal agencies in February 2001 to assess their programmes and policies relating to people with disabilities, and to identify how they would support the objectives of the NFI. The objectives include:

- Increasing access to assistive technologies
- Expanding educational opportunities
- Promoting increased access into the community, and
- Increasing access to employment.

The NFI promotes federal interagency coordination to solve the complex social policy issues that impact employment for people with disabilities. The NFI recognizes that many aspects influence the ability of people with disabilities to seek and keep meaningful employment. These issues are broad-based, and involve many government entities.

For instance, the Department of Transportation needs to ensure that people with disabilities have a way to get to work. The Department of Education needs to ensure that people with disabilities have the requisite education and effective processes to transition from school to work. The Department of Health and Human Services needs to ensure that people with disabilities have access to health care. And the Social Security Administration needs to ensure that social security programmes provide the flexibility and incentive for people with disabilities to leave the public assistance roles and participate in the workplace.

The Department of Labor is charged with preparing the American workforce for new and better jobs, and ensuring the adequacy of America's workplaces. The Department is responsible for the administration and enforcement of over 180 federal statutes. DOL programmes, services and benefits are intended for all employers and workers across the nation, including individuals with disabilities.

Under the strong leadership of Labor Secretary Elaine L. Chao, the Department of Labor, through the Office of Disability Employment Policy, has been given a significant share of the responsibility for fulfilling the promise of the President's New Freedom Initiative.

Established just two years ago, ODEP has committed millions of dollars to fund various experimental programmes to eliminate employment barriers in the public and private sector.

The workforce development system, which links people looking for jobs with available jobs, does its work in nationwide programmes named One Stop Career Centers. ODEP's funds help these one stop centers to use effective methods to link people with disabilities and jobs. Such methods benefit both young people and adults with disabilities coming from all ethnic and racial backgrounds.

ODEP funds are focused on finding ways to better link employer demand with skilled labour supply. I offer you several examples of our work.

JAN – the Job Accommodation Network

- Provides free telephone and Internet technical assistance on making workplace accommodations.
- Is used both by employers and employees to determine effective accommodations.
- Provides personalized attention to approximately 32,000 workplace accommodations in any given year.

EARN – the Employer Assistance Referral Network

- Provides free telephone and electronic assistance to employers seeking to hire people with disabilities.
- Connects employers to local resources that have qualified job candidates with disabilities.
- Worked with some 2,000 employers in its first year.

The President and the Secretary of Labor recognize and reward those organizations, businesses and individuals who establish the most effective policies and practices increasing the employment of people with disabilities. For the first time in November 2002, the Secretary of Labor saluted winners of the New Freedom Initiative Award.

Our work includes refining methods of supplying skilled labour to the workplace. I again offer you several examples.

Telework/Telecommuting Research

- This project is intended to test and assess the feasibility of telework or telecommuting for persons with severe disabilities. The research is using federal agencies as pilot sites.

Customized Employment

- Customized employment means individualizing the employment relationship between employees and employers based on a determination of the strengths, needs, and interests of the person with a disability. It may include job development or restructuring strategies. Customization of employment is especially important for people with severe disabilities.

Youth

- We support programmes that develop effective school to work strategies. In addition, we help launch and expand programmes that provide mentoring and work experience for young people with disabilities interested in technology fields.

Technical Assistance

- ODEP also funds three national technical assistance centers. Two provide technical assistance to One Stop Career Centers in order to assist them to serve youth and adults with disabilities more effectively. Another center provides technical assistance to community rehabilitation providers.

Collaborative Efforts

- One promising approach finds the Department of Labor collaborating with the Social Security Administration and the Department of Health and Human Services. We established a position named a "navigator" in the One Stop Career Centers to help people with disabilities to find their way through the maze of state and local services essential to living independently in the community.

Perhaps you have heard of Social Security's "Ticket to Work." It provides incentives for people with disabilities to return to work by:

- Allowing people with disabilities to choose their own support services, including vocational education and rehabilitation
- Extending health coverage for Social Security pension beneficiaries (people with a former workforce attachment) so they can return to work without the fear of losing health benefits, and
- Expanding health coverage for certain people with severe disabilities who decide to go to work. They will continue to receive health benefits at the same time income rises or medical condition improves.

Improving the employment results of people with disabilities requires the cooperation of the federal government, state and local governments, the private sector, service providers, and advocacy organizations.

The President has said, "Government likes to begin things – to declare grand new programmes and causes. But good beginnings are not the measure of success. What matters in the end is completion. Performance. Results."

We must work together to develop strategies for success. We must determine what barriers act as roadblocks – and we must remove them.

As we move further into the 21st century, we are faced with new challenges.

New opportunities for employment are opening as scientific and technological advances give rise to new industries and occupations unheard of only a few decades ago. At the same time, many traditional job opportunities are disappearing as industrial operations become increasingly automated and the nation's economy as a whole becomes increasingly globalized.

The transformation we are currently undergoing creates a great opportunity in terms of employment for people with disabilities. Together we must make sure that the result is a society – a world – that affords opportunity for employment and community participation to all people.

The French Government's Perspective on Disability and Employment

Jean-Yves Hocquet

Today's meeting is an important one from our perspective, as France has undertaken a major review to overhaul its system.

Year after year, the situation of disabled people and their families is becoming a real challenge for society, and one area in which society is judged in particular is how it treats people with disabilities.

Passed just over 25 years ago, the Act of 30 June 1975 was a milestone. For the first time, the disabilities issue was addressed comprehensively and in terms of rights. France placed disabilities on its collective responsibility and social welfare agenda. It asserted the nation's duty of mutual responsibility and specified what form the government's commitment would take. People with disabilities were awarded regularly upgraded benefits. Towns and cities, public transport and large retailers had to start providing suitable access. And, although there is still some way to go on this issue, the right to education for disabled children and adolescents was acknowledged to be a necessity.

A further Act adopted on 10 July 1987 completed the legislation by making it mandatory on the State and enterprises to employ disabled people.

Today, we have to review the very foundations of our policy, shifting away from a uniform system of support towards a new rationale that takes fully into account the needs of each individual.

What is at stake is the very principle of equal opportunities. This is why the President of the Republic has made our disabilities policy one of the major projects of his five-year term of office. The initiative is part of a broader drive to bolster national cohesion. The report under discussion here today provides some particularly stimulating food for thought.

We view this approach as part of a raft of initiatives at different levels of international cooperation, the latest being the European Year of People with Disabilities. A second generation of national action plans will cover inclusion, a topic now under discussion in our Social Welfare Committee.

1   What of the Disabled and Employment?

It is apparent that the very notion of disability has changed. Anyone with an interest in access to jobs for the disabled will tend to focus on a highly specific and relatively small group of disabled people as defined by the Act of July 1987, i.e. people who, in order to find or keep a job, apply through COTOREP (*Commission technique d'orientation et de reclassement professionnel*) or other channels for official recognition of their disabled status.

But this excludes disabled people who have given up work and others who, in spite of some degree of disablement, have entered the labour market directly, without going through the channels mentioned above.

There is a larger but lesser known group covering all those of working age who suffer to some degree from health problems – physical or mental impairments – resulting in disabilities. People in this group may or may not apply for disabled status, depending on the severity of their health problems and consequent disabilities, their educational attainment and the situation in the labour market. Taking both groups into account gives a better grasp of how the job market works for those with health-related disabilities. The HID survey on disabilities, disablement and dependency (*Handicaps, Incapacités, Dépendance*) covers the entire working-age population, regardless of whether people are disabled or not. It provides an overview of disabled workers as defined by the 1987 Act and, for the first time, places this group in the broader setting of people with impairments or disabilities, regardless of whether or not they have been officially awarded disabled status. It improves our understanding, for instance, of what typifies, constitutes and serves as input to the "disabled" category, as defined in the 1987 Act.

1.1 People with Disabilities, as Defined in the 1987 Act

Disabled workers, under the 1987 Act, include anyone with an officially recognised disability in one of the following four categories:

* Disabled workers officially recognised as such by a COTOREP commission, i.e. holders of an RQTH certificate (*Reconnaissance de la Qualité de Travailleur Handicapé*).
* Victims of work accidents with a degree of permanent disablement exceeding 10%.
* People on invalidity pensions.
* Disabled ex-servicemen/women and those in a similar category.

Of the 31 million people in the 20-59 age group in France, 1.4 million have an official "disabled worker" status and, of the 25.5 million people making up the labour force, 701,000 fall into this category, i.e. a total of just under 2.8% of the labour force.

Only 547,000 of the disabled labour force are in work. This puts the employment rate in this group at only 39.1%, as against 73.5% for the 20-59 age group. Unemployment stands at 24% compared with only 10.6% for the labour force as a whole.

1.2 Disability

The HID survey has identified a group that extends beyond the definition in the 1987 Act to include anyone declaring health problems – physical or mental impairments – as a disability.

What HID measures is someone's "employability". Working involves movement, physical exertion (heavy weights, fast repetitive movements), and the use of intellectual, behavioural or interpersonal skills.

While employability – the likelihood of a person being able to work – does depend to some extent on the degree of disability and other characteristics, it cannot be reduced to those aspects alone; it is also contingent on the efforts made by the employer, or society as a whole, to accommodate that person.

Access to work varies with the type of disability. A severe disability preventing physical exertion (affecting 1.4 million people), the inability to move around (1.2 million) and severe learning impairments (0.5 million) are

the greatest barriers in terms of access to work. Conversely, impaired behavioural and communication skills seem to be less of a handicap, with
employment rates of around 50%.

We therefore have a group of several million people that overlaps with
the group of officially recognised disabled (1.4 million according to administrative data) but the two groups do not match. Adressing this problem requires new solutions.

1.3   Avenues to Explore

The HID survey is therefore a valuable source of insight into access to work
for the disabled, whether this means people registered on support schemes
or a larger group. The disability factor combines with skill level and age in
restricting disabled persons' access to work and leads them to register with
official disability schemes.

But apart from access to work, there may also be the question of the
type of work (stability, pay) and type of employer (major enterprises covered by the 1987 Act or very small firms, private sector, voluntary sector,
sheltered employment). So one welcome initiative is that of Eurostat to
launch a Europe-wide survey in 2002, backing up the jobs survey conducted
by INSEE, the French Statistical Institute.

2   What Will Our Policy Lines Be?

The first goal is to make up lost ground: there will be 3,000 extra places in
sheltered employment centres (*centres d'aide par le travail*) and over 2,000
places in special care centres this year, i.e. double the planned rate of increase.

And then, of course, there is educational inclusion. As this is one of the
government's concerns, the number of classroom assistants will rise to 6,000
for the next school year, i.e. triple the 2002 figure.

The government has also introduced a special scheme providing immediate support for the very severely disabled who opt to live at home.
Increased support will be available in 2003. Within the next 12 months, we
shall have created 5,000 jobs for care workers. Finally, we have launched a
reform of the guardianship system (currently offering legal protection to
60,000 people).

These measures will be accompanied by an in-depth reform which will build up a customised system of support, tailored to individual needs, that will make labour-market and social integration for the disabled a priority.

After consolidating the social welfare system phased in over the past 20 years, there is now a need to provide customised support for the disabled, tailored to the person's profile and life plan.

Customisation means first of all assessing the abilities, potential and needs of disabled people in their own environment.

Customisation also means endeavouring to compensate people, under a new right to compensation, for the impact of a disability – e.g. the additional cost of living and working – as distinct from the minimum income entitlement guaranteed by more general provisions.

Customisation means considerably simplifying benefits, combining current schemes without doing away with any advantages but improving their accessibility and hence their effectiveness.

Last, customisation means taking into account the fact that a disability evolves over a lifetime, acknowledging for instance that someone with a disability is still disabled after the age of 60 and should continue to receive special support. There is a more general problem of transition from one system to another; transfers are not necessarily automatic or advantageous for those concerned.

There are several ways of achieving this goal:

- People with disabilities could have their own personal adviser to tailor solutions to their needs.
- A network of centres for the disabled could be set up across the country.
- The centres could be coordinated by a national agency for the disabled. These centres could provide people with disabilities, and their families, with all of the information they require. They could also draw up, with the disabled person, the family and a multidisciplinary team of professionals, a personal plan covering every aspect of daily life including education, training, accommodation, working life, paid carers, technical assistance and service animals. They should, of course, take into account the person's ability to pay.

Back at the training stage, too, it is important to explain the issues to trainee architects, engineers and other professionals and raise awareness about the adjustments they should spontaneously be making to ensure that their plans are suitable for everyone.

There should also be greater emphasis on support functions such as those performed by care workers, whose skills should be given more recognition and taught on diploma courses.

Finally, technical assistance is still too hard to obtain and finance. This is the main obstacle to independence and needs to change. The community should cover the cost of a wider range of equipment. Also, disabled people should be given better access to the assistance now available thanks to ever-advancing technological change.

Besides this customisation of our support system, there should be a further goal to reform, i.e. to give people with disabilities the means of building a real career path. It is up to society to adapt to their needs.

This begins with education and training, which are crucial if the disabled are to find their place in society. The principle of non-discrimination makes it mandatory for the national education system to accept any disabled children who can be integrated, and to form the necessary ties with special-needs education which also plays a vital role. This obligation must be respected. We must make this possible by developing facilities for the disabled, from the childcare stage through to university, by mobilising and training staff ready to work in this field and making more use of human and technological support.

Then labour-market integration should be facilitated by expanding existing schemes that cover both the ordinary and sheltered work environments.

An initial step forward has been made with changes to the way COTOREP functions. Commission members include independent specialists whose names are put forward by the institutions managing rehabilitation/sheltered job centres, by associations representing disabled adult workers and by trade unions.

The Commission has always operated in two separate sections, one dealing with work-related decisions and the other with social measures. It has support from a secretariat and is backed up by a multidisciplinary technical team.

Since 1994, the recommendation has been for the two sections to operate more closely together and take a comprehensive approach to employment and social security.

With regard to technical resources, the focus has been on upgrading premises, electronic document management at a number of sites, and work to back up the information system.

Doctors are now more involved in assessing the circumstances of people with disabilities, hence the need to formalise the organisation of medical duties, the roles and responsibilities of each practitioner (including the coordinating doctor) and the necessary operational resources during the medical assessment process. Provision has been made for new training initiatives and more networking, one innovation being the appointment last year of a doctor (*médecin référent*) to coordinate the national network.

COTOREP has also been asked to improve the way it receives people with disabilities.

The unification of COTOREP should continue and eventually lead to a single Commission.

The Commission itself needs to position its work better. It could then devote more time to formulating or upgrading its policy and discussing difficult cases; a faster procedure could be used to validate proposals from the technical team on specific issues.

The scale used to assess the degree of disability, introduced by decree in 1993, is updated by a standing committee. It now needs to be supplemented with further tools that allow other factors affecting personal circumstances to be taken into account.

*

*   *

This is why discussions have recently been launched on the elaboration of tools to enlighten COTOREP members about proposals coming from the technical team regarding the award of "disabled worker" status and the granting of a disabled adult allowance to people with less than 80% disability; after all, work-related issues concern both groups equally. The approach consists in defining what disabled people can do, rather than what they cannot do.

The reform should also help to improve the interface between COTOREP's work and that of other bodies (including the *Commissions départementales de l'éducation spéciale pour les enfants*, or CDES [commissions in each French *département* that deal with the education of children with special needs], departmental schemes providing independent housing, schemes promoting labour-market integration and, in particular, departmental programmes for the employment of disabled workers [PDITH], and local information and co-ordination centres for the elderly [CLIC]). The aim is to set up a real partnership network.

Furthermore – and this is a priority – the authorities must create more sheltered structures, consolidate their work, confirm the rights of those with sheltered places and promote innovative projects. This will enable people to build real career paths. The goal should be to allow suitable candidates to move from jobs in sheltered employment centres out into sheltered workshops or the open labour market, although they must have the option of moving back if necessary.

As for integration into the open labour market, the goal set by the 1987 Act is far from being achieved, particularly in government departments. The Act stipulates that people with disabilities must make up 6% of the workforce in enterprises employing 20 people or more. Employers can obtain partial exemption if they place orders with or sub-contract to the sheltered employment sector, launch initiatives as stipulated in industry-specific agreements, or donate to institutions that assist enterprises (41%), individuals (22%) and operators (37%).

In spite of all this, there is still scope for further work to combat discrimination against disabled people, backed up by the European Union's approach based on Article 13 of the Treaty of Amsterdam and the relevant policy instruments. Once the employment Directive has been transposed into French law, the social partners will be better able to negotiate the ways and means of improving working conditions for people with disabilities. French legislation already contains legal and even criminal provisions to this effect, but they are not necessarily enforced and it will be interesting to see how they are evaluated within the framework of the European Union. Finally, people with disabilities should be given the opportunity to combine income from work with their benefits, as a means of promoting access to work.

Customised support, access to the world of work: these are our two priorities for reform. The aspect of our approach that relies on information exchange is the drive to revamp the law and enhance it with new ideas while implementing a programme covering every aspect of a person's life, and tackle the employment issue to make a comprehensive impact on a person's environment.

Extending the rights of disabled people and ensuring that they are really respected also means acknowledging that a person with disabilities has responsibilities like any other member of society.

What Do We Mean by "Being Disabled"?

Key Issues

1. Whether a person is disabled or not can mean various things. Assessments, involving both medical and vocational judgements, have several different but related objectives: to define needs, to determine eligibility for services, and to regulate access to transfer payments.
2. Assessment problems and cross-country differences in assessment procedures and eligibility criteria are reflected in often high and dissimilar benefit rejection rates.
3. There is a striking lack of permeability between being disabled and not being disabled, which fosters benefit dependence. People avoid risking the loss of their benefit through attempting to work, which contributes to very low outflow rates from disability benefits. Not being entitled to disability benefits can exclude people from receipt of necessary services.
4. To distinguish full from partial and permanent from temporary disability is notoriously difficult, and there is no uniform response to these two problems across countries.
5. Different procedures, medical and occupational requirements are applied to assess shorter-term sickness and longer-term disability. The result can be confusion and injustice. There are also different responsible authorities in most countries.

OECD Policy Conclusions

- "Disabled" can refer to a medical condition, labour market prospects or benefit receipt. These should be determined independently.
- The term "disabled" should no longer be automatically equated with "unable to work". Disability should be recognised as a condition but it should be distinct from eligibility for and receipt of benefits, just as it should not automatically mean an obstacle to work.
- This approach would allow beneficiaries to "risk" taking up work even if they are not sure to be fit for work. The disability status itself should be the basis for certain benefits that are designed to compensate the extra costs of the disabling condition, e.g. for medication, care, or mobility. Benefits for these purposes should not be related to the work status of the disabled person, should not be means-tested, and should be paid as long as the costs arise.
- The disability assessment should be repeated at regular intervals. If a review finds considerable health improvement or if the vocational outcome of a stable health condition is judged differently, intervention strategies should be re-adapted.
- This "unbundling" of disability and benefit receipt would help to ensure that the full range of disability-related benefits and services is available to every person with a disability, according to individual needs but regardless of the work situation, the insurance status or benefit receipt.

Measuring Disability and Measuring the Impact of Living with a Disability

Adele D. Furrie

> We have certain rights. What I need from you
> is only my rights and not a lot of sympathy.
> Mutinda Kimilu, Dublin Elementary School, age 9

1   Overview of the Paper

The early 1980s – with the 1981 International Year of the Disabled and the United Nations' International Decade of the Disabled (1983 to 1992) – marked a turning point in how countries viewed their citizens with disabilities. There was movement away from the paternalistic view of persons with disabilities as individuals who need help – seeing the disability before the person – to one that acknowledged that persons with disabilities were citizens that have the right to full participation in their society – seeing the person before the disability.

Countries have responded to this attitudinal change by introducing disability policies that have been translated into a myriad of programmes and services – all of which purport to meeting the objective of full participation. However, the question remains: What is the impact of these programmes and services?

The short answer is that persons with disabilities are still struggling to achieve their rights, and many continue to face societal barriers that prevent or impede their full participation. This is the case in countries around the world.

Understanding what barriers still exist and what accommodations have been obtained is an essential component of understanding the disability policies that should be enacted and the programmes and services that should be implemented. Another critical component is the establishment of an information system to monitor the impact of any initiatives that are undertaken. However, before any of this work can be done, you need to determine the characteristics of your population with disabilities – who they are and the impact that living with a disability has on their everyday activities.

For the past 18 years, I have worked with government officials in both developed and developing countries to assist them with the design of their disability information systems. Two current projects provide examples of this work, and both of these projects complement the work that we are here to discuss at this conference: working with the US Bureau of Labor Statistics to develop a set of questions to operationalize the *Americans with Disabilities Act* (ADA) definition of persons with disabilities and working with a group of researchers to create a Barriers and Accommodations Index (BAI) that measures the impact of living with a disability.

Life would be simple for a disability data manager if, within a particular country, there was one definition of disability, one set of questions that operationalized that definition and one data collection methodology that could be used to collect the information from survey respondents. Life is not that simple. In fact, the opposite is true. In most countries, there are multiple definitions of disability, a variety of questions are used to operationalize those definitions and numerous collection methodology can be employed – each of which has an impact on the results. Therefore, a major difficulty facing economists when they attempt to undertake an analysis of the social and economic impact of living with a disability is the lack of comparable date across data sets.

This is the situation being faced by the United States. The Bureau of Labor Statistics has been tasked with producing regular and ongoing measures of the employment of Americans with disabilities. Their starting point is clear. The 1990 ADA was designed to provide a clear and comprehensive national mandate for the elimination of discrimination against individuals with disabilities. The ADA also includes the definition of disability that must be used for this initiative.

The survey vehicle that appears to be the most appropriate is the monthly Current Population Survey (CPS), which currently provides monthly employment data. The task that remains is to identify a small set of questions that could be used to operationalize the ADA definition. In this paper, I will describe the process that is underway to develop this set of questions.

While measuring disability is indeed the first step, measuring the impact of living with a disability provides the information that is needed by policy analysts to determine the extent to which a disability policy is meeting its objectives. Canada has had the opportunity to undertake four surveys that collected information on the population with disabilities with respect to type, severity, age of onset, and underlying health conditions and health problems. Canadian economists and statisticians were fortunate to be able to build on the work completed by the OECD working group[1] that operationalized the functional definition of disability. These questions provided the starting point for developing the screening questions that were used to identify the adult population with disabilities. While these questions worked well in identifying those individuals who were limited in their activities as a result of a physical or sensory impairment, they did not work well in identifying those adults who experienced a limitation in their activity because of a developmental anomaly or a mental health condition or as a result of labelling by others because of a disability.

Through consultations with Canadians with disabilities, advocates, and organizations of and for persons with disabilities, support was obtained for use of the functional model of disability to identify the population with disabilities. This support was forthcoming with the proviso that the survey include questions to explore both the accommodations obtained from society to eliminate or reduce barriers to full participation as well as the barriers encountered that had not been removed. It was agreed that the barriers and accommodations questions should cover the spectrum for full integration: financial, societal, physical, personal, employment, education and transportation. All four surveys included these questions; however, there was a considerable increase in focus on employment barriers in both the 1991 Health and Activity Limitation Survey (1991 HALS) and the 2001 Participation and Activity Limitation Survey (PALS).

As a result of a recent initiative on the part of Statistics Canada and Canadian academics, micro-data from Statistics Canada's surveys are now available in research centres across Canada.[2] This has afforded researchers with the opportunity to explore the barriers and accommodations data from the 1991 HALS.

Using my experience with the design and conduct of the 1991 HALS – along with the human rights background of the principal investigator and with input from other team members – we have created a BAI that meas-

69

ures the impact of living with a disability and that complements the objective measures that are usually used (e.g. employment status, income levels, sources of income). This index places the onus on society rather than the individual with a disability. In this paper, I will describe in more detail the process used to develop this index, and I will provide some of our initial results.

Measuring disability and measuring the impact of living with a disability are exercises that are both culture-bound and definition-bound. The set of questions used to measure disability in the United States may or may not be completely applicable in other countries because they are designed to operationalize a specific definition of disability within a specific context (i.e. American culture, value and norms). However, the process used to arrive at a set of questions might be worth considering as countries begin to further contemplate their own data collection activities. In a similar way, the BAI reflects the Canadian situation; however, the process used to arrive at the BAI might prove to be a useful model for other countries.

2 Measuring Disability in the Past

Measuring disability in surveys offers some unique challenges for even the most experienced survey methodologist. Determining who comprises the population with disabilities is the first challenge. Once determined, the second challenge is to determine what questions could be used that will allow individuals with those types of disabilities to identify themselves. However, this second challenge also has to address what survey vehicle will be used to collect the data since it is the survey vehicle that determines the number of questions that can be used.

Canada and the United States have been collecting data on the population with disabilities at regular intervals during the past two decades using a number of survey vehicles. The number of questions used to identify the population with disabilities and what questions were used has varied with each data collection activity. The following provides an overview of selected survey initiatives from the two countries.[3] Disability rates generated from each survey are included to demonstrate the impact of the use of different questions, different numbers of questions and different survey vehicles.

2.1 United States

2.1.1 The Census of Population

Conducted by the U.S. Census Bureau, Department of Commerce, the 1990 and 2000 Censuses of Population included two questions – each with multiple parts – designed to measure the prevalence of disability in the American population.

The 1990 Census included two questions. The first question dealt with limitation in the workplace because of a physical, mental or other health condition. The second question had two parts: the first part dealt with an individual's ability to go outside alone and the second part dealt with an individual's ability to take care of his/her own personal needs.

The 2000 Census also included two questions – questions that were different from the 1990 Census. The first question had two parts: the first part dealt with seeing or hearing impairments and the second part dealt with limitation in physical activities. The second question had four parts. The first two parts were asked of all ages, and they dealt with difficulty in learning, remembering or concentrating and difficulty with basic physical activities. The second two parts were for persons aged 16 or older, and they dealt with the ability to go outside (same question as in the 1990 Census) and the ability to work at a job or business (similar to the question asked in the 1990 Census; however, the wording is slightly different).

In both the 1990 and 2000 Censuses, every fifth household in the United States was given the long questionnaire, which included the disability questions.

Table 1: Disability Rates by Age and Gender, 2000 Census

Age Group	Male	Female	Both Sexes
16–20 years	14.5	12.0	13.3
21–64 years	20.2	18.2	19.2
65–74 years	33.1	31.6	32.3
75 years and older	51.1	55.1	53.6

The 2000 Census[4] disability questions resulted in a disability rate of 13.3% for the population aged 16 to 20 years. This rate increased to 19.2% for persons aged 21 to 64 years. Males across all age groups recorded a higher disability rate than females. The employment rate was higher among non-disabled persons age 21 to 64 years than for persons of the same age reporting a disability – 77.2% compared to 56.7%.

2.1.2 Survey of Income Program and Participation (SIPP)

SIPP is a multi-panel longitudinal survey of adults that measures their economic and demographic characteristics for a period of 2.5 years. SIPP provides both a cross-sectional view of respondents' lives at discrete points in time as well as a longitudinal history of changes to the economic circumstances and household relationships.

In addition to the core set of data collected every four months, most interviews include additional sets of questions (called topical modules). These modules give SIPP the flexibility to accommodate topics on emerging issues on relatively short notice.

Disability is addressed in the Health and Disability topical module, which extends the coverage to include questions to identify children with disabilities. The Personal History topical module includes a work disability history module.

All interviews are by personal visit, although follow-up, if needed, is done by telephone. The interviewer collects demographic information about all persons in the sample, regardless of age, from a household member aged 15 years or older. Each person 15 or older is then asked to provide information about him-/herself; if someone is not available at the time of the interview, another adult is asked to provide information about that person (providing a "proxy" response).

In the 1990s, two panels included disability. The first data were collected in the period October 1993 to January 1994 and were combined with data collected in the period October 1994 to January 1995. The second data were collected from August to November 1997 and were combined with data collected in the period August to November 1999.

SIPP used seven sets of questions in the 1994/95 survey to identify the population with disabilities, as follows:
1. three questions that covered the use of technical aids for persons with a mobility disability;
2. a functional approach using six questions that covered seeing, hearing, communication and mobility functions in everyday living;
3. six questions that covered selected activities of daily living (ADLs), including mobility within the home and personal care;

4. six questions that covered selected instrumental activities of daily living (IADLs), including mobility outside the home, light housework, preparing meals, keeping track of finances, taking medication and using the telephone;

5. five questions, including the presence of selected conditions such as developmental disabilities, mental retardation, learning disabilities, and dementia, including Alzheimer's disease, and a general question on mental and emotional conditions;

6. two questions that covered general limitations in specific activities – work and housework; and

7. one question that covered the receipt of disability benefits.[5]

Based on the responses to the questions noted above, SIPP developed a severe disability definition that included individuals who answered "Yes" to one or more of the following:

1. were unable to perform one or more of the functional activities;
2. required personal assistance to perform one or more ADLs or IADLs;
3. used a wheelchair;
4. used a cane, crutches or walker for six months or more;
5. had a developmental disability;
6. had Alzheimer's disease;
7. were unable to do housework;
8. were unable to work at a job or business; and/or
9. were receiving disability benefits.[6]

Table 2:   Disability and "Severe" Disability Rates by Age Group, SIPP

Age Group	Disability Rate	"Severe" Disability Rate
15 years	6.7	4.4
16-24 years	10.2	5.3
25-34 years	12.9	5.8
35-44 years	17.2	8.5
45-54 years	24.2	12.3
55-64 years	36.8	23.8
65-74 years	44.9	29.8
75 years and older	65.1	52.7
15 years and older	**23.6[7]**	**14.2**

SIPP estimated that there were 47.814 million persons with disabilities in the United States who were aged 15 and older. This means that almost one out of every four adults has some level of disability (23.6%).

Disability increases as age increases. An estimated 257,000 individuals aged 15 answered "Yes" to at least one of the screening questions, thereby resulting in a disability rate of 6.7%. Among adults aged 45 to 54 years, the disability rate rises to 24.2%, and among older adults aged 75 and older, the disability rate jumps to 65.1%.

When one applies the "severe" disability definition, the numbers reduce significantly – from 47.814 million with all levels of disability to 28.825 million with a "severe" disability. This results in a drop in the disability rate from 23.6% to 14.2%. As with the total population with disabilities, the "severe" disability rate increases as age increases – rising from 4.4% for persons aged 15 to 52.7% for persons aged 75 and older.

While the older age groups – persons aged 65 to 74 and persons aged 75 and older – showed some reduction in the overall rate between all levels of severity and "severe" disabilities, the most notable differences were noted among the younger age groups. For persons aged 25 to 34, the application of the "severe disability" criteria reduced the disability rate from 12.9% to 5.8%. Among persons aged 35 to 44, the rate dropped to 8.5% from 17.2%.

2.1.3 National Health Interview Survey on Disability (NHIS-D)

The National Health Interview Survey (NHIS) is a multi-stage probability sample survey that permits continuous sampling of the non-institutionalized civilian population in the United States. This national survey has been operational since 1957. The U.S. Census Bureau, Department of Commerce conducts the survey on behalf of the National Center for Health Statistics, Center for Disease Control.

Using the NHIS sample, the 1994-95 NHIS-D was the first comprehensive survey of persons with disabilities of all ages ever conducted in the United States. The Phase I Disability questionnaire was administered at the same time as the NHIS core questionnaire, and it collected information about all members of the NHIS households. As with the NHIS core questionnaire, the NHIS-D Phase I questions were answered by any available adult in the household who was knowledgeable about the health of other household members. The Phase I questionnaire collected basic data on disability and was used as a screening device to determine eligibility for the second phase of the survey.

An important goal of the NHIS-D was to develop a database that would provide a useful set of measures of disability while maintaining a balance between the social, administrative and medical perspectives involved in the measurement of disability. Eleven major partners collaborated to develop the survey instruments that would enable analysts from each of the different programme areas to define their population of interest through the combination of variables in order to meet the specific needs of their particular programme. Through this flexible approach, the content of the survey was able to meet researcher requirements and to enable researchers to develop public health policy, produce simple prevalence estimates of selected health conditions and provide descriptive baseline statistics on the American population with disabilities.

There were 113 criteria used to select adults (those aged 18 and older) for inclusion in the second phase of the NHIS-D. These criteria were derived from responses to single questions on the NHIS core questionnaire (activity limitation) and the NHIS-D Phase I questionnaire.

The analysis that follows is based on 81 of the 113 criteria. Information on regular doctor visits and receipt of disability benefits were not available for the analysis. The 81 criteria were grouped into 25 categories as follows:

1. Seeing – legally blind or difficulty seeing expected to last 12 months or longer
2. Hearing – used a hearing aid and/or trouble hearing expected to last 12 months or longer
3. Communication – difficulty communicating with family members and/or persons outside the family
4. Understanding – difficulty understanding people when they talk or ask questions
5. Learning – serious difficulty with age-appropriate learning
6. Technical aids, including selected mobility aids, a brace and an artificial limb
7. Dizziness – that has lasted for at least three months
8. Balance – that has lasted for at least three months
9. Ringing, buzzing, roaring in ears – that has lasted for at least three months
10. Selected health conditions, including learning disability, cerebral palsy, cystic fibrosis, Down syndrome, mental retardation, spina bifida, autism, hydrocephalus and polio
11. Activities of daily living – responses (a lot and unable) for reference period of 12 months
12. Activities of daily living – needs reminder or person close by

13. Activities of daily living – needs special equipment to do
14. Instrumental activities of daily living – responses (a lot or unable) for reference period of 12 months
15. Instrumental activities of daily living – gets help or supervision
16. Functional activities – responses (unable) for reference period of 12 months
17. Functional activities – responses (a lot of difficulty with two or more)
18. Mental health, including frequently depressed or anxious, difficulty making/keeping friendships, getting along with others in social/recreational settings, trouble concentrating, serious difficulty coping with day-to-day stresses, frequently confused, disoriented or forgetful, and have phobias or unreasonably strong fears
19. Mental health – specific mental/emotional conditions (past 12 month reference period), including schizophrenia, paranoid or delusional disorder (other than schizophrenia), bipolar disorder, major depression, anti-social disorder, obsessive-compulsive disorder, or any other severe personality disorder, Alzheimer's disease/another type of senility disorder, alcohol abuse disorder, drug abuse disorder, and other mental/emotional disorders
20. Mental health – (past 12 month reference period) take prescription medications for ongoing mental or emotional condition
21. Mental health – condition causes trouble in finding/keeping a job
22. Services and benefits, including participated in sheltered workshop, transitional work training or supported employment, goes to a day activity centre for persons with disabilities, received physical therapy (during past 12 months), received occupational therapy (during past 12 months), ever received vocational therapy, have a case manager (during the past 12 months), needed a case manager (during the past 12 months), and has a court-appointed legal guardian
23. Perceived disability of self or other family member and others consider self or other family member to have a disability
24. Activity limitation – limited or unable to work and limited in other activities
25. Health status – poor

Approximately 85,000 households participated in the NHIS in 1994 and 1995. There were approximately 218,000 individuals in those households and, among those, 8,800 persons aged 18 and older responded "Yes" to one or more of the disability screening criteria.

While the NHIS is an annual survey, the two phases of the NHIS-D have only been conducted once. At this juncture, there are no plans to conduct this survey again.

Table 3:   Disability Rates by Age Group, NHIS-D 1994-95

Age Group	Disability Rate[8]
18-24	7.9
25-34	8.9
35-44	11.6
45-54	16.4
55-64	21.3
65-74	26.2
75+	36.6
18 years and older	**15.6**

Based on the 81 selected criteria as described on the previous two pages, there were an estimated 29.903 million adults with disabilities in the United States. This means that 15.6 out of every 100 adult Americans had a disability as defined by the selected criteria.

Disability increases as age increases. An estimated two million young adults aged 18 to 24 were classified as having a disability – resulting in a disability rate of 7.9%. Among adults aged 45 to 54, the rate more than doubles to 16.4%, and for seniors aged 75 and older, the rate more than doubles again to 36.6%.

2.2   Canada

2.2.1 The Canadian National Disability Database

Obstacles – the 1981 report of the Special Parliamentary Committee on the Disabled and the Handicapped – directed Statistics Canada to build and maintain a national database on the issues facing Canada's population with disabilities. Statistics Canada responded with the conduct of three surveys in the following decade: the 1983/84 Canadian Health and Disability Survey (CHDS), the 1986/87 Health and Activity Limitation Survey (1986 HALS), and the 1991 Health and Activity Limitation Survey (1991 HALS).

1983/84 CANADIAN HEALTH AND DISABILITY SURVEY (CHDS)

The CHDS was the first attempt to collect national data on the prevalence of disability in Canada. The survey was completed in two stages. The initial stage was conducted as part of the regular monthly labour force interview that provided at that time – and continues to provide today – the monthly employment figures on the size and composition of the Canadian labour force. At the time of the survey, it was the largest monthly survey of households and it utilized a cadre of experienced interviewers. The disability questions were added to 5/6ths of the monthly sample of households in October 1983, and in June 1984 they were added to 5/6ths of the monthly sample of households in six of the 10 provinces.[9]

Nineteen screening questions were added as a supplement to the regular labour force survey questionnaire, including 12 questions that covered activities of daily living as indicators of physical disability, five questions concerning hearing, seeing and speech problems, one question dealing with general limitation in activity, and one question that was included to identify persons with developmental delays. This last question was only asked when the interview was being completed by a proxy respondent.[10] No attempt was made to explicitly cover persons with a disability as a result of a mental or emotional condition because of concerns that such questions might negatively affect the response rate to the labour force survey in subsequent months.

All persons for whom a positive response was obtained to one or more of the 19 screening questions were contacted approximately one week after the initial contact. The 19 screening questions were asked again, and those respondents who answered positively to one or more of the 19 questions during the interview were asked additional questions to explore both the accommodations obtained from society to eliminate or reduce barriers to full participation as well as the barriers encountered that had not been removed.

Of the 127,000 individuals residing in 65,800 households, approximately 15,850 persons aged 15 and older indicated some disability in the second interview and completed the questions on barriers and accommodations.

1986/87 HEALTH AND ACTIVITY LIMITATION SURVEY (1986 HALS)

The 1986 HALS was the second major disability survey undertaken by Statistics Canada. It was also the first post-censal survey conducted by Statistics Canada. The two disability questions added to the long questionnaire of the 1986 Census of Population – the one completed by every fifth household in Canada – were used as the sampling frame for persons residing in households.[11] The first disability question on the Census dealt with general limitation in activity at home, at school or at work, or in other activities such as transportation to and from work or leisure activities. The second question asked if the individual had any long-term disabilities or handicaps.

The results of the testing of the two Census questions prior to their inclusion on the 1986 Census questionnaire indicated that not all persons with disabilities would respond positively to the Census disability questions. Therefore, the 1986 HALS sample included a sample of persons who responded positively to one or both of the Census disability questions as well as a sample of individuals who answered negatively to both disability questions.

The 1986 HALS[12] used the same 12 questions covering activities of daily living as indicators of physical disability as well as the same five questions concerning hearing, seeing and speech problems that were used in the 1983/84 CHDS. In response to the limitations in the data identified by users of the CHDS, the 1986/87 HALS split the general limitation question in two – with one question dealing with limitation in activity because of a physical condition or health problem and the second question dealing with limitation in activity because of a long-term emotional, psychological, nervous, or mental health condition or problem. Two other questions were added: one to identify individuals with a learning disability and the other to identify individuals with developmental disabilities or a disability as a result of a mental health condition.

If a respondent answered positively to one or more of these screening questions, they were asked additional questions to explore both the accommodations obtained from society to eliminate or reduce barriers to full participation as well as the barriers encountered that had not been removed.

Because the sample was selected from the 1986 Census, the resulting database included not only the information from the HALS questionnaire but also all of the Census data for the individual as well. Also, some family and household income data were included from the Census.

Approximately 112,000 individuals who answered "Yes" were selected to participate in the 1986 HALS. Of those, 11,735 were non-respondents and 22,040 answered "No" to all of the HALS screening questions and, as a result, were classified as non-disabled. The remaining 78,225 were classified as having a disability.

Approximately 72,500 individuals who answered "No" were selected to participate in the 1986 HALS. Of those, 5,270 were non-respondents and 3,910 responded "Yes" to one or more of the HALS screening questions and, as a result, were classified as having a disability. The remaining 63,320 were classified as non-disabled.

1991 HEALTH AND ACTIVITY LIMITATION SURVEY (1991 HALS)
The same sample design and sample allocation was used for the 1991 HALS. The 1991 Census question was identical to the one used in the 1986 Census.

The majority of the screening questions remained the same as the 1986 HALS, with some minor changes. There was continued criticism that persons with learning disabilities, developmental disabilities and disabilities as a result of a mental health condition could not be differentiated in the survey. As a result, the learning disability question was expanded to include some examples of learning disabilities. Two additional questions were added after extensive consultation with the Canadian Mental Health Association, the Canadian Association for Community Living and People First. Both examined the issue of labeling – one in the context of difficulty learning and the other because of a specific mental health condition.

If a respondent answered positively to one or more of these screening questions, they were asked additional questions to explore both the accommodations obtained from society to eliminate or reduce barriers to full participation as well as the barriers encountered that had not been removed. Employment was of particular interest in the 1991 HALS since these data formed the basis for the availability data that were used to monitor employer's compliance with the relatively new *Employment Equity Act*.

As important was the in-depth questioning that was included about disincentives to employment. In 1986, the participation rate for persons with disabilities aged 15 to 64 was 47.5, as compared to 77.9 for the non-disabled population. What was missing from the 1986 survey was an answer to why so many persons with disabilities had opted out of the labour force. Through consultations with disability organizations, service providers and adults with disabilities, we developed a series of questions that examined the barriers encountered when employment was being sought. Questions were included on the nature and extent of accommodations that would be required to enable adults with disabilities to obtain employment. Examples of the barriers questions included a "Yes" or "No" response to a series of statements such as "you would lose some or all of your current income if you went to work" and "you would lose some or all of your current additional supports such as your drug plan or housing if you went to work".

Again, because the sample was selected from the 1991 Census, the resulting database included not only the information from the 1991 HALS questionnaire but also all of the Census data for the individual as well. Also, some family and household income data were included from the Census.

Approximately 35,000 individuals who answered "Yes" were selected to participate in the 1991 HALS. Of those, 7,000 answered "No" to all of the HALS screening questions and, as a result, were classified as non-disabled. The remaining 28,000 were classified as having a disability.

Approximately 113,000 individuals who answered "No" were selected to participate in the 1991 HALS. Of those, 5,600 responded "Yes" to one or more of the HALS screening questions and, as a result, were classified as having a disability. The remaining 107,400 were classified as non-disabled.

Table 4:   Disability Rates by Age Group and Health Survey

Age Group	1983/84 CHDS	1986/87 HALS	1991 HALS
15-24	3.8	4.5	4.5
25-34	5.3	6.7	6.8
35-54	9.9	11.7	13.7
55-64	24.7	26.1	27.1
65 and older	38.6	45.5	46.3
15 and older	**12.8**	**15.4**	**15.6**

The 1983/84 CHDS reported a disability rate of 12.8% for the population aged 15 and older. The difference between this rate and the two post-censal survey rates can be attributed to two major factors. The first factor is the additional screening questions to identify persons with learning disabilities, developmental disabilities and disability as a result of a mental health condition. The second factor is the inclusion of a sample of persons who answered "No" to the initial screening questions. In the 1983/84 CHDS, one respondent was asked to respond to the screening questions for all family members. The follow-up survey was conducted only with those individuals for whom a positive response was received in the initial interview. This differs from the sample selection for the two post-censal surveys. For these two surveys, a sample was selected from the "Yes" responses to the Census disability questions as well as from persons who answered "No" to both disability questions.

2.2.2 The National Population Health Survey

The NPHS is designed to collect information related to the health of the Canadian population. The first cycle of data collection began in 1994, and it continues every second year thereafter. The survey collects not only cross-sectional information, but also data from a panel of individuals at two-year intervals.

The household component includes household residents in all provinces, with the principal exclusion of populations on Indian Reserves, Canadian Forces Bases, and some remote areas in Quebec and Ontario.

The selected person in each household will be followed at two-year intervals as part of the longitudinal component. Interviewing one respondent simplifies the longitudinal follow-up. Each time the respondent is re-surveyed, the same basic health-related information will also be collected for all members of the household in which he/she is then living.

Proxy reporting of the health component was allowed for the selected respondent only for reasons of illness or incapacity. Such proxy reporting accounted for 2.7% of the information collected for respondents aged 12 years and older. On the other hand, all interviews for selected respondents under 12 years old were done by proxy.

Functional health status was measured using eight questions that dealt with seeing, hearing, communicating, mobility, dexterity, pain, cognition and emotion. Data from three cycles have been published based on these questions.

Table 5:   Disability Rates by Age Group, NPHS 1994-1999

Age Group	1994-95	1996-97	1998-99
15-24	8.9	5.1	9.4
25-34	9.6	6.4	9.8
35-54	13.2	10.3	14.3
55-64	20.2	18.2	21.1
65 and older	31.9	27.4	35.2
15 and older	**15.2**	**12.0**	**16.5**

The disability rate for 1994/95 was very similar to the 1991 HALS rate, but the 1996/97 rate dropped to 12.0 followed by a large increase in 1998/99. These rate fluctuations require further analysis because the context within which the questions were asked, the placement of the questions and the control for proxy responses remained constant over the three time periods.

2.2.3 2001 Participation and Activity Limitation Survey (PALS)

The 2001 Census of Population included two disability questions that were different from those included in the 1986, 1991 and 1996 Censuses. The first question dealt with difficulties performing daily activities and the second question asked about reduction in activities at home, at work or at school, or in other activities.

The sample design for PALS differed significantly from the two previous post-censal surveys. A sample of approximately 43,000 individuals was selected from those individuals who answered "Yes" to one or both of the 2001 Census disability questions. No sample was selected from the population who answered "No" to both census disability questions. This decision was made based on testing of the new Census questions prior to their inclusion in the Census. The test showed that the new Census disability questions performed better than the disability questions on the previous Censuses and that the population with disabilities missed by these new questions would have mild disabilities.

The third change introduced in PALS was the screening questions. Many remained the same as those used on the 1991 HALS. However, a question was added about pain and discomfort and another about having difficulty learning with examples of attention problems, hyperactivity and dyslexia. More specific examples were added to the question concerning developmental disability as well as the general limitation question as a result of an emotional, psychological or psychiatric condition.

Table 6:   Disability Rates by Age Group, 1991 and 2001

Age Group	1991 HALS	2001 PALS
15-24	4.5	3.9
25-34	6.8	5.1
35-54	13.7	10.8
55-64	27.1	21.8
65 and older	46.3	40.5
15 and older	**15.6**	**14.6**

As with the three previous disability surveys, persons who identified as having a disability with a positive response to one or more of the PALS screening questions were asked additional questions to explore both the accommodations obtained from society to eliminate or reduce barriers to full participation as well as the barriers encountered that had not been removed.

Again, because the sample was selected from the 2001 Census, the resulting database included not only the information from the PALS questionnaire but also all of the Census data for the individual as well. Also, some family and household income data were included from the Census.

The disability rate for the population was 14.6 – lower than the 15.6 reported from the 1991 HALS. In fact, the disability rates for all groups were lower. I believe that the major factor that caused this difference is the dropping of the "No" sample. Clearly, further analyses of the data are required. The information on barriers and accommodations as well as employment details will be released later this year. It is expected that these data will provide some additional insights as to the population differences between the 1991 HALS and the 2001 PALS.

3 Measuring Disability to Establish an Employment Rate for Persons with Disabilities

Executive Order 13078 requires the Bureau of Labor Statistics (BLS), in conjunction with the Bureau of the Census and other agencies, to develop and implement an accurate and reliable methodology for determining the employment rate for adults with disabilities. These data can also be used by several other agencies, including the Equal Employment Opportunity Commission, the Social Security Administration and the Department of Education, to assist in their efforts toward improving the employment of persons with disabilities.

The *Americans with Disabilities Act* (ADA) definition is the definition that must be operationalized. The three criteria that are present in the ADA definition of a person with a disability are as follows:

i)   A physical or mental impairment that substantially limits one or more of the major life activities of such individual

ii)   A record of such an impairment

iii) Being regarded as having such an impairment

Major life activities are defined through a set of examples such as caring for oneself, performing manual tasks, walking, seeing, hearing, speaking, breathing, learning, working and participating in community activities.[13] These examples, while not meant to be exhaustive, appear to cover the span of what researchers in the field have labeled activities of daily living, instrumental activities of daily living and the environment outside of the home over which the individual has no control.

As a first step in the development of the screening questions that could be used to operationalize the ADA definition, I was contracted to develop an annotated bibliography – its purpose was to inform the BLS as to what questions are available for identifying the adult population with disabilities and the degree to which these questions have been tested for reliability and validity. This bibliography was completed and submitted to the working group in June 1999.

The next step was an analysis of the major data sets available in the US. These data sets included the 1994/95 SIPP, the NHIS on Disability, the Behavioral Risk Factor Surveillance System (BRFSS), the 1998 N.O.D./Harris Survey of Americans with Disabilities, the WHO-DAS II, the 2000 Census disability questions and the Indiana Independent Living Survey. The data from these surveys were analysed and the results were reported in the report entitled *The Effectiveness of Disability Screening Questions in Identifying the Adult Population with Disabilities – May 22, 2000.*

Through an arrangement with the team responsible for the new National Co-morbidity Survey (NCS), we included a set of questions similar to those that had been used in previous surveys to identify the population with disabilities. A preliminary analysis of these data has been conducted and a sample of 270 individuals has been selected based on their responses to the disability questions as well as other health and lifestyle questions.

Our research plan includes four more activities as follows:
1. a review of some of the information provided by the respondent during his/her NCS interview to determine what – if any – additional information is required to determine that individual's disability status;
2. follow-up interviews with those respondents for whom additional information is required;
3. a Delphi panel to determine disability status based on the NCS and follow-up information using the same profile as in Activity 1; and
4. based on the Delphi outcome, a statistical analysis of the full NCS database to establish the small set of questions.

We are approaching individuals from throughout the US who are willing to help BLS identify survey questions to identify the disability population by providing expert opinion in Activities 1 and 3. Each profile will be sent to two experts, thereby providing two opinions as to the need for additional information. We will also include the ADA definition along with the EEOC definitions of specific words that are included in the definition.

Follow-up interviews will be conducted by a team assembled by BLS to collect the information indicated as necessary to identify the profiled individuals' disability status. In actuality, only about 60 interviews will be conducted; the initial 270 cases were drawn from the sample for this purpose because we anticipate that as many as two-thirds of the respondents may choose not to participate in the re-interviews.

After the rich information from the interviews is gathered, it will be added to the existing profiles and circulated to the Delphi panels. The Delphi panels will provide their opinions as to whether or not the individuals captured by the profiles have a disability. We expect to repeat this process of collecting the panels' responses and re-circulating them to the panels on approximately three occasions.

Lastly, as indicated in activity 4 above, we will take the individuals' disability classifications that emerge from the Delphi process and combine them with survey respondents whose disability status is unambiguous (i.e. clearly with a disability as defined in the first prong of the ADA and clearly with no disability because they said "No" to virtually all of the candidate disability questions) and run an analysis that will determine if a small set of questions exists in the NCS that will identify the individuals with a disability.

4   Measuring the Impact of Living with a Disability

Through consultations with Canadians with disabilities, advocates, and organizations of and for persons with disabilities, support was obtained for use of the functional model of disability to identify the population with disabilities. This support was forthcoming with the proviso that the survey include questions to explore both the accommodations obtained from society to eliminate or reduce barriers to full participation as well as the barriers encountered that had not been removed. It was agreed that the barriers and accommodations questions should cover the spectrum for full integration: financial, societal, physical, personal, employment, education and transportation. All four Canadian surveys included these questions; however, there was a considerable increase in focus on employment barriers in both the 1991 Health and Activity Limitation Survey (1991 HALS) and the 2001 Participation and Activity Limitation Survey (PALS).

As a result of a recent initiative on the part of Statistics Canada and Canadian academics, micro-data from Statistics Canada's surveys are now available in research centres across Canada.[14] This has afforded researchers with the opportunity to explore in detail the rich data sets that had to date only been available to Statistics Canada employees.

Using my experience with the design and conduct of the 1991 HALS – along with the human rights background of the principal investigator – the research team of the Geography of Literacy and Disability project has developed a new index that promises to provide a powerful tool for disability activists, policy-makers and advocates in Canada.

This index applies the human rights model of disability to the analysis of the 1991 HALS. The Barriers and Accommodations Index places the locus of disablement on environments, systems of support and the exercise of rights, rather than on the functional limitations of the individual.

Our research team used the HALS questions pertaining to barriers and accommodations to create the new index for our study of literacy and disability. This new index, the Barriers and Accommodations Index, measures the severity of barriers experienced and the degree of accommodations received – the experience of persons with disabilities in social environments, rather than the qualities or limitations of the person.

Further, it provides an overall measure of people's experiences in terms of the accessibility of their environments. Rather than only looking at barriers and accommodations in one segment of an individual's life – within the home, at work, etc. – this index examines the impact across all activities. It demonstrates that environments accessible to all people, regardless of their diverse physical, intellectual or psychological qualities, are framed as a social responsibility, rather than as a "special interest" measure.

To create the Barriers and Accommodations Index, our research team reviewed HALS, which was organized by major life activity, and selected those questions that identified barriers and accommodations.

Barriers are grouped into six broad categories: 1) aids and personal services; 2) modifications to structures; 3) transportation; 4) employment; 5) financial; and 6) attitudinal. A barrier is identified when something, such as specialized equipment or training, is needed but not available (e.g. not receiving adequate training, negative perceptions by the employer create barriers to employment). Lack of finances is a barrier to taking courses, travelling, participating in leisure activities or making modifications to homes. Attitudinal barriers are encountered in all aspects of life. This includes being labelled by others and having difficulties travelling because of unsupportive staff.

Accommodations are grouped into four broad categories: 1) aids and personal services; 2) modifications to structures; 3) transportation; and 4) employment. The financial and social categories are only included in the barriers section. The aids and personal services category looks at a series of questions relating to the current use of any aids, services, specialized equipment or devices, any physical or communication therapy received, and any assistance received to perform daily activities.[15]

Table 7:   Perception of Barriers in Daily Activities by Adults with Disabilities

Persons Reporting ...	% Reporting
... no barriers encountered and no accommodations received	13.4
... some barriers encountered but all barriers removed through accommodations	9.6
... some barriers encountered and some removed through accommodation but others remain as barriers	49.5
... some barriers encountered and none removed through accommodations	27.5

Our preliminary findings using this index show that at the Canada level, 13.4% of adults with disabilities reported that they encountered no barriers in their daily activities. An additional 9.6% stated that they had experienced some barriers but, through accommodation, all barriers had been removed.

Forty-nine per cent of adults with disabilities reported that they experienced barriers and that some – but not all – of those barriers had been removed through accommodation. 27.5 per cent of adults with disabilities – just over one out of every four – reported some barriers were encountered and none had been removed through accommodation.

These preliminary findings only touch the surface of the powerful new index. Further analyses will be done as part of the report and atlas that will be produced as deliverables for the research project. Plans are underway to create a similar index using the PALS data, and an article will be forthcoming in spring 2004.

5   Conclusion

The search for a small set of questions to identify the population with disabilities began for me some 18 years ago when I assumed the responsibility for the Canadian national disability database. The search continues in a number of venues throughout the world. The Bureau of Labor Statistics has a research plan. The Washington Group – part of a United Nations Statistical Division initiative – has held two meetings on the subject. One of the products of the first meeting was the development of a matrix that cross-classifies the purpose that a general disability measure is supposed to address (i.e. the use that the data will be put to) with a typology of question characteristics that addresses concepts such as domain, severity, etiology and duration. Work on both this conceptual matrix as well as an empirical matrix is currently underway by a team with members from Italy, the United Nations and the United States. There is this OECD initiative and there could well be others.

This paper demonstrates that you get different answers depending on the definition of disability used and the way in which the definition is operationalized. The SIPP experience (US) provides a good example of an instance where the disability rate using one set of questions is 23.6% and it then drops to 14.2% when another set of criteria are applied. The 1991 HALS and PALS comparison (Canada) shows how the use of two screening questions to identify the sample population can result in dramatically different results if false negatives are not factored into the design.

But measuring disability is only one half of the equation – albeit an important half, because one has to use the right questions in order to identify the population for whom the disability policy and programme interventions are being directed. However, for disability policy and programme interventions to be truly effective, one has to understand the impact of living with a disability and the extent to which full participation in society is prevented or impeded. The barriers and accommodations data that form an integral part of the Canadian national disability database provides an opportunity to explore this issue. The new Barriers and Accommodations Index – created as part of a research project that explores the relationship between literacy and disability – measures the severity of the barriers experienced by persons with disabilities rather than the severity of the disability in terms of the nature and extent of the limitations experienced by the individual him-/herself.

Therefore, response to the question "What do we mean by being disabled?" requires two steps: we need to know who to talk to and we need to understand what society needs to change so that the nine-year old Mutinda's of the world can exercise their rights as full and participating members of their communities.

Notes

1   McWhinnie, J.R. (1981) *Disability Indicators for Measuring Well-being*. Paris: OECD Social Indicators Programme.

2   These data are available for research projects that receive approval through a research vetting process, and all data retrievals are subject to the stringent release criteria imposed by Statistics Canada's review process.

3   There are many other surveys that have included questions to identify the population with disabilities. The surveys selected represent the surveys most often referenced in discussions concerning the characteristics of the population with disabilities.

4   P42. Sex by age by disability status by employment status for the civilian non-institutionalized population. http://factfinder.census.gov/servlet

5   This criterion is not included in the analysis because the data were not available.

6   Ibid.

7   The denominator used in the calculation of the disability rate is the estimate of the population as generated by SIPP.

8   The denominator used in the calculation of the disability rate is the population estimates for 1994 as derived by the U.S. Bureau of the Census.

9   The June 1984 sample was added so that provincial estimates could be produced.

10   Different screening questions were used for the population aged 0 through 14 inclusive. This paper describes the questions used for the adult population aged 15 and older.

11   A survey of residents of health-related institutions was conducted in the spring of 1987. The sampling frame was a list of institutions provided by the 1986 Census.

12   Different screening questions were used for the population aged 0 through 14 inclusive. This paper describes the questions used for the adult population aged 15 and older.

13   US House of Representatives, 1990, p. 51.

14   These data are available for research projects that receive approval through a research vetting process, and all data retrievals are subject to the stringent release criteria imposed by Statistics Canada's review process.

15   A complete description on the questions used to create the Barriers and Accommodation Index is available on request to the author of this paper.

References

Health and Activity Limitation Survey – 1986 Users' Guide. Statistics Canada.

Health and Activity Limitation Survey – 1991 Users' Guide. Statistics Canada.

Furrie, Adele/Coombs, John (1990) *A Profile of Persons with Disabilities in Canada*. Statistics Canada – Catalogue 98-126.

Adults with Disabilities: Their Employment and Education Characteristics – 1991 Health and Activity Limitation Survey (1993) Statistics Canada – Catalogue 82-554.

Highlights: Disabled Persons in Canada – the Health and Activity Limitation Survey (1990) Statistics Canada – Catalogue 82-602.

A Portrait of Persons with Disabilities – Target Groups Project (1995) Statistics Canada – Catalogue 89-542E Occasional.

Report of the Canadian Health and Disability Survey, 1983-1984 (1986) Statistics Canada – Catalogue 82-555E.

Obstacles – *The Report of the Special Committee on the Disabled and the Handicapped* (1981) Canada House of Commons.

The Search for a Minimum Set of Questions to Identify the Adult Population with Disabilities – June 13, 2000: Presentation to NCHS Workshop on NHIS-D, Minneapolis, Minn., USA.

A Profile of Disability in Canada 2001 (2002) Statistics Canada, Catalogue 89-577-XIE.

2001 Participation and Activity Limitation Survey – A Profile of Disability in Canada (2002) Statistics Canada – Catalogue 89-579-XIE.

What Do We Mean By Being Disabled?
A WHO Perspective

Irene Hoskins

The theme of this conference is how can we transform "disability" into "ability" and, very rightly, the first question that is asked within this context is "What do we mean by being disabled?" In response to this question, I would like to give a brief overview of how disability is being viewed, defined and measured at WHO. More specifically, within the context of looking at how "disability" can be turned into "ability", this means:

- Viewing disability from a "health" rather than a "disease" perspective.
- Rejecting the view that disability is a defining feature of a separate minority of people.
- Being able to measure the different components of disability and their consequences.
- Creating an enabling environment based on the principle of inclusion rather than exclusion, derived from the diagnosis of a medical condition.
- Analysing the primary reasons for disability at various stages of the life course and how they can be prevented.

Further, I would like to expand this discussion by adding two additional points which are important to the discussion on the future occurrence of disability in our societies:

- Beyond the focus on policies for the management of disabilities and the administration of disability benefits, we need to determine the risk factors and primary causes that contribute to disease and disabilities. More specifically, what policies are necessary to prevent disabilities or the worsening of disabilities? In this connection, the question needs to be raised: Is it possible to link disability policies to the larger efforts of health promotion and prevention?

- What are the linkages between population ageing and disability? As populations age, chronic diseases are significant and costly causes of disability. Societies in OECD countries continue to age rapidly. How can this challenge be met?

Defining and Measuring Disabilities

According to the Preamble of WHO's Constitution adopted in 1946, "health" is defined as "a state of complete physical, mental and social well-being and not merely the absence of disease or infirmity". Based on this broad understanding of health, it is vital to recognise that disablement is not simply a defining attribute of a minority of people but rather a universal feature of humanity, manifested for everyone in different levels of functioning and at different stages of life.

Quoting WHO's Director General, Dr Gro Harlem Brundtland, "improving the health of an individual, or the population as a whole, is not merely a matter of reducing premature death due to disease and injury. Health is also about human functioning, the capacity of individuals to live a full life as an individual and as a member of society".

It was not until the 1990s that WHO tried to capture this important paradigm shift which eventually led to a biopsychosocial understanding of human functioning and disablement. It has resulted in several revisions of the ICIDH (International Classification of Impairments, Disabilities and Handicaps), a classification of human functioning at the physical, personal, and societal levels that goes beyond a mere medical diagnosis and takes into account the social and environmental context within which people live. Finally, this led to the publication in 2001 of a new international standard that describes and measures health and disability, the ICF (the International Classification of Functioning, Health and Disability). The ICF provides, notably, operational tools for both measurement and comparison.

ICF describes disability as an overarching term covering the experience of functional limitation at the level of the body or organ system as well as the person in society. Disability is the outcome of the interaction between a person's health condition and the context within which he/she finds him-/herself. The "context" is made up of personal factors (e.g. age, sex, race and education) and external environmental factors (e.g. attitudes, physical environment, assistive technology, policies, services, environmental and personal support).

Disability is described from three different perspectives or levels:

- Body functions and structures where the experience of a disability is termed an *impairment*, e.g. the lack of muscle tone, lack of speech or intellectual impairment.
- Personal activities where the experience of a disability is called an *activity limitation* (e.g. inability to walk, to communicate or to care for oneself).
- Societal (or person within society) where an experience of a disability is called a *participation restriction* (e.g. not working because the work environment is inaccessible or not communicating because people do not engage in communications with the individual concerned). In other words, a person may be unable to do certain things but can still participate because the environment facilitates participation. On the other hand, he/she may have the ability to do something but be prevented from doing it because of a lack of opportunities, an enabling environment or negative attitudes towards disabilities.

Currently, common clinical usage of the word disability refers to something close to activity limitation and tends to also include some elements of participation restriction.

These measurements are extremely important not only for documenting the prevalence of chronic disability but also for forecasting current and future needs for long-term care and health system planning.

Global Increase in Chronic Diseases

WHO regularly undertakes studies on what is called the *Global Burden of Disease* to determine the age- and sex-specific prevalences of a large number of disease diagnoses by geographic regions or country groupings. For example, the Global Burden of Disease projections have clearly demonstrated the so-called "epidemiological transition", that is the move from infectious to non-communicable diseases which is currently underway in the developing world – a world where chronic illnesses, such as heart disease, cancer and depression, are quickly becoming the leading causes of morbidity and disability. For example, in 1990, 51% of the global burden of disease in developing and newly-industrialised countries was caused by non-communicable diseases, mental health disorders and injuries. By 2020, the burden of the non-communicable diseases in theses countries will rise to approximately 78%.

Established market economies, i.e. OECD countries, have already undergone the epidemiological transition and chronic non-communicable diseases and injuries continue to be significant and costly causes of disability.

This leads to the urgent question of how policy-makers can transform disability into ability, i.e how can they address and eliminate some of the risk factors contributing to disability and morbidity in the first instance? These risk factors relate to *environmental* risks, such as sanitation, hygiene and air pollution; *occupational hazards*, such as industrial accidents, ergonomic stressors causing, for example, lower-back pain, a major cause of absence from work; work-related noise, one of the most common occupational hazards causing hearing loss; and finally the *behavioural* risk factors.

With regard to the latter, behavioural risk factors, WHO estimates that in the developed countries of North America, Europe and Asia Pacific, at least one third of the disease burden is attributable to the following five risk factors: tobacco, alcohol, blood pressure, cholesterol, and obesity. The tobacco epidemic alone kills about 2.4 million people every year in industrialised countries and disables many more through respiratory diseases. The risks arising from high blood pressure and cholesterol, strongly linked to heart attacks and strokes, each cause millions of deaths annually and are closely related to the excessive consumption of fatty, sugary and salty foods. They become even more dangerous when combined with tobacco and excessive alcohol consumption.

The lack of physical activity, a growing phenomenon in the age of the automobile and the computer, is in itself a serious health risk. While it is easy to blame behaviour on the individual it would in most cases be more appropriate and effective to promote population-wide prevention strategies aimed at reducing these risks to health. Governments should seek a more joined-up approach, including concerted action by many different agencies across society, for policies that promote health and prevent disability.

Disability – A Challenge for Ageing Societies

Last, but certainly not least, when discussing disabilities, we need to refer to the ageing of populations which brings with it an increased risk of developing disabilities, including mobility and cognitive impairments that often occur at older ages. An older person's independence is threatened when physical or mental disabilities make it difficult to carry out the activities of daily living. Furthermore, people with disabilities, as they grow older, are likely to encounter new and additional barriers related to the ageing process. But, in fact, the disabilities related to the wear and tear of the ageing process could in many instances have been prevented in the first place.

The good news is that, as longevity increases in OECD countries, there is evidence of a decline in severe disability among the older population. Bio-technologies offer earlier diagnoses and new treatments, including the replacement of lost functions. Among such promising developments has been the actual decline in disabilities among older Americans between 1982 and 1999, compared to the projected rates if disabilities had remained stable over the same time period. England, Sweden and some other countries have shown similar trends. The critical question is therefore not only whether these trends will continue, in spite of increasing numbers of nonagenarians and centenarians, but also whether the increasing numbers of persons 60 plus will remain active and whether, at the same time, working life can be extended and age discrimination can be attenuated. Clearly, age discrimination and discrimination against the disabled remain powerful deterrents to participation and inclusion and thus continue to contribute to the rising social cost of disability.

To counter such negative developments, WHO advocates the life course perspective on ageing and the decline in functional capacity. The life course approach underpins all multi-sectoral actions on active ageing. Functional

Functional Capacity over the Life Course

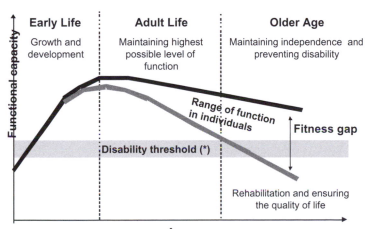

Source: WHO/NMH/HPS, 2000

capacity (such as ventilatory capacity, muscular strength and cardiovascular output) increases in childhood, peaks in early adulthood and is eventually followed by a decline. The rate of decline, however, is largely determined by factors related to lifestyle – such as smoking, alcohol consumption, levels of physical activity and nutrition – as well as external and environmental factors. The gradient of the decline may become so steep as to result in premature disability. However, the rate of the decline can be influenced and may even be reversible through individual or public policy measures at critical junctures of the life course. Moreover, it has to be realised that the disability threshold is not stationary but rather moves up or down depending on the interaction of the individual with his/her environment. Thus, making the environment more friendly and manageable for older persons and persons with disabilities will inevitably decrease the number of disabled persons and increase personal and societal well-being.

98

References

OECD (2002) *Biotechnology and Healthy Ageing*. Paris: Organisation for Economic Co-operation and Development.

WHO (2001) *International Classification of Functioning, Disability and Health*. Geneva: WHO.

WHO (2002) *World Health Report*. Geneva: World Health Organization.

WHO (2002) *Current and Future Long-Term Care Needs*. Geneva: WHO.

WHO (2002) *Active Ageing: A Policy Framework*. Geneva: WHO.

What Do We Mean by Being Disabled?
A Regional NGO Perspective

Vladimir Kosic

In April last year, in Trieste, Italy, the World Health Organization (WHO), in conjunction with the Ministry of Health of Italy and the Regional Government of the Regione Autonoma Friuli-Venezia Giulia, held the International Conference on Health and Disability. I quote this event not for geographical reasons but, according to me, because during the Trieste Conference a milestone was marked on *how disability should be considered*. Let's try to understand why.

A Scientific Approach

During the Trieste Conference, which lasted from 17-20 April 2002, a new World Health Organization publication was presented to classify the functioning, health and disability of people across the world which challenges mainstream ideas on how we consider health and disability. ICF (International Classification of Functioning, Disability and Health) is the name given to this classification, and it changes our understanding of disability for many reasons. The most important are:

1)   While traditional health indicators are based on the mortality (i.e. death) rates of populations, the ICF shifts focus to *"life"*, i.e., how people live with their health conditions and how these can be improved to achieve a productive, fulfilling life. It has implications for medical practice; for law and social policy to improve access and treatment; and for the protection of the rights of individuals and groups.

2)   Disability is *not* presented as a problem of a *minority group*, nor just of people with a visible impairment or in a wheelchair. For example, a person living with HIV/AIDS could be disabled in terms of his/her ability to participate actively in a profession. In that case, the ICF provides different perspectives as to how measures can be targeted to optimize that person's ability to remain in the workforce and live a full life in the community.

3)   The ICF takes into account the *social aspects* of disability and provides a mechanism to document the impact of the social and physical environment on a person's functioning. For instance, when a person with a serious disability finds it difficult to work in a particular building because it does not provide ramps or elevators, the ICF identifies the needed focus of an intervention, i.e. that the building should include those facilities and not that the person be forced out of the job because of an inability to work.

4)   ICF puts *all disease and health conditions on an equal footing irrespective of their cause.* A person may not be able to attend work because of a cold or angina, but also because of depression. This neutral approach puts mental disorders on a par with physical illness and has contributed to the recognition and documentation of the worldwide burden of depressive disorders, which is currently the leading cause, worldwide, of life years lost due to disability.

In other words, for the person involved, disability is conceptualised as a multi-dimensional experience that can be related to organs or body parts, such as impairment of the mobility of joints or bones, or the function of muscles. There may be effects on certain activities, for instance lifting or gripping objects with the hand. There may be consequences for a person's participation in aspects of life, such as education, work or leisure. Participation can be facilitated in various ways; for instance, by the provision of assistive technology or environmental modifications. What must be stressed is the fact that physical and social environmental factors play a significant role in the "creation" of disability.

Put in this way, the word disability is used as an *umbrella term* which includes:

* impairments;
* activity limitations;
* participation restrictions.

In order to understand better what should change by adopting the ICF to classify disability and which are the new fields and topics involved I think a comparison with the traditional way of considering disability might help.

DISABILITY	Old paradigma	New paradigma
Definition	A personal problem caused by functional limitations due to psychical or physical impairments.	The result of *psychical or physical impairments* and of the social and cultural obstacles which hinder the process of integration and which may concern any citizen.
Strategies for intervention	Limit or eliminate the functional deficit by active intervention on the individual.	Remove barriers, facilitate the access to services, promote the well-being and health of citizens.
Methodology for intervention	Take care that there are medical services, rehabilitation, school, work and psychogical support for disabled people.	Overcome a sectorial vision of the needs and support both the persons involved and their families by offering different instruments and services, promoting, at the same time, processes of social change.
Subjects involved	Doctors, rehabilitation and social professionals.	The participation of professionals involved both in social and health fields is a component which must be added to the participation of other disabled people, other consultants who can offer information, and new subjects we are able to involve.
Reasons to act	The disabled citizen benefits from grants and services according to the seriousness and the cause of his/her impairment.	Services and grants are justified as the necessary condition for the disabled person in order to benefit from the complete rights of his citizenship.
Role of the disabled person	Object of intervention, patient, a person who benefits of something, object of research.	A liable and active subject in taking decisions, involved in research, client.

101

The choice to consider disability as one of the main problems in social policy, in medical practice and in law, in order to improve access to services and treatment, and for the protection of the rights of individuals and groups, means that we both recognize the extent of the consequences due to disability and the required attention we must pay to face it properly. We are not anymore interested neither in the cause nor in the type of disability or the life cycles. To act in order to overcome the consequences of disability so that the disabled person might benefit from his/her citizenship rights, as we have shown in the above table, implies an idea of planning society which involves all, or nearly all, the fields in which public administration acts. But the value of a unitary approach towards disability gives us the possibility to propose shared models of intervention, to develop services and invest shared resources, trying to improve the whole organization of the society we live in, stressing the fact that we are not dealing with a problem of a minority group but that we are pursuing a general interest. To properly evaluate the consequences of disability is fundamental for the future development of health and social services since the "burden of disease" is much more linked to the disabling consequences than to its treatment in the acute phase. This way of considering the problem implies, as we like to stress again, a multi-dimensional vision, as the answers to disability cannot be given only by the health and social system, but housing, transport and even leisure might assume, sometimes, even a greater relevance not only to improve the quality of life but even to properly spend financial resources.

102

The Regional Consulting Committee of the Associations of Disabled People of Friuli-Venezia Giulia

It might be useful, at this point, to explain the role and the activities of the Steering Committee I am heading. It has been founded in 1985 but it was legally recognized as the representative of all disabled people of the region, with a specific law, in 2001. We can say that it expresses a kind of a third level of democracy, as in our region, which is divided in four provinces, in each province there is a Committee which includes the associations of that area. The four Committees choose two delegates each who constitute the Regional Steering Committee, so we have eight members plus the president.

What we are trying to ensure for the disabled people of our region are the so-called four rights:
1) The right to lead an autonomous life.
2) The right to lead a healthy life (prevention, treatment and rehabilitation for each specific disability).
3) The right to education.
4) The right to work.

We are trying to ensure the same standard of services for the whole regional area, which is not so simple, though the region has the same laws and financial resources. An important role is played by the local committees and the most active associations which are able to check the situation more directly. For this reason we have about 10 Steering Committee meetings each year. Every local Committee expresses the problems of the area and we try to support the most difficult situations. One of the main goals is to link and to strengthen the collaboration and comparison among the four committees so that the Steering Committee is able to make shared proposals to the Councillor who plans the health and social policies. We are also trying to affirm that every disabled person should have a life project, as it is provided by a regional law already approved in 1996.

Our headquarters are in the same building where the Councillor for health and social policy of our region resides, better to say, my office is next to his. We collaborate with the Councillor trying to plan the regional health and social policy foremost. We have succeeded to realize some of the goals we had planned even in other fields. The collaboration with the public and private institutions dealing with disability, including problems of housing, school, work etc., is daily routine and quite often we have to face new challenges. We are consulted when new bills are proposed and discussed in the regional parliament and I must say that our proposals are always considered and often accepted. We have succeeded in convincing our politicians that if we want to face the problems of disabled persons wisely we must invest both financial resources and intelligence. It is not worthwhile to keep people in hospitals or in old people's homes, as it would cost more with no satisfaction for the people concerned. I am sure that if we try to remove disability from society, from our life, we waste money, time and happiness. Disability means being alive with some problems we have to share with the community we live in, because by giving the proper answers to disabled people we improve the standard of society and we provide values for a worthy existence. Disability can be accepted if we alleviate it, if it is shared by the community and if we succeed in giving it a meaning.

103

Ability Assessment in Pre-pension and Flex Job Schemes

Steen Bengtsson

The reform of the Danish system of pre-pension (disability pension) originated in the research on disability pensions (with the 1984 reform called pre-
pension) that took place at the Danish National Institute of Social Research
in Copenhagen from the 1960s. In this decade, the labour market participation of physically disabled persons was surveyed and the main result, i.e.
that people with disabilities are very well able to work if only they had
enough self-confidence, was used as the basis of legislation for vocational
rehabilitation. In the 1970s, the problem of an increasing number of disability pensioners became the inspiration for research in this area. In the 1980s,
a new reform was introduced, the pre-pension reform, which included both
disability pensions and some social pensions.

The research on regional differences – in terms of awarding pre-pensions –incidentally discovered that the way local authorities administered
pre-pensions and other provisional benefits was decisive for the number of
awarded pensions. At that time, this result was not expected because a
number of central government boards had the authority of awarding these
pensions and the local authorities had no formal influence. Disability was
generally considered as something to be evaluated only by medical experts.
How could it be that local authorities' administration had an impact on how
to assess individuals' disability?

This was in support of the rehabilitation philosophy. As mentioned
above, vocational rehabilitation was established during the 1960s. The system seemed, however, to have been destroyed by decentralisation (rehabilitation was moved from the regions to the municipalities) in connection with
the Social Assistance Reform in 1976. Some argued that it would take years

to rebuild that kind of expertise that was now divided among 275 municipalities instead of among the 12 centres where it used to be concentrated. In
the 1980s, however, a new dimension – the economic incentive – turned up
in terms of relations between the central government and the local authorities. If local authorities began rehabilitating disabled individuals, pre-pension might be avoided. This resulted in quite a new policy in this area.

In the 1990s, local authorities little by little got the responsibility for
awarding pre-pensions, and in return they had to pay an increasingly higher
proportion of the pre-pensions. In 1992, they paid 50% of pre-pensions and
all other maintenance benefits as well, which meant that they did not any
longer have an incentive for awarding a pre-pension. In 1998, they paid 65%
of these pensions, whereas they paid 50% of the provisional maintenance
benefits and 35% as wage support to the new flex jobs. The system now
became action-oriented, i.e. the incentives for the local authorities were now
to choose the most active possibility.

At the same time local authorities acquired more instruments for vocational rehabilitation and activation of clients on sick pay, unemployment
benefit, rehabilitation benefit and social assistance. Rehabilitation benefit was
reformed in 1990 and unemployment benefit in 1994. Social assistance was
gradually replaced during the 1990s, more or less by activation. In 1995, an
earlier scheme was updated into the so-called 50/50 scheme offering a permanent 50% wage support to individuals with only 50% working ability. In
1998, this scheme was changed into a more flexible form, thereby creating
the so-called flex job scheme including support rates of 33%, 50% or 67%
according to an individual's working ability. The very same year, a special
law enhanced disabled individuals' possibility of getting a job. The law included both support when starting a job as well as the possibility of getting
some personal assistance. By these initiatives, the local authorities had gained
a number of new instruments for administering the cases in a more active
way.

With the 1998 legislation the new ability assessment was introduced,
not yet directly formulated in law texts but in an indirect way. This was ef-
fected by making the application for pre-pension something that could not
simply be done by the citizen him-/herself, but should be decided by the
municipality and only when all possibilities of vocational rehabilitation or
flex jobs had been exhausted. Hence, a person that could be rehabilitated to
a job or a flex job could not apply for a pre-pension, even if he/she should
be medically "bad enough" to get it. With the pre-pension reform of 2003

the new principle has been made official, and its application has been pre-pared by courses for caseworkers all over the country.

We are not yet certain whether this is the background to the decline of pre-pension awards during the 1990s. I am preparing a project to throw light on this. Another possibility is that the individuals who would earlier have got a pre-pension are now "parked" on social assistance. But, anyhow, the number of pre-pension awards has drastically declined in the period 1994-2000, from around 28,000 in the beginning of this period to 13,000-15,000 by the end. So there has been a decline of about 50% in pre-pension award in the late 1990s, and the number of social assistance receivers has not grown in the same period. If this is a genuine activation policy it so far (2003 in-cluded) saved the country for some 200,000-pension years, which is some 4 billion euro. Even if activation is costly too, one can at least conclude that we get more value for money in this way because we know from research that nearly all persons prefer flex jobs or other supported employment for pre-pension. If persons are just "parked" on social assistance, however, there would have been no gain from this policy.

Table 1: Pre-pension Awards, 1990-2000

	1990	1992	1994	1996	1997	1998	1999	2000
High (w.a. near 0%)	3,357	3,241	5,014	2,441	2,308	2,205	1,806	2,114
Middle (w.a. -33%)	8,878	7,801	7,884	7,189	6,868	6,900	5,140	6,034
Low, health rel. (w.a. 50%)	7,392	8,440	8,026	8,621	8,714	6,843	4,155	3,698
Low, mixed	3,403	3,830	2,599	2,354	2,240	1,838	1,163	930
Low, purely needs related	4,507	4,397	2,952	2,527	1,798	1,339	711	698
Total	27,537	27,709	26,475	23,132	21,919	19,125	12,975	13,474

Note: w.a. = working ability.

Source: Førtidspensioner Årsstatistik 2000.

During the 1990s, the award of the highest and middle pre-pension (corre-sponding to a loss of working ability of 100% and 67%) has decreased by about 35%, the award of the lowest health-related pension has decreased by 50%, whereas the award of the purely needs-related pre-pension has de-creased by as much as 85%. So the decline was concentrated in groups with the highest working ability. There may be two reasons for that. One is that these persons are most likely to profit from vocational rehabilitation to or-dinary jobs or to wage-supported jobs. Another reason may be that when obtaining pre-pension was easier, a number of those pensions went to individuals who would anyhow stop working, and who had health problems or social conditions which by that time would have entitled them to the pension. With more severe conditions for obtaining pensions these individuals will have to finance their withdrawal themselves.

It is too early to say whether the 2003 reform of the pre-pension system – making ability assessment official and explicit – will change anything. It is possible that we have already gained what can be gained by this new principle because it in fact has been applied for the last five years in this indirect way as I have mentioned. It is furthermore possible that the reform makes casework more bureaucratic because the new law demands a certain formal procedure. This procedure is described in a manual and has been taught to all caseworkers. Our latest research shows that municipalities who administer in a rule-oriented and formal way are awarding more pre-pensions, whereas municipalities that administer in a specific way and are using networks of employers, education places and medical doctors are awarding fewer pensions. Perhaps the reform will install a bureaucracy, which draws in passive direction.

108

The following Table from Bengtsson (2002) shows the results of a linear regression, where the dependent variable is an index of pre-pension awards, and the independent one a number of social qualities of the municipality (which are not shown in detail here) and answers from a questionnaire on the municipal administration in the areas of sick pay, social assistance, rehabilitation and pre-pension. As the index is 100 when the number of pre-pensions that could be expected from the age composition is awarded, the parameter shows by how many per cent the variable may influence the award.

Table 2:   Linear Regression of Pre-pensions Index

Variable	Parameter	p
- - - - - - - - (social background variables of municipalities) - - - - - - - - - - - -	- - -	- - -
Isolated administration: norms decided by Social Committee	+ 10	0.00
Formal administration: use of prognoses of social assistance	+ 8	0.00
Network administration: cooperation with medical doctors organisation	- 4	0.05
Specific administration: in vocational rehabilitation	- 20	0.00

Source: Bengtsson, 2002.

Linear regressions of pre-pensions from sick pay, from social assistance, health related, needs related and a number of other subgroups give similar results, showing that isolated and formal administration mean a higher number of pre-pensions, whereas network and intersectorial administration mean a lower number of pre-pensions awarded. These results comply with Michel Crozier's (1967) theory of Bureaucracy as characterised by formality and isolation, impeding goal attainment, in contrast to the Dynamic Organisation characterised by networking and intersectoriality.

The Danish pre-pension reform with its orientation towards integration on the local level and a less medical concept of disability is rather unique in Europe. Other countries trying to limit the awarding of disability pensions, have often centralised the control and restricted the pensions to a strictly medical diagnosis. Here the local and nearby authority has developed into an organisation that works through local partnerships to integrate people in employment if possible. The so-called local coordination committees deserve to be especially mentioned. They were established in 1999 in every municipality, and include representatives from the municipality, employment office, social partners, local medical doctors and organisations of disabled people. Research has shown that some of them are making a great difference whereas others are achieving less.

Municipalities are different, too. This is no new phenomenon. Huge municipal differences existed already before 1992 when the old central government boards had the right to award pre-pensions. Quite a few are pensioning the double number of what should be expected from population composition, unemployment and other relevant background variables, and quite a few are pensioning half the expected number. Even if the expected number has been calculated on the basis of research and published since 1995, the municipalities have not used this statistics to become more equal. The development goes in fact in the opposite direction. It seems that local differences – for the time being at least – are the price to be paid for decentralizing the right to award pre-pensions to the local authorities.

This is illustrated in Table 3, where municipalities are classified according to the results of a nine-year regression from official statistics, where a parameter alpha is estimated to characterise the level of pre-pensioning in the municipality, and a parameter beta is estimated to characterise the development in pre-pensioning award in that period. It can be seen that low-level municipalities more often show a relative decrease, whereas high-level municipalities more often have an increase in their award of pre-pensioning during the nine-year period. Both things naturally considered relative to the overall decrease in award of pre-pensioning during the period.

Table 3:   Municipalities Classified According to Award of Pre-pensions and
             Development of Award of Pre-pensions, 1992-2000

		Development in award of pre-pension seen in relation to the development in other municipalities	
		Decrease (beta negative)	Increase (beta positive)
The level of award	Low level (alpha neg.)	81	60
of pre-pension	High level (alpha pos.)	46	88

Note: * alpha and beta are the estimates given in Førtidspensioner Årsstatistik 2000, Table 14. OR =
               2,58.

As can be seen from this description there is no ability assessment in the
traditional sense in the Danish pre-pension and flex job schemes. Instead,
pre-pension and flex job are two possible outcomes of a rehabilitation process, where the primary goal is rehabilitation into a regular job. The disability pension case has been replaced with the rehabilitation process administered in local networks of municipal agencies and partnerships. The weak
point of this system is the many municipalities who do not develop a dynamic style of functioning, but instead are pre-pensioning many more than
they should be expected to. Unfortunately, the pre-pension reform which
has come into force this year (2003) does not seem to address this point, and
therefore should not be expected to contribute to pursue the development
of the late 1990s.

References

Bengtsson, Steen (2002) *Bestemmer forvaltningen om du får førtidspension* (Does Administration
       Decide if You Get a Pre-pension?). Socialforskningsinstituttet report 02:15.
Crozier, Michel (1967) *The Bureaucratic Phenomenon*. Chicago: The University of Chicago Press.
Førtidspensioner Årsstatistik 2000 (Pre-pensions Yearly Statistics 2000). Den sociale Ankestyrelse.
       www.dsa.dk.

What Do We Mean by Being Disabled?
Session Report

Joakim Palme

To engage in the endeavour to define disability, in a serious and fruitful way, we need first to answer the question why we need to define disability. The answer may be less self-evident than would perhaps be assumed. One could actually argue against the desirability of spending much time and resources on definitions since disability is a source of human variation, which, as such, is enriching society. However, we must also recognise the empirical fact that many members of society are disabled of their ability to participate as full members of society, by their physical or psychological impairments. They might be dependent on special services in order to be engaged in gainful employment, or simply be unable to earn an income and hence be dependent on cash benefits of some kind, mostly paid by the state. What, in the end, is at stake here is the welfare of citizens and how the (welfare) state may enhance and secure the welfare of its citizens by providing various sorts of benefits and services, and designing them properly.

It can moreover be argued that any discussion on disability requires a minimum definition of the concept. This is also true if we want to turn disability into something different, like, as is the case in the present context, ability. Here, administrative and scientific requirements might appear different. There are, however, as will be claimed in the following, obvious reasons for pursuing scientifically informed definitions also in disability policy.

The session offered different perspectives on disability. This is due to the fact that the participants in the discussion not only represented different countries but also different roles with regard to both disability and disability policy. What follows is an attempt both to highlight some of the is-

111

sues that were discussed in the session, and to present a few reflections of my own on the report and how it was received.

The Report

Disability programmes definitely have specific characteristics but they also share common traits with other social security programmes. The way they are treated by the OECD in the current report not least reflects the commonality. Thus, some of the analysis and some of the perspectives applied, follow "trends" that have become visible (fashionable) in the treatment (by the OECD as well as other organisations) of other programme areas. This is most obvious and explicit with regard to unemployment policy. What the report in fact calls for is consistency in the policies pursued in different areas. This means that the relevance of the report, as well as the critique of it, is likely to be applicable beyond the disability policy area.

112
What appears particular about disability is that it is associated with such a diversity of benefits and services, and that these programmes are subject to huge variation among countries. This has of course contributed to the fact that there is relatively little comparative research carried out in this field. That the OECD now has made a serious attempt to map the situation, and also to analyse the nature and consequences of the institutional diversity, is only to be welcomed. The difficulty of the task implies that descriptions, as well as analyses, are bound to be incomplete, and that more work remains to be done. Seldom has the old slogan "more research is needed" appeared more appropriate.

For comparative research, the effort by the OECD to compile information about disability policy programmes in the member countries will no doubt be of great value. What the OECD together with the European Centre has achieved would have been virtually impossible for research teams without this institutional backing. The main – as well as the background – reports fill important gaps in our knowledge about an area in society where there are a number of reasons why we would benefit from more knowledge. The programmes are very costly and the costs are likely to increase with population ageing. The prevalence of impairment and disability indicated by the receipt of benefits indicates that many members of society experience welfare problems.

The policy conclusions of the report entail recommendations both about definitions and about policy design. As described elsewhere, a core idea is to decouple the definitions of disability (or, more properly, impairments) from those of work incapacity. Disability and work incapacity is simply not the same. One set of policy conclusions concern the balance between rights and responsibilities of persons who claim benefits. What is recommended in the report are new obligations for disabled people, including sanctions, which are intended to foster a culture of mutual obligations. Several recommendations concern the programme administration, where early intervention, case management and activation come out as keywords. Another so-called "trend" that is visible in the policy recommendations is, what I would label, "partnership with employers". The OECD usually tries to promote best practices in its policy conclusions. Here, they have failed to identify good enough practices, which is disappointing as such, yet not entirely convincing. Why do policy-makers fail in this area but not in all other programmes?

While the aim of this session was to scrutinise the definitional aspects of disability, it is clear that this is related to other aspects of the conclusions of the report. Hence, issues of rights and responsibilities, case management, as well as partnership came to surface in the various interventions.

The Panel

The panellists come from different countries but also from different positions within their own societies. They represent state-financed research, consultancy, social security administration, regional organisations working with disability issues and multilateral organisations. Despite these differences, there were also common viewpoints expressed. There appeared to be a general consensus that disability should not be equated with work incapacity. This is also the underlying notion of the entire report. My impression is that the various suggestions made in the report are intended to avoid putting people with disabilities in benefit traps. This concern is likely to have been driven, not only by the fear that persons with disabilities might be excluded from the labour market but evidently also by worries about the increased costs for income maintenance programmes.

Definitions of disability reflect our perspective on both disability and ability, i.e. an underlying paradigm. The World Health Organisation (WHO) has recently made a useful contribution to this core issue, by working out a new classification system, which is bringing definitions in tandem with how we want to address disability. This system ICF (the International Classification of Functioning, Health and Disability) delivers a system for both measurement and comparisons based on a bio-psycho-social (holistic) approach to health and body functions. The ICF is intended to work across cultures. It is however contextualising impairments with an orientation to participation restrictions. In 2002, the assembly of the WHO accepted the new definitions.

Hoskins also took up the question of social security and disability from a "very" early intervention perspective. How can social security prevent disability? Here she promoted the perspective applied by the WHO, which is basically a "risk factor approach". Hoskins distinguished between occupational, environmental and behavioural risk factors of relevance from a preventive perspective. The fact that a lot can be gained from reducing work and environment hazards should not refrain us from focusing on the behavioural damages from, for example, smoking.

In her intervention Hoskins brought the issue of "population ageing" into focus, and here she promoted the life course perspective taken by the WHO. What this boils down to is to "slow down the observed health decline" that is putting such large pressures on the public system of care and income support. While she underscored that the "disability threshold" is largely dependent on the context, this should not prevent us from pursuing policies that have the potential of reducing the impairments of the population over their life courses. This has the potential both of reducing the financial burden on the public purse and of bringing about more public revenues by enabling more persons to be taxpayers during more years over their life course.

Adele Furrie's perspective is influenced both by her background as analyst at Statistics Canada, where she worked with surveys of disability, and her present work as consultant, where she is directly involved with different actors (in the North American context). With her long experience in this field she emphasised the importance of past work of the OECD in the 1980s when it delivered standardised definitions of disability. By working out conceptual frameworks and standardising measurement, the work of international organisations obviously has the potential to improve the possibilities of doing fieldwork, not least with surveys. While Furrie argued for applying a multitude of questions, she also recognised that the survey approach often sets strict limits on what can actually been carried out due to the potentially negative effects on response rates. This is evident in her work with the Current Population Survey (CPS) in the U.S.

Furrie furthermore advocated a medical and functional definition of impairments, and for contextualising disability. Consequently, a major concern in Furrie's work has been about different barriers facing people. From the perspective of the disabled she has identified different kinds of limitations and barriers: physical and attitudinal, and a frustration with ineffective policies that do not deliver the intended output. From the employer's perspective she has seen that legislation has been imposed without consultation. When it comes to the Canadian system of workplace quotas various kinds of problems have emerged, and not only about increased costs. Successful integration is double-sided; once a person with disabilities is considered fully integrated in the workplace, a new person with disabilities needs to be taken on. Partnership between government, employers and disabled is badly needed to overcome the present barriers.

Furrie summarised her position briefly as follows: Employment for those who can work requires personalised services to respond to the heterogeneity of the impaired population. It also demands partnership with employers. She thus came very close to the guidelines of the OECD report. In addition, she underlined the importance of providing income security when necessary, and personalised employment-oriented services to fit the different needs individuals may have.

In his intervention, Vladimir Kosic, president of the regional steering committee on disability in Trieste, Italy, put his strongest emphasis on the importance of a scientific approach, both to definitions and to policy evaluation. The way Kosic described the work of the steering committee, how it is set up to represent all disabled persons in the region and to interact with regional government, as well as with the local level, suggests that there are good practices with regard to "participation". The need to encourage such policies was warranted by the OECD report and by several speakers in the discussion.

Kosic endorsed the ICF approach to impairments, and the framing of activity limitations and/or participation restrictions imposed by it. This gives a natural focus on the fundamental goals of disability policy; how to secure the rights of all persons to work, to education etc. Since there are a number of reasons why people are disabled from exploring their full potentials as citizens, there has to be a multitude of approaches to tackle these different situations. In practice it demands personalised social services, even individual life plans including different functioning. This means that not only the medical aspects have to be covered by the services but housing, leisure etc. The ICF has the potential of being a good tool to improve access to services. We are, in this context, not interested in the causes but in how citizenship rights can be secured.

Kosic further urged for the necessity of gathering more data in order to establish a scientific ground for comparing and evaluating different policy experiences. If this is not done, the goals will not be reached. He warned for the kinds of policy discussions that are based on ideological assumptions and anecdotical evidence, and instead argued for the search of pragmatical solutions. Kosic also argued that political consensus of involved actors needs to be found in order to establish a long-term commitment of society. Here an investment perspective is useful. If the necessary investments are made this will help to control costs because poor disability policy results in very expensive hospitalisation etc. Moreover, disability policy should be the concern of all people because it is related to fundamental democratic aspects of society. This is why, in Kosic's view, a unitary approach is so useful, and why these policies are not a minority interest but a majority question.

Two of the panellists explicitly dealt with decentralising reforms in the administration of disability programmes, one from the point of view of research and the other from the perspective of the social security administration:

Steen Bengtsson discussed the Danish experience in the 1990s. During this period, municipalities got increased responsibilities for people with disabilities. The award of pensions is now determined at the local level. This has implied an increased financial burden on the municipalities but also increased resources for rehabilitation. The increased local variation in the award of pensions, also when structural factors are accounted for, raises questions of justice, i.e. whether benefit claimants are treated in the same way regardless of their domicile. Recently, the government has introduced standardisation of methods as a response. Bengtsson is however not convinced that this will work, at least not with regard to the goal of increasing activation. Previous research has shown that the more bureaucracy, the less activation, which suggests that the recent standardisation might result in decreased activation. What is clear, however, is that the total award rate of early pensions has gone down quite dramatically. What is not yet examined is whether the total benefit dependency has gone down.

In relation to the OECD recommendation of "early intervention", the Danish case gives an interesting example (possibly a good practice). The Danish government has observed that once a person has applied for a disability benefit, the applicant will sooner or later get it. Early intervention has then to be about how to prevent possible applicants from starting to claim the benefit and instead first try rehabilitation. It should be noted, though, that in the Danish system of pre-pensions no health test is required. In any case, Denmark is a typical case for the kind of policy consistency propagated by the OECD. The country has pursued a broad reform work in the spirit of activation across the board during the 1990s.

The Swiss case, as reported by Bruno Nydegger, shares the decentralisation experience with Denmark. The Swiss reform also entailed changes with regard to definition. A strict independence between disability and earnings capacity is now applied, and, furthermore, a causal link between health problems and restricted earnings capacity is also required before a claimant is granted the right to a cash benefit. The decentralisation of decision-making in the cantonal system produces large variation across the nation. This is again similar to the Danish situation.

What, in addition, is characterising the development in Switzerland, is the increase of multiple and mental diagnoses. As was pointed out in the subsequent discussion, this is not unique to the Swiss case. The current reform of the Swiss administration is intended to cope with increased complexity of the multiple diagnosis cases so that they are not trapped in lengthy legal procedures and that, instead, the potentials for rehabilitation are explored.

In his paper, Nydegger made what I see as a controversial claim when he argued that the basic problem, also in this policy area, is how to distribute scarce resources. I would argue that a fundamental aspect of social policy is that the budget size is not fixed but rather dependent on how you organise the policy programmes. What I mean is that if policies related to impairment are made universal, and in the interests of the entire population, the budget for disability is likely to be more generous. What has been found in this context, not least when we compare countries, is that there are good reasons for seeing the resources allocated to a policy area partly dependent on how polices are designed, particularly with regard to the inclusion of a majority of the population. This is of course not to argue that the access to resources is not setting restrictions to what we can achieve.

In the discussion that followed the interventions of the panellists, issues were raised in connection to the earlier interventions but new questions were also put forward. It was started off by David Morris who pointed out that definitions of concepts may entail elements that are offensive to people with disabilities, most notably in terms of not recognising their full citizenship rights. Aurelio Fernandez Lopéz followed up to this and criticised the discussion for representing steps backward in failing to distinguish between persons and their disability.

Another issue that was raised by Delia Lattanzi concerned the question of sanctions in relation to the test of work capacity of people with impairments, and also suggested that classification of degrees of disability could be useful in this context. Vladimir Kosic claimed that while there should be a responsibility to work, sanctions should not be used because there is a risk that authorities become oppressive of vulnerable persons. He argued for a sensitive approach to each person, disabled or not. Adele Furrie argued against classification of degrees of disabilities, since it does not acknowledge that the consequences of impairments are dependent on the context.

The question about the role of the medical profession attracted the attention of several speakers. Vappu Taipale, with a background as child-psychiatrist, pointed to the dominance of the medical in the definition of disability, and asked if there is a proper balance between medical and contextual definitions of disability? Adele Furrie meant that the medical profession has a role but only one role, and that other professions like social workers potentially are important players. Moreover, stigma and attitudes should be recognised on par with medical functional definition. Steen Bengtsson pointed out that the medical profession often has a control function and that this is related to deservingness, and might entail oppressive elements. He argued that we need to develop new techniques of control also involving the people with disabilities by direct representation.

In response to a question concerning the assessment of mental disabilities, raised by Han Bakkum, Bruno Nydegger urged for developing new and better techniques. The insurance medicine needs to be developed with regard to these diagnoses. Again, the relevance of Vladimir Kosic's urge for more science, and more evidence-based policy was very clear. Without a scientific approach, resources and people will not be enough. This is valid beyond the OECD countries. Daniel Mont, from the World Bank, extended the perspectives on disability to the development world and pointed to the great challenges and lack of resources. Here, Irene Hoskins pointed to an ongoing transition in these countries where the importance of accidents and non-communicable diseases, like psychiatric diagnoses, are increasing in relative importance. The burden of disease is increasing tremendously. This is of course a very different situation with regard to the general lack of organisation. There is also stigma and less self-organisation, which need to be overcome.

The Knowledge Gaps

While it can be argued that the OECD report has filled important gaps in our knowledge about disability policy cross-nationally, there is little doubt that it left many old questions without a satisfactory answer. But it has also raised new questions, or, to put it differently, it is helping us to ask questions more properly.

I would argue that one of the clearest messages from the panel was that scientifically-based knowledge is of great importance if we want to turn disability into ability, i.e. if we want to improve the welfare of citizens with functional impairments. I would like to emphasise Adele Furrie's point about the importance of past contributions of the OECD when it comes to definitions and methods of surveying disabilities, and Vladimir Kosic's call for more comparative analysis. Here, we are obviously still in an early stage of the work.

While a lot of attention is given to the cash benefits programmes, to my mind, the access to benefits in kind is much more important for actually turning disability into ability. This is of course an area where comparisons are even more difficult to make. When it comes to "case management", the difficulties of systematic analysis are also evident upon analysing the development in single countries.

Concluding Remarks

The costs of disability policies are huge. With aging populations they will increase if nothing is done about the causes of disability and/or the design of benefit programmes. To address the causes we need to invest in both working conditions and the environment, to follow Hoskins' distinctions. To

119

change people's behaviour is more delicate from an ethical point of view, and is very difficult in any case. That education plays an important role for hazardous habits like smoking points to the possibility of actually changing things for the better. It is not without costs and to make it an attractive option, it requires that state and other organisations change, or rather extend their time frame for "accounting".

In reforming the benefit programmes, we have to be careful not to create new or reinforce old divisions of welfare. We have to recognise the important differences in public health that have been identified. We should simply avoid to create different "Nations of Welfare", to use Richard Titmuss' terminology, one nation of people without impairments and one with those who not only suffer from different impairments but also struggle with less resources, and, hence, restricted possibilities to act as full citizens.

The decisions of the public and private employers appear critical if we want to turn disability into ability to earn one's living on the market. In a market economy, the room for manoeuvre is restricted. This implies that, if people with physical or psychological impairments have lower productivity, it requires that the state provide subsidies, invest in physical adjustments of workplaces or simply define quotas for all employers. But the decisions not to hire a person with impairment might simply be based on prejudice. Also here, the importance of education should be given high priority. The discrimination of persons with a disability, is in such cases not only a loss for the person, who is disabled to earn his/her living, but also a loss for society at large.

I would like to return to the question why *no best practice* could be identified. Why do all policies fail in this area and not in others? Which policy instruments are missing? I would claim that the lack of good practice warrants a more thorough explanation. What can be offered here are only a few personal reflections. I would argue that the lack may well be explained by the lack of good enough data and analysis. Here, it is important to underscore that different strategies may entail "good practice". Has the OECD made any mistakes in their assessment of best practice? Above, I have pointed to elements of good practice, when it comes to protecting the incomes of disabled persons and engaging persons with impairments in the political process.

We are all victims of our own contexts. The usefulness of learning from the trials and errors in single countries are always restricted by the different contexts in other countries. This notwithstanding, I would like to refer to a few examples from my own country, *Sweden*.

One of the most ambitious programmes for people with severe impairments, the so-called "assistance reform" was implemented in the first part of the 1990s. The programme is intended to enable persons with very severe and often multiple impairments to live a normal autonomous life by providing "around the clock" personal assistant(s). The evaluations of this programme suggest that it has made possible a different and better life for those who are entitled to the services. It should also be recognised that for most persons who are covered by this programme there are small possibilities of getting engaged in gainful employment. If we are interested in promoting the abilities of people with disabilities to live as normal citizens then it is in any case of great importance. Yet the programmes struggle with problems of "cost control" and this suggests that there are problems of sustainability.

The importance of engaging persons with impairments and their organisations in the implementation and administration of policies was underscored several times during the session. From a Swedish historical perspective, there can be no doubt that the organisations of disabled persons have been very important for the promotion of their interests. How are the disabled persons organised? Does the focus on medical diagnoses also in the organisation of disabled persons hamper an effective impact on general policies and policies that promote employment?

In some way we need to create institutions that are sustainable over the business cycle, even if the cycle exhibits dramatic changes. In the 1990s, Sweden went through a severe economic recession. This affected all spheres of society. What is striking is how dependent vulnerable groups are on *macroeconomic conditions*. Even if the decades meant that the political ambitions increase, both before and during the crisis, for the majority of people with disabilities it was a lost decade in terms of improving the welfare of these people. It is probably of little comfort that the welfare of people with disabilities did not worsen more than that for other people. This suggests that if we want to be successful in promoting the integration of persons with disabilities it is probably critical if the demand for labour can be kept high. I suspect that this is also critical for engaging employers. To base the partnership with employers on their self-interest as regards the supply of labour appears to be a more solid strategy than to base it on their altruism.

*

*   *

For the 21st century, it may be enlightening to take the perspective of the Japanese Nobel laureate Kenzaburo Oe, who in connection with the receipt of the prize reflected on the upcoming 21st century. He did it from the perspective of his son who suffers from multiple impairments. Despite his disabilities the son is an appreciated composer. He is an example of how it is possible for all citizens to contribute to society if the right opportunities are given. But Kenzaburo Oe was pessimistic about the prospect for his son in the 21st century. This was based on the fact that the ability of the father to help his son would end some day. He lacked faith in society, whether it would be strong enough to step in and secure the welfare of the son. For me this is one of the great challenges of our time, to build strong enough institutions that we can entrust with the care of the weakest members of society, also to the extent that they can function as full citizens.

What Rights and Responsibilities for Society and for Persons with Disabilities?

Key Issues

1. Most societies accept their responsibility to offer special support to persons with disabilities. But too little effort is made to (re)integrate or keep disabled workers, in particular older disabled workers, in the labour market. Instead, income-replacing cash benefits are deemed sufficient.

2. Not everybody who is fully and permanently disabled receives adequate disability benefits. Many of those who have never been integrated into the labour market or who have been out of the labour market for too long are not entitled to any (or only to a relatively low minimum) benefit, or maybe to a household means-tested non-contributory disability benefit.

3. Disabled people are treated as if they were unable to work. Hence, little is expected from them in terms of contributing to their successful labour market integration. In some countries, certain groups of (insured) disabled people are obliged to go through vocational rehabilitation or training before any benefit could be awarded. However, age-specific data on programme participants suggest that this obligation is only applied for people below age 45.

4. While disabled people tend to have few obligations, they also have few rights, e.g. to get their workplace accommodated. Anti-discrimination legislation, which is spreading quickly, has yet to prove its effectiveness in this context.

5.   Too often, disability benefit programmes have become a "catch-all" ben-
      efit replacing long-term unemployment, social assistance, or early re-
      tirement payments. Governments have tightened eligibility criteria, in-
      troduced "mutual obligations" and sometimes reduced benefit levels
      for these other benefits.

OECD Policy Conclusions

124

- The focus of policy should not in the first place be on granting entitlement to income-replacing benefits but on providing individually-tai-
  lored assistance aiming at reintegration into the labour market.
- Income support should be provided to the extent necessary while these
  efforts are underway, unless integration measures are inappropriate
  due to the severity of the disability.
- If society obliges authorities to make efforts to reintegrate people, so
  should cooperation be expected from the disabled person. Failure to
  make an effort to participate in the (re)employment process should
  result in sanctions in the same way that failure of society to provide
  work should result in an obligation to pay the disabled person a cash
  transfer. Such "mutual obligations" should be handled sensitively; there
  should be no question of people being forced to accept inappropriate
  work.
- Introducing the notion of mutual obligations of both society and the
  disabled person would move disability policy closer to the philosophy
  of unemployment programmes, which also expect an active contribution and effort from beneficiaries. Lessons should be drawn from recent changes in unemployment and social assistance programmes.
- In means-tested disability schemes the method of household income
  testing may have to be reconsidered if such an approach of mutual obligations is applied. A disabled person not entitled to any transfer payment because of other household income sources cannot easily be
  obliged to participate in integration programmes.

The OECD Perspective on Mutual Obligations

Peter Scherer

Introduction

The OECD Report *Transforming Disability into Ability* took its current form because its authors were confronted with a fundamental paradox in policies in many member countries:

- Disability support is awarded on the basis of demonstrated inability to work.
- Disabled people want to be enabled to participate in society, which includes in particular access to work.

This implies that income support is granted provided disabled people demonstrate they cannot work. That is, they are given support for demonstrating they cannot work, not for finding out how they can. The Report documents at length the result of these policies: very small rates of outflow from disability benefit, despite wide-ranging programmes to encourage it.

In looking for a way out of this dilemma, we have drawn on the growing experience with policies directed at other groups, and particularly at the unemployed.

Unemployment Policies

Historically, policy for the unemployed was based on a similar (but different) dilemma. Unemployed people were seen as victims of the labour market, and policies that required action on their part were condemned as "blaming the victims". Yet the whole basis of unemployment insurance was that it was there to subsidise job search: that is, actions to find a new place in the labour market.

The persistence of unemployment at times when overall employment rates have grown has led to a revision of policy in most countries – a revision which the OECD encouraged in its "job strategy" published in 1996. The unemployed are now increasingly *required* to make "active" steps to find work as a condition for receiving income support. This applies whether they are receiving such support on the basis of unemployment insurance, and also if they have become reliant on means-tested social assistance.

No one claims such polices are a panacea. Our own analysis shows that some "active" policies – such as classroom training of unemployed people for particular vocations – do not help much in actually getting into the labour market. Some types of employment – such as fixed term public sector jobs – can isolate participants from looking for more permanent jobs in the "regular" labour market, so those emerging from such work can be worse off – in terms of employment access – than those who were searching more widely during the same period.

While it is sometimes alleged that these new policies amount to "blaming the victims" of malfunctioning labour markets, this need not be the case. Some countries which have been most fervent in implementing such policies – such as Australia and the UK – base most income support on assistance principles, and put no time limit on receipt. However, this income support, while potentially unlimited in time, is not unconditional. It is based on the obligation to take up opportunities as they arise, and not to wait until the "perfect" job is on offer.

Disabled People and Employment

Disabled people who try to find a place in modern labour markets operate at a double disadvantage. They face the same challenges of structural change and job insecurity as other labour market participants. And their disability makes it more difficult to find a place.

Table 3.6 (see Annex to this paper) in the Report shows that, overall, less than half of those reporting a disability are employed. In general, they do not receive income support: apart from some social insurance based systems (such as that of Sweden), receipt of benefits and having a job are mutually exclusive. Benefit receipt is seen as being associated with exclusion from the job market, whether or not this is the intention of policy-makers.

Hence it is important to admit at the start that it would be foolish to pretend that there exists a magic formula which will enable disabled people to have just the same access to the labour market as others. But this is not the same as saying that there is nothing that works. On the contrary, the Report we are discussing contains some very strong clues in this regard. In particular, when we disaggregate these figures by age (Table 3.4 in the Report, see Annex) , however, the story is very different. Overall employment rates turn out to be very poor guides to possibilities and the potential of disabled people to participate economically.

In particular, a number of countries have succeeded in achieving a relative employment rate of over 80% on the part of those *under age 50*: it is 87% of the rate for the non-disabled in Switzerland, and above 80% in a number of other European countries. In general, these are countries that require applicants for disability benefits to participate in rehabilitation efforts, and only allow them once to access disability benefits (which assume that they cannot work) if those efforts have failed. Quotas for employers to employ a certain percentage of disabled people seem to contribute. There is, then, an implicit mutual obligation in these cases: society will provide income support for those who cannot work, but will require those who apply for such help to test stringently whether this inability is really the case. And it works: relative employment rates are not perfect, but they are much higher than would happen if disability benefits were awarded on the basis of nothing but "objective" medical evidence.

In the overall picture, however, many of these countries do poorly by disabled. This is because of the other feature of their policy that is documented at length in the Report: above age 50, the disability benefit programme has been converted into an early retirement route, and all efforts to rehabilitate are abandoned. This is a part of a broader attitude to older people under which, in return for income support, they are encouraged to regard themselves as obsolescent and to get out of the way of the labour market. Income support systems underwrite this attitude, but they do not cause it: similar attitudes to older workers can be observed in countries (such as the UK and Australia) with much more meagre levels of public income support in retirement. In Australia, the US and the UK, the ratio for older people is lower still, so that the difference (of about 20 percentage points) between older and younger disabled people is similar over all the countries for which we have data.

A counter example is Sweden, where income support is generous, but has resisted (while not completely avoiding) this drift to treating older workers as expendable. It would be better to explicitly put in place explicit early retirement programmes and recognise their cost than to use disability programmes for this purpose, as it can easily result in all disability beneficiaries being treated as people who have prematurely aged.

But this poor performance overall should not be allowed to hide the lesson that the experience of these countries shows: that a policy of mutual obligations can work, and is effective improving employment rates of disabled people.

The lesson is that active policies to promote employment of disabled people can have an effect. If applied to younger age groups, they can counteract (through retention in employment) the effects of discrimination against hiring of older disabled people, though in no country is such discrimination corrected: the employment ratio is always lower for older people. The rate for older people is, nonetheless, higher in European countries that have relatively high employment rates for younger workers than it is in those countries for which employment rates for younger people is already low.

The Insurance Principle

When this principle was first proposed by the OECD, a number of countries reacted by saying that it violated the basic principle on which social insurance is based: in return for paying a premium, those covered by social insurance are entitled to unconditional recompense if the condition against which they are socially insured occurs. Making receipt of disability benefits conditional on fulfilling further mutual obligations is, it was argued, a violation of this contract. It is fair to say that this attitude is not confined to countries which rely on contribution-based social insurance models. Disabled people are recognised as requiring protection even where there has been no opportunity to contribute, or where (as in Australia) social protection does not rely on contribution records.

On this point I would argue that the analogy that is implied with an ordinary insurance contract is not valid. Social insurance is of its nature compulsory, and so the design of the system has to take account of the social and economic externalities that the system design involves. An individual or even group contract with an insurance company for (for example) compensation in the case of certain defined accidents does not need to be subject to such scrutiny. But social insurance cannot escape it.

The issue I have in mind here is the social consequence of signalling that disabled people are not expected (unlike the unemployed) to make a contribution to society. The implication is that they have little of economic value to contribute, and so society is better off without their services. But it is not their fault, so we should compensate them.

It is sometimes agued that this issue can best be addressed by making opportunities available to disabled people, forbidding discrimination against them by employers, but in neither case imposing compulsion. By such an approach, it is argued, the insurance principle can be honoured and opportunities for them can still be created.

The basic problem with this approach is that it fails to recognise the basic facts of labour market economics. Most jobs are not particularly enjoyable. Individuals undertake them in return for the compensation they receive. If disabled people are to be integrated into society, they face the same challenge.

On this understanding, the income support disabled people receive is not a "compensation" for their condition. It is their wage for social participation. Their participation in integration activities is therefore the counterpart for that compensation, just as work is the counterpart of a wage.

It is also true that "disability" is essentially a social construction: it is a category into which people with very different physical and mental capacities are placed in different societies (and at different times in the same society). Medical criteria are needed to define entitlements to support, but their definition and specification cannot be reduced to a "scientifically" precise set of criteria. This is another reason that a policy or legislation which identifies disability with inability to work can over time lead to the exclusion from the labour market (and thus from full participation in society) of people who do have a contribution to offer.

The Mutuality of the Obligation

I pass now to the other side of the bargain. The "integration" principle discussed in chapter 6 of the Report (alongside the compensation principle) is (with the exceptions mentioned above) largely observed in the breach. Almost nothing is done to integrate older disabled people into the labour market, and even for younger people the offers are often few and inadequate.

Clearly disabled people only have an "obligation" to participate if an activity is offered to which they can realistically respond: one that builds on their talents and adjusts for their disability. Failure to offer such an opportunity is not a ground for denying the income support that is necessary. Unemployment insurance programmes do use the time-limited nature of income support as an incentive to push recipients into taking their job search obligations seriously. In the case of severe disability, a threat that such support is withheld is clearly unacceptable.

Of course, many disability benefit schemes do include compensation for "partial" disability, or include partial disability in an overall guarantee. It is clear that in such cases, providing participation opportunities will be less costly – and requiring beneficiaries to take them up will be even more appropriate. In practical terms, this is clearly the place to start.

However, reforms that go in this direction may be resisted if unemployed people (or those in receipt of social assistance) are themselves denounced for failing to find work. In such circumstances, disabled people will fear being doubly castigated, and may resist any "reform" which would put them into the same administrative category as unemployed people. Therefore, introducing mutual obligations into the systems providing support for disabled people may require the re-adjustment of the way other recipients of social support are treated.

For those who are severely disabled, voluntary participation will always be the only real option: compulsion will be counter-productive. But here the mutual obligation principle operates on the side of the beneficiary. Proper implementation of this proposal would require a large expansion of support resources beyond those currently on offer. If there are some people for whom it is indeed the case that the cost of support completely outweighs the contribution they could make, it will be necessary to formulate clear criteria for making that judgement.

Transforming Disability into Ability

It follows from these considerations that the transformation of disability programmes into labour market programmes will require a fundamental change in their nature, and often in the legislation on which they are based. It will be necessary to abandon the idea that only those who "cannot work" are entitled to compensation. This approach, common to many countries, is self-defeating, since it essentially sends signals to medical practitioners and to potential applicants that they should commit labour market euthanasia and suicide (respectively) to get the compensation they need.

Instead, the object of the screening must become the determination of the degree and nature of integration support and compensation each client needs. Society may then decide that some integration support is too expensive, and rely on compensation alone. But unless we change direction, the tendency will continue to be to make this judgement for *all* those labelled as disabled.

Annex: Tables 3.4 and 3.6 from the OECD Report

Table 3.4: Higher Relative Employment Rates for Persons of Prime Working Age and with Higher Educational Attainment

Relative employment rate of disabled over non-disabled persons, by age group, gender and educational attainment, late 1990s

	All	Age group		Gender		Educational attainment	
	age 20-64	20-49	50-64	Men	Women	Lower	Higher
Australia	0.55	0.66	0.45	0.54	0.56	..	..
Austria	0.60	0.85	0.55	0.60	0.59	0.49	0.67
Belgium	0.54	0.73	0.30	0.59	0.52	0.46	0.64
Canada	0.72	0.80	0.62	0.71	0.73	0.64	0.77
Denmark	0.61	0.74	0.42	0.61	0.62	0.44	0.73
France	0.72	0.83	0.67	0.75	0.69	0.71	0.83
Germany	0.67	0.84	0.65	0.69	0.62	0.57	0.71
Italy	0.60	0.84	0.52	0.59	0.63	0.48	1.02
Korea	0.74	0.82	0.66	0.66	0.69	0.73	0.89
Mexico	0.77	..	..	..	..	..	..
Netherlands	0.60	0.70	0.52	0.61	0.64	0.55	0.63
Norway	0.72	0.81	0.62	..	..	..	..
Poland	0.29	0.32	0.35	..	..	..	..
Portugal	0.59	0.70	0.56	0.59	0.62	0.58	0.85
Spain	0.41	0.53	0.36	0.43	0.37	0.41	0.57
Sweden	0.69	0.78	0.56	0.77	0.64	0.64	0.72
Switzerland	0.79	0.87	0.68	0.84	0.75	..	..
United Kingdom	0.53	0.64	0.42	0.51	0.56	0.41	0.65
United States	0.58	0.66	0.48	0.55	0.61	0.40	0.66
OECD (19)	0.62	..	..	..	..	..	..
OECD (14) [a]	0.61	0.75	0.52	0.62	0.61	0.54	0.74
EU (11)	0.60	0.74	0.50	0.61	0.59	0.52	0.73

Note: .. Data not available. a) Age, gender or educational attainment not available for Australia, Mexico, Norway, Poland and Switzerland.

Source: See Annex 1, Table A1.1.

Table 3.6: Work and Benefit Status of Disabled Persons

Distribution of disabled persons by work-benefit status, percentages, late 1990s

	Employed total	of which: no benefits	benefits	Non-employed total	of which: no benefits	benefits
Australia	41.9	39.1	2.8	58.1	15.7	42.4
Austria	43.3	26.4	16.9	56.7	14.2	42.5
Belgium	33.4	15.1	18.3	66.5	16.2	50.3
Denmark	48.2	25.7	22.5	51.8	6.3	45.5
France	47.9	30.0	17.9	52.1	11.7	40.4
Germany	46.1	30.5	15.6	53.8	11.9	41.9
Italy	32.1	25.4	6.7	68.0	28.8	39.2
Korea	45.9	40.1	5.8	54.0	49.5	4.5
Mexico	47.1	44.8	2.3	52.9	52.5	0.4
Netherlands	39.9	23.3	16.6	60.1	19.5	40.6
Norway	61.7	56.5	5.3	38.3	12.2	26.1
Portugal	43.9	26.0	17.9	56.0	20.9	35.1
Spain	22.1	16.8	5.3	77.9	28.0	49.9
Sweden	52.7	14.8	37.9	47.3	1.1	46.2
Switzerland	62.4	52.0	10.4	37.6	14.2	23.3
United Kingdom	38.9	23.5	15.4	61.1	9.1	52.0
United States [a]	48.6	42.0	6.6	51.4	18.8	32.6
OECD (17)	44.5	31.3	13.2	55.5	19.4	36.1
ECHP (11)	40.8	23.4	17.4	59.2	15.2	44.0

Note: Family benefits are considered as no benefits.
           a) Benefits are disability benefits only.

Source: See Annex 1, Table A1.1.

Disability, the Organisation of Work, and the Need for Change

Colin Barnes

There is considerable historical and anthropological evidence that impairment is a human constant and that cultural responses to perceived abnormalities of the body and mind vary across time, culture and place. It is equally evident that throughout recorded history western society has systematically discriminated against or excluded various groups of people on the basis of perceived biological inferiority, and that this exclusion became systematic following the material and ideological changes associated with capitalist development.

The combination of industrialisation, urbanisation, and associate ideologies including: liberal utilitarianism, Social Darwinism, and Eugenics, provided "scientific" legitimacy to ancient myths, fears and prejudices, and the gradual but intensifying commodification of everyday life. As a result "work" became almost exclusively associated with wage labour and paid employment. This precipitated the development of an employment infrastructure geared to the needs of those deemed "capable" of this type of activity.

Hence, those considered incapable of work, and labelled "disabled" were, apart from in, and immediately following, times of war, excluded from the workplace. This legacy remains with us today. Discrimination against disabled people is therefore institutionalised in the very fabric of western society; consequently, disabled people encounter a whole range of material, political and cultural barriers to meaningful mainstream employment and social participation.

Moreover, despite the introduction of a range of measures said to address this unfortunate and unacceptable situation, often generated by the

133

social obligation felt towards those who acquired impairment/s during wartime, including in some states such as the USA and Britain, anti-discrimination legislation, barriers remain largely unchecked. As a result, unemployment and underemployment are a constant feature of the overwhelming majority of disabled people's lives. This has obvious and well-documented negative economic, social and psychological implications for disabled people themselves, their families and, indeed, society as a whole.

This is especially important given that the more technically and socially sophisticated a society becomes the more impairment and disability it creates. There are more disabled people today than there ever were in the past, and the numbers are likely to increase substantially over the coming decades due to a variety of factors including medical advances, ageing populations, the spread of terrorism and war.

The barriers remain because, hitherto, legislation has been weak and piecemeal and, without exception, is founded, one way or another, on an individualistic rather than a holistic approach to the problem of disability. To-date, the overwhelming bulk of the policies introduced to address the problems encountered by disabled workers in the workplace have centred mainly on the supply side of labour: namely, disabled workers, in the form of training schemes, subsidised wages and so on. All of which, though not always unwarranted, to varying degrees, reinforce rather than undermine the traditional assumption that disabled workers are somehow not equal to non-disabled peers: the very opposite of what is needed.

Moreover, policies based on notions of "mutuality", that aim to focus on both the supply side (disabled workers) and the demand side (the workplace) of labour, invariably gravitate toward the former, because of national governments' subjugation by international corporate interests, and their ongoing support for, and propagation of, ideologies and cultures that prioritise profit over people.

It is evident therefore that if governments are serious about addressing the employment problems experienced by disabled people then anti-discrimination policies must adopt a more holistic approach, be strengthened and rigorously enforced. Barrier removal in the workplace is only possible by the development and adoption of policies with a clear and unambiguous focus on the demand side of labour – the social organisation of work – and the economic and social infrastructures that support it. This includes: education systems, health and social support services, transport systems, and the built environment, housing, and leisure industries. All of which are geared to the needs of the non-disabled majority and, consequentially, compound the difficulties encountered by disabled people in the labour market.

Where legislation exists enforcement must be properly funded and made highly visible; naming and shaming those who act in discriminatory ways. Where legislation is currently being considered, governments must make the appropriate arrangements to ensure enforcement commissions are properly in place and that individual responsibility is not left to disabled people themselves.

It is worth considering, too, that unemployment and underemployment are not experiences exclusive to disabled people. These are increasingly common phenomena in most countries across the world. These problems can only be resolved through increased government intervention in the labour market. Appropriate policies could include a substantive reduction in the hours worked, job share schemes, wage regulation, reduction in retirement age and so on.

But whilst such policies appear to fly in the face of recent trends, it is important to remember that government intervention in the way the labour market operates is a well-established feature of western development. Since at least the Industrial Revolution successive governments across Europe and North America have played a major role in structuring and restructuring the labour market through grants and tax concessions for industrialists and employers in order to sustain economic growth and maintain political stability.

135

Moreover, with regard to the employment of people with ascribed impairments, various "demand side" initiatives were successfully implemented during and immediately following the 1939/45 war in many European states to include this section of the workforce in the world of work. In most cases these were only tentatively enforced and often abandoned as the memory of war diminished and the political climate changed. But if governments are serious about getting disabled people into work then similar policies might be re-introduced.

However, this is not to suggest that everyone with an accredited impairment can or should be expected to work at the same pace as "non-disabled" contemporaries or that all disabled people can or should work in the conventional sense. As is increasingly recognised, to expect people with "severe" physical or cognitive conditions to be as productive as non-disabled peers is one of the most oppressive aspects of modern society.

But to reiterate, work, as we understand it today, is an outcome of the Industrial Revolution: a social creation. Thus, what is considered work at one point in time may not be perceived as such in another. Furthermore, to radically reconceptualise the meaning of work beyond the rigid confines of waged labour is not unprecedented in the modern context. For instance, in their attempt to assert the role of women in a predominantly patriarchal society, the Women's Movement has successfully redefined the meaning of work to include unpaid labour: namely, housework and child care.

Furthermore, since the emergence of the disabled people's movement, independent living, disability arts and culture, the concept of a "disabled identity" has taken on a whole new meaning which in many ways serves to undermine traditional assumptions about disability, dependence, and work. In the UK, for example, the coming of direct and indirect payment schemes enabling disabled people to employ personal assistants (PAs) or helpers has meant that many disabled people, although formally "unemployed" are now employers themselves. Many PA users employ as many as five or six people over the course of a week.

The recent unprecedented expansion of user-led involvement in the development and delivery of services has also meant that more and more disabled people now spend their "free" time actively involved in service provision of one form or another. The coming of the disability arts movement has precipitated the generation of a whole range of cultural activities involving both disabled and non-disabled individuals which, taken together, constitute meaningful alternatives to the various "non-disabled" cultures which continue to permeate late capitalist society.

A further corollary of these developments is the need for a re-evaluation of "disability"-related benefits and pensions within the workings of the economy. Escalating benefit costs are due to a variety of factors: demographic, economic, political and cultural; not least of which is ongoing government failure to address the structural barriers to disabled people's meaningful involvement in the conventional workplace. At present, disability-related premiums are fundamental to modern societies that are geared almost exclusively to non-disabled lifestyles.

But rather than being viewed as a drain on national economies they should be considered an indicator of collective social responsibility. It should also be remembered that disability-related benefits are not passive in the sense that they go straight into the recipients' pockets, they are circulated throughout the economy in terms of generating goods and services. Furthermore, there is ample evidence that in many western societies increasingly large sections of the workforce are employed in the service sector, and that they are "dependent" on disabled people and other disadvantaged groups for their very livelihood. Rather than stigmatise and penalise those in receipt of disability benefits, politicians and policy-makers should be striving to develop a more equitable and less stigmatising disability benefits system.

All of this may be located within the growing realisation amongst scholars and policy-makers that the continued development and, therefore, future stability, of a "western style" economy such as that of Britain is inextricably linked to the complex and ever-changing relations between production and consumption. This should be coupled with the recognition that, regardless of their role within the "conventional" labour market, disabled people are both producers and consumers of a vast array of services upon which many non-disabled people depend; they are, therefore, a fundamental component within this equation.

Finally, as the boundaries between what is and what is not considered a socially acceptable condition become evermore blurred, as they most surely will if only because of the changing demography of European society and recent developments in genetic medicine, changes that are evident throughout much of the "western" world, the significance of this realisation will become ever more obvious.

Recommended Further Reading

Abberley, P. (1996) 'Work, Utopia and Impairment', in Barton, L. (ed.), *Disability and Society: Emerging Issues and Insights*. London: Longman.

Barnes, C. (1991) *Disabled People in Britain and Discrimination: A Case for Anti-discrimination Legislation*. London: Hurst and Co., in association with the British Council of Organizations of Disabled People.

Barnes, C. (2000) 'A Working Social Model? Disability, Work and Disability Politics in the 21st Century', *Critical Social Policy*, 20 (4): 441-457.

Barnes, H./Thornton, P./Maynard Campbell, S. (1998) *Disabled People and Employment*. Bristol: The Policy Press.

Bauman, Z. (1998) *Work, Consumerism and the New Poor*. Buckingham: Open University Press.

Beck, U. (2000) *The Brave New World of Work*. Cambridge: Polity Press.

Burchardt, T. (2000) *Enduring Economic Development: Disabled People, Income and Work*. York: The Joseph Rowntree Foundation.

Hyde, M. (1998) 'Sheltered and Supported Employment in the 1990s: The Experience of Disabled Workers in the UK', *Disability and Society*, 13 (2): 199-216.

Lunt, N./Thornton, P. (1997) *Employment Policies for Disabled People in Eighteen Countries: A Review*. York: University of York, Social Policy Research Unit.

Oliver, M. (1996) *Understanding Disability: From Theory to Practice*. London: Macmillan.

Roulstone, A. (1998) *Enabling Technology: Disabled People, Work and New Technology*. Milton Keynes: Open University Press.

Russell, M. (1998) *Beyond Ramps: Disability at the End of the Social Contract*. Monroe, Maine: Common Courage Press.

Stone, E. (ed.) (1999) *Disability and Development: Learning from Action and Research in the Majority World*. Leeds: The Disability Press.

WHO (2001) *Rethinking Care from Disabled People's Perspectives*. Geneva: World Health Organisation. (Also available on: www.leeds.ac.uk/disability-studies/archiveuk/index.)

(Other relevant literature can also be downloaded free for the Disability Archive UK on: www.leeds.ac.uk/disability-studies/archiveuk/index.)

Towards Mutual Responsibilities:
A Dutch Blueprint

Philip R. de Jong

The OECD study advocates "mutual obligations" as a critical element in the design of disability policy. This concept should guide the design of the relationship between disabled citizens and the state as well as between employers and disabled employees.

Both relationships have been the subject of recent changes in Dutch disability policy. These changes have reinforced the responsibility of both the state and employers to promote (re)-employment of disabled workers. Since 1996 employers bear a large financial responsibility when their employees fall ill. The effect was a 15% reduction in sickness absenteeism. Since 1998 premium rates for disability insurance differ according to the disability risk at the level of the individual firm. These employers' incentives were not matched by equally strong incentives for employees. In that sense "mutuality" was, until recently, absent.

Stressing the responsibilities of the disabled is a new concept in Dutch disability legislation, which used to be biased towards income security as opposed to job security. In April 2002 a new regime was introduced defining the actions to be taken by employers and employees during the first months of sickness. These actions aim at early intervention, and prevention of avoidable disability benefit dependency. The adequacy and sufficiency of the actions are tested by the Social Insurance Institute, when a disability claim is filed. If the actions are judged insufficient the claim will not be processed. Employees who refuse to cooperate with reasonable efforts of employers to help them back to work, can be fired.

This policy direction is underscored by proposals for a new disability insurance scheme put forward by a National Commission on Disability

Policy (named after its chairman the "Donner" commission). The proposed scheme puts even more emphasis on the mutual obligations of employers and employees with respect to each other.

These proposed and enacted changes are placed against the long-standing disability problem in the Netherlands, where 10% of the labour force is on disability benefits.

An employment-oriented disability policy, based on mutual obligations between the disabled, employers and the State, requires disability (benefit) and reintegration schemes that are consistent with that orientation. These schemes follow from a number of premises and principles, which I list first. Then I derive a set of programme characteristics, partly from the proposals of the Donner Commission. I conclude with some pros and cons of this blueprint. An asterisk (*) indicates which parts of this blueprint have already been enacted or for which a Bill has been drafted by the Dutch government.

Premises (based on a wide body of research)

1. For a given impairment the claim of being unable to engage in gainful activity is a matter of external (medical, cultural, institutional, economic) conditions that cannot be influenced by the impaired individual, and of his/her preferences.

2. External conditions affect the disability behaviour of the impaired and of those parties (employers, doctors, programme administrators) that determine the employability of impaired workers.

3. Public intervention may change external conditions and the behaviour of those involved in the process that leads from impairment to disability.

4. Most impairments start during working age, while in employment. Therefore, employers can play a central role in creating the appropriate conditions for continued employment.

5. Early intervention to contain absenteeism is key to prevention of long-term benefit dependency. Careful design of short-term sickness benefits, therefore, is at least as important as that of long-term disability benefits.

Principles

1. Public interventions should limit benefit dependency as much as is socially acceptable.
2. Public interventions should promote productive employment of workers with disabilities as much as possible.
3. Public interventions should reward employers who reduce non-employment of the disabled.
4. A clear distinction should be made between entitlement to disability benefit and to rehabilitation (to what the OECD denotes as "participation packages"). Complaints about low resumption rates among disability beneficiaries point to inconsistent design.
5. Clever combinations of rules and incentives should reach these goals.

Mutual Obligations between the State and the Disabled

Characteristics of an Employment-oriented Cash-benefit Scheme   **141**

1. Disability benefits are only available for those who pass a stringent work incapacity test. These benefits are an individual entitlement to indemnity of productivity loss. They are wage-related and not tested for other income sources.
2. The test should be so stringent that return to work options can be considered unrealistic. Beneficiaries, therefore, are exempt from mandatory rehabilitation but may apply for a "participation package".
3. Those who are denied a benefit may reapply if their health deteriorates.

Characteristics of an Employment-oriented Rehabilitation Programme

1. Impaired persons who do not pass this test are offered a "participation package" including a temporary rehabilitation benefit. Those who are without employment after lapse of the rehabilitation period, and those who are not interested in a package, are treated as regular unemployed and eventually end on means-tested welfare.
2. (*) Impaired persons, other than those who are denied a disability benefit, can apply for a participation package. Apart from in-kind provisions and services aimed at accommodation of workers and workplaces the package may supply a wage subsidy that compensates for productivity loss.

3. An independent body should process applications for a participation package. This "body" may be part of the social insurance agency but operates independently from it (to make an institutional distinction between the disability and the disability beneficiary status).

Mutual Obligations between Employers and Employees

Employers' Obligations

1. (*) The employer is mandated to continue payment of (70% of the) wage during sickness of an employee. This payment serves as a rehabilitation benefit.
2. (*) The employer is obliged to do everything necessary in terms of prevention and swift return to work.
3. (*) "Everything" includes contracting vocational health care, support, conflict mediation and job mediation if an employee cannot return to his/her current employer.
4. (*) If, two years after reporting sick, the employee is still without employment, the employer may end the employment contract, while the employee is entitled to unemployment insurance.
5. (*) Dismissal after two years of sickness is only legitimate if the social insurance agency judges the reintegration efforts of the employer as sufficient. If the efforts are judged insufficient the employer is obliged to continue wage payment.
6. Employers are obliged to call upon their sick employees to collaborate with reintegration plans.

Employees' Obligations

1. Providing information on the causes and severity of their limitations.
2. (*) Collaboration with action that promotes a timely return to one's job.
3. (*) Readiness to accept other, accommodated, work while recovering.
4. (*) Readiness to accept other work, if functional limitations prevent one from taking up one's old job.
5. (*) Readiness to accept other work in another firm, if the old firm cannot provide commensurate work.
6. Employees may not turn down jobs earning 70% or more of their previous wage.

142

7. Employees are obliged to call upon their employers to make present employment opportunities available.
8. Employees who refuse to collaborate with their employers' reintegration efforts can be fired.

Beneficial Effects

1. Employees with sufficient residual capacities are motivated, more strongly than before, to return to work because the disability benefit route is closed, and unemployment leads to means-tested welfare. They will put pressure on their employers to adapt workplaces or create commensurate work.
2. Employers who are financially responsible for paying sickness benefits get an instant return on investment in containment of absenteeism and swift reintegration of sick workers. They will put pressure on their employees to return to work as soon as possible.
3. Disability beneficiaries will not be bothered with reviews and rehabilitation demands.
4. Disability benefit expenditures decrease, as will contributions with beneficial effects for the labour market.
5. Aggregate employment will increase.

Adverse Effects

1. A stringent definition of disability that is both valid and reliable is difficult to implement and administer.
2. The design and administration of participation packages is even more complex.
3. A stringent definition of disability is likely to provoke social pressure for high benefits (the Dutch Social-Economic Council recommends replacing 75% of lost earnings) and for inclusion of excluded health problems. Such pressure may jeopardise its sustainability.
4. Assessment of insufficiency of employers' reintegration efforts is likely to be considered arbitrary and will be met with strong protest.
5. More than before, employers will screen new job applicants as well as their current manpower on health risks.
6. A more adversarial system induces increased litigation.
7. Aggregate unemployment will increase.

143

Should We Establish a System of "Mutual Obligations" for Persons with Disabilities?

Kenneth S. Apfel

This new OECD report (*Transforming Disability into Ability*) provides valuable new information on the urgent need for enhanced policies to promote work for persons with disabilities. Few will disagree with the central OECD policy conclusion that far too little is being done to reintegrate or keep disabled workers in the labour market and that efforts in particular fall short for older workers. The key question before us is not whether we need to expand efforts to promote work but how best to expand efforts, and in particular, what should be the responsibilities of government, employers, and persons with disabilities in this process.

The central OECD policy recommendation is to promote work through the establishment of a system of "mutual obligations" for both society and for persons with disabilities, somewhat analogous to systems that have already been established for persons receiving unemployment insurance or social assistance payments. While the report makes a compelling case in this area and while I have been a long-standing supporter of many efforts to strengthen "mutual obligations", I have serious reservations about establishing stronger sanctions mechanisms on individuals with disabilities. Until reintegration assistance has first been vastly strengthened and shown to produce solid and sustained results, a system of "mutual obligations" is – at best – premature for the United States.

Persons with disabilities in the United States still face enormous obstacles in their efforts to work. My deep fear is that a "mutual obligations" strategy that includes individual sanctions in practice would end up combining (1) modest government efforts to reduce barriers and/or encourage work, (2) nearly non-existent efforts to expand the responsibilities of employers, and (3) tough sanctions on persons with disabilities who too often cannot overcome the barriers and return to work. Such a strategy sets the stage for a set of unacceptable outcomes: a reduction in government income support for the disabled, a shift to more individual responsibility to meet work and income needs and a new paradigm that blames persons with disabilities for the absence of work.

A very recent piece of evidence increases my concerns in this area. Legislation was recently introduced in the US Senate (S.5) that could dramatically transform the US Supplemental Security Income programme, which is the primary social assistance programme for persons with disabilities. If this legislation is enacted, all individuals on the disability rolls may be required by States to participate in work, education or rehabilitation activities, and failure to comply can lead to total elimination of all government-provided income and health support. This punitive legislation, which incidentally includes no increases in support by government or by employers, significantly changes the paradigm by blaming persons with disabilities for the absence of work. It is my fervent hope that the current Administration will oppose legislation in this area.

US Experience With Welfare Reform

The US experience with welfare reform provides some useful lessons and gives us reasons to be both somewhat optimistic as well as very cautious about a system of "mutual obligations". What are our "mutual obligations" in the US in this area of social policy?

The US welfare system provides support primarily to poor single parents with children. In 1996, the US established very tough work requirements and sanctions for the vast majority of welfare beneficiaries, and the culture of welfare offices significantly changed to promote work rather than welfare. The majority of states (37) established "full family" sanctions, meaning that the entire cash assistance grant can be eliminated for failure to work. Caseloads dropped by half, food stamps participation by almost a third, and about 5% of families are receiving sanctions in any given month.

What about employers? The use of "employer obligations" in the US to assist former welfare beneficiaries is virtually non-existent. There are no requirements and only very modest incentives to provide jobs, and working poor families and people leaving welfare to work receive vastly less in terms of employer-provided health coverage, pension benefits, and other worker benefits than the general population. For example, three quarters of the working poor do not have access to employer-provided sick leave, compared to only 40% of workers with income above 200% of poverty. Large proportions of working poor families who leave welfare and government-provided health insurance do not receive employer-provided health insurance.

What about "government obligations" in this area? Government support for work support programmes has been vastly increased in recent years. Work supports amounted to only $6 billion per year in the late 1980s and now amounts to about $50 billion a year. Most of the significant increases predated the enactment of welfare reform. The key expansions are in the earned income tax credit, child care assistance and health insurance coverage for working families not on welfare. While major gaps still exist for many, many families, it is clear that US policy has taken substantial steps to try to "make work pay". If it was not for this dramatic increase in support that mostly predated welfare reform, I would have been very opposed to the imposition of the work requirements and individual sanctions in this area.

However, even with this significant increase in support, the case for tough sanctions is debatable. On the positive side, the move to a system of tough work requirements and sanctions as well as added government support for work has greatly increased work, and modestly reduced poverty (by about 10%) for single parent mothers. However, even with these new levels of work support, some very needy families have been hurt by the sanctions policies and work requirements. Studies show that a third to a half of welfare "leavers" found no work, and only a fifth to a half of sanctioned families found work. Many sanctioned families still face multiple barriers to work, including health difficulties. I should point out that these sanction policies cover many persons with some level of disabilities, since over 40% of TANF recipients report having some level of physical or mental impairment, a proportion almost three times the level of the general population.

A Similar System for Disability?

The OECD report concludes that a sanctions system makes sense within the context of a much stronger societal support system. What do these support systems look like now in the USA and what is the potential for change?

EMPLOYERS

The centerpiece of employer responsibilities in this area revolves around the Americans with Disabilities Act. The ADA, a very important civil rights law, has broadened access in a variety of ways and has served to change public perspectives of persons with disabilities. The remedies in the ADA banning discrimination and requiring reasonable accommodation in the workforce appear to have been somewhat effective for higher-skilled workers, particularly those connected to employers, but employers largely have avoided employment for lower-skilled persons with disabilities who make up the vast majority of federal disability beneficiaries. Currently, employers receive very modest tax incentives to help them comply with ADA barriers and a very modest tax credit to help subsidise the wages of individuals on disability insurance or persons referred from vocational rehabilitation agencies.

What would a system of mutual obligations mean for US employers? As is the case with welfare, I believe the answer would end up being "very little". Discrimination-based enforcement through mechanisms such as the ADA has yet to show major results, and a government system of numerical targets for hiring the disabled would have no chance of enactment in the US. Employers will continue to resist hiring disabled persons for a variety of reasons. While it is possible that a much stronger regime of tax incentives might help somewhat, I fear that pervasive discrimination against hiring the disabled will be hard to overcome. Moreover, without broad access to jobs, I question the moral basis for imposing a sanctions system on persons with disabilities.

GOVERNMENT

What about added government responsibilities in this area? Earlier in this conference, W. Roy Grizzard from the US Department of Labor discussed the progress being made in expanding the government's commitment to assist the disabled in returning to work. I applaud these efforts and will only take time to briefly review these initiatives at this point.

The major new reform in this area relates to bipartisan legislation enacted during the Clinton administration that is just now being phased in. This legislation provides "tickets" – an outcome-based voucher payment system – to employment networks to assist persons with disabilities to return to work. In addition, health insurance coverage for persons receiving social insurance payments and returning to work has been significantly expanded, and coverage for persons receiving social assistance payments and returning to work has been modestly expanded. Finally, US "one stop" work centres are starting to expand efforts to serve persons with disabilities.

These are all very important actions, but frankly, it will take years for these initiatives to be fully operational. And it may very well take added resources for those "tickets" to have a major impact, but more time is needed before a fair assessment can be made in this area. Even after full and successful implementation of these important initiatives, substantially more comprehensive steps are needed in at least four areas – creating a "culture" of work, establishing much more comprehensive assessment measures, developing major expansions in early intervention strategies, and vastly expanding efforts to "make work pay" for persons with disabilities. All need considerable increases in government commitments if we want a system that truly serves to transform disability into ability.

1)   Organisation Culture

The primary work of Social Security offices in the US is to determine eligibility for benefits. Up until 1996, eligibility determination was also the primary work of local welfare offices. In the case of welfare, the shift to work necessitated a shift of roles in the local welfare offices – in effect, the "culture" of local welfare offices had to change. As part of a comprehensive effort to shift more focus on work and reintegration for persons with disabilities, the culture of Social Security offices must also somewhat change. As a first step, substantial numbers of work incentive specialists are needed to work with persons with disabilities and with other public and private organisations to encourage integration activities. In addition, the culture of US "one-stop" work centres will need to evolve to become much more receptive to assisting persons with disabilities.

2)   Assessment

The OECD Report makes abundantly clear the difficulties in assessing what constitutes disability and work incapacity. In practice, we all know that it is exceedingly difficult to distinguish those who are able to work from those who are not. Virtually everyone in the disability field believes that more disability beneficiaries can and should work. While medical and technological advances give us a somewhat better understanding of how medical conditions affect the ability to work, we certainly do not yet possess the supreme knowledge to be able to know with any certainty who can or cannot work. Moreover, no consensus exists on the overall proportions of persons with disabilities who should or can work or be subject to sanctions. Much better assessment measures are clearly essential in this area.

We are quite a ways away from having these measures. And without much more comprehensive assessment measures, what moral basis would we have to establish a system of individual sanctions? Which persons, for example, with schizophrenia would we sanction, and who would be exempt? Which persons with substantial mobility impairments? Until we establish a much more comprehensive assessment system, I strongly question the moral basis for imposing a sanctions system on persons with disabilities.

3)   Early Intervention

The OECD Report also makes abundantly clear the importance of expanding early intervention initiatives, even before people become eligible for disability benefits. Early intervention efforts are clearly needed and these initiatives should supplement and not replace income assistance. This will require new government resources, but it is well worth the outlay of resources. And as we move forward with efforts to strengthen the government role in early intervention and reintegration, I recommend that extra efforts be targeted towards two groups – older teenagers and older workers. Both are at very high risk of a lifetime of income assistance if targeted efforts are not instituted.

There are currently 1 million children on the disability rolls in the USA. To oversimplify, the current "assessment" process conducts a re-determination of eligibility when the beneficiary turns 18; benefits at this point are either continued or curtailed. Much more is clearly needed. As youths move from childhood to early adulthood, their expectations are being formed of themselves and their future links to the labour market. Unless we invest heavily in integration activities at this stage, those expectations will likely solidify around a lifetime of income assistance and little or no work. We let these young people down if we do not dramatically increase government responsibilities in this area.

The second group is made up of older disabled workers. I believe we let these individuals down in two ways. First, many older persons who are presently not on the disability rolls should be receiving disability benefits. About 10% of early retirees would likely qualify for larger disability benefits if they applied, and many more individuals with major disabilities are screened out because they either do not meet current rigid disability eligibility guidelines or have no recent work experience. In addition, the two-year waiting period for health insurance coverage after receipt of disability payments creates real hardship on older persons. We need policies to help more of these individuals receive income support and immediate health insurance coverage.

A second issue relates to persons who are applying for disability assistance or are already on the rolls but receive no real assistance to return to work. As the OECD Report makes painfully clear, there is a striking age bias in integration programmes. We need to significantly step up assistance in this area or the vast majority of these individuals who apply for disability assistance will never work again.

4)   Make Work Pay

It makes little economic sense for a person on the disability rolls to leave the rolls to take a job at low wages, and it makes no sense to leave the rolls to return to work if such a step means losing health insurance. We need much more comprehensive policies to "make work pay" for persons with disabilities. While we have made some progress in "making work pay" for welfare families, only smaller steps have been instituted for disabled beneficiaries, particularly older individuals. The current work incentive scheme is cumbersome and very hard for beneficiaries to understand. We need reform in this area. And we need substantially greater efforts to increase support for work through a combination of partial benefits when coupled with some work, the establishment of a sizeable disabled workers tax credit similar to the earned income tax credit and continued expansion of health insurance coverage for persons who return to work. Unless we truly make work pay, a sanctions system merely ends up penalising persons who have disabilities.

Role of US Disability Insurance in Income Support

One final reason for caution in the area of individual sanctions relates to the growing importance of the US disability system – and the diminishing role of a variety of other assistance programmes – in providing income support for the working age population, particularly workers with less education and lower skills.

The US unemployment insurance system, which provides only short-term (6-9 months) assistance, provides benefits to a dwindling share of unemployed workers. During the 1990s, only a third of unemployed workers actually received unemployment benefits, down about 20% from the levels in the 1960s and early 1970s. Currently, only one third of less-skilled men and only 15% of less-skilled women separated from their jobs qualify for unemployment assistance. In addition, the proportion of families eligible for traditional US cash welfare assistance and food stamps has declined by a third to a half in recent years. Lastly, the United States has no general relief programme as a fallback for most of the poor.

Disability beneficiaries face numerous obstacles to securing jobs – obstacles above and beyond their disabling conditions. Indeed, about two thirds of disability beneficiaries have no more than a high school degree and will find diminishing opportunities in the US labour market.

Unlike most of the European income support systems, the US disability benefit system is often the only potential source of support for individuals with major impairments, and this is especially true for older workers and for persons with lower skills. We need to be very careful before we impose benefit reductions on persons reliant on the disability programmes.

Conclusion

Some day, a system of strong individual sanctions may make sense for the United States, but not today, and not for some time into the future. First, let us take down more of the barriers and encourage work so that persons with disabilities can take full advantage of a tightening labour market in the years ahead. And let us create some real incentives to make work pay for persons with disabilities. And let us create real job opportunities by at least reducing the barriers for employers to hire persons with disabilities. And let us see some real success for our efforts. We should not even consider establishing a framework of "mutual obligations" through a system of individual sanctions for persons with disabilities until we have truly enhanced government and employer responsibilities in this area. Without the establishment of much stronger societal systems, we would be establishing a new paradigm – one that blames persons with disabilities for the absence of work. That would be very, very wrong for society and for persons with disabilities.

"Escape into Disability": The Polish Transformation Country Experience

Stanislawa Golinowska

1) The serious problem of the state social policy pertaining to disability and the reaction of society in this respect in the transformation countries is a phenomenon of the so-called "escape to disability" that can be especially observed in difficult life situations and intensification of social changes. Analysed from the time perspective, the problem in question has two different causes. The first cause is the heritage of the past and the second one is the transformation of the labour market during the transition period.

153

The post-communist countries are still bearing the consequences of the socio-economic policy of the previous system. The policy of full employment or even "compulsory labour" or perhaps, stating it more delicately, compulsion to a determined kind of labour often resulted in a reverse reaction – looking for the possibility of avoiding this pressure, at the same time assuring oneself another source of income, different from regular work salary. Such a possibility has been created by the system of disability pensions. Escape into disability instead of undertaking a job or remaining in the labour market is a typically Polish phenomenon, which has lasted for over a quarter of a century (1970s, 1980s and half of the 1990s).

Which elements of the socio-economic system contributed to this situation?

- A low and poorly differentiated remuneration system, limiting the motivation to work.
- The control of labour relations by political authorities.
- Limited possibilities of changing the career path in case of life problems.

- Underdevelopment of educational care and nursing institutions (for children and the elderly) motivating women to take advantage of disability pensions faced with the necessity to provide nursing and educational care to the family.

Which elements of the social security system contributed to the easy access to disability pensions?

- Liberal medical certification (medical assessment) of a disability level, using only a medical definition of disability – health impairment (instead of inability to work) together with the lack of disability standards and any accountability (medical, financial, social) of a commission (collective body) responsible for the medical certification of the effects of the decisions taken.
- A similar level of disability pension in comparison to work remunerations and the old-age pension.
- An insufficient system of control and verification of the state of ability of people who receive a disability pension.

On the other hand, the pressure on the system of disability pensions during the transformation period was mainly due to a bad labour market situation:

- The outbreak of transition unemployment, related to the introduction of market economy and the changes in the economic system, in conjunction with the changes of trends and principles in international collaboration and the modernisation of industry (decline of old industries and dynamic increase of labour productivity in branches using modern technologies).
- Underdevelopment of educational and adaptation programmes allowing for the change of professions or additional training.
- Barriers to mobility, allowing for a change of workplace such as: underdevelopment of contractors, housing market, transport and communication infrastructure.

At the same time the social insurance system was still in place offering disability pensions and allowing for easy access to the system (a reform of the pension system was carried out in 1996). Which elements of the disability pension system contributed to the pressure of entering the system during the transformation period?

- The introduction of automatic indexing of long-term social benefits (under high inflation conditions) with a sharp decrease in the level of remunerations.

- Separating the social security institution for farmers under the supervision of the Ministry of Agriculture from the internal disability certification system, allowing for easing a difficult social situation in the country by the system of disability pensions.
- Lack of control of the farmwork safety system resulting in a high accident rate in the agricultural sector.
- No reform of the social insurance system, in which disability pensions played the role of early old-age pensions, allowing older workers to pass the change of the system and the introduction of market economy in a less shocking way.

2) Under conditions of introducing market mechanisms, promotion of competition and effectiveness and the existence of a large-scale unemployment rate, work for the disabled as an alternative solution to pension benefit is not sufficiently understood in the transition countries. The disabled are not able to find work in the open market, despite the introduction of motivation instruments for employers. On the other hand the development of sheltered workplaces is very expensive and requires reimbursement from public funds. It results in an approach that is limited only to income support.

155

3) Although disability pension benefits are more attractive than unemployment or pre-old-age pension benefits they loose in relation to wages due to the changes in the indexing rules introduced in the second half of the 1990s (price indexing instead of wage indexing). Such a situation is conducive to undertaking work in the so-called grey sphere by some pensioners which does not result in the decrease of the benefit due to undertaking a job. The employer is also interested in employing a pensioner because he/she does not need social insurance and agrees to be unofficially employed. In view of this fact a number of pensioners is de facto *employed* and the phenomenon is socially tolerated.

4) Social policy with respect to the disabled has elements of a policy with problems to leave the "magic circle" of difficulties. Its next steps will include:
- Limiting easy access to the system of disability pensions by changes in the medical certification system (one-person certification instead of a commission, change of the definition – giving up the medical definition and introducing the definition which reflects the fact of ability/ disability to work).

- Introducing a system of pre-pension prevention (compulsory medical rehabilitation, occupational rehabilitation together with granting the training before the decision on a disability pension).
- Developing different forms of activities for the disabled, which support the professional and social rehabilitation process, and especially so-called sheltered workshops and rehabilitation groups.
- Analysing the effectiveness of the current employment solutions for the disabled on the open labour market and looking for possibilities of increasing this kind of employment.
- Introducing changes in the employment system of the disabled in the "sheltered" institutions by supporting different forms of such employment (legislature on social employment is being developed in Poland).

5) The introduction of social policy changes pertaining to disability is carried out on the basis of a dialogue with organisations of the disabled having the following characteristics:

- Putting high priority on securing income for the disabled that are outside of the social insurance system (persons born disabled, disabled from childhood and early adolescence) and subsidising their families in the system of social assistance.
- Avoiding the problem of employing disabled people because of a great number of problems connected with the restructuring of the economy and strong social pressure on job creation in general and even more for the young than for any other "special" participants at the labour market (if prioritising).
- Strong defense of protected (sheltered) workplaces by the lobby of the disabled organisations even if only monitoring of the functioning of such firms is involved for better transparency connected with the flow of public funds.

6) The subject of mutual obligations of society and the disabled has a lot of aspects. One of them is the scale of the redistribution of income for the social benefits for the disabled, another one is the relationship between benefits in cash and services and subsidies for education and institutions to facilitate the employment of the disabled (the policy of active and passive support analogically, as it is the case in supporting the unemployed).

- The opinion polls in Poland show the social acceptance for the redistribution of income in favour of the benefits for the disabled under the condition that the access to the pension system be limited.
- The change of social policy with respect to employing the disabled in the direction of differentiated and individually tailored programmes of social inclusion requires some promotional and educational work. That is why not only bigger public sources are needed but also openness on the part of the disabled to the changes. Since a strong attachment to the existent solutions may be observed.

Annex

Figure 1:   Beneficiaries of All Schemes of Social Security for Disabled Persons

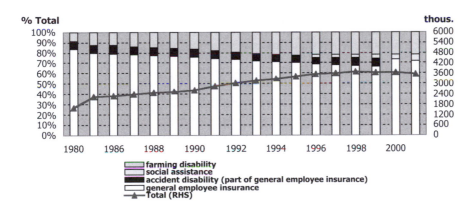

Figure 2:   New Beneficiaries in the Employee and Farmers' Disability System

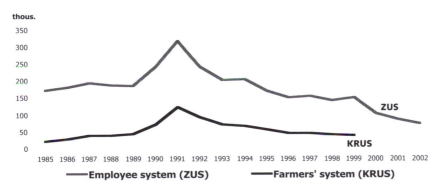

Figure 3:   Expenditures for Total Disability Transfers

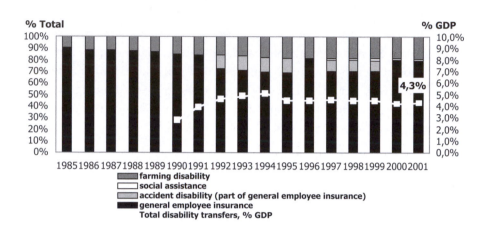

% Total   **% GDP**

farming disability
social assistance
accident disability (part of general employee insurance)
general employee insurance
Total disability transfers, % GDP

What Rights and Responsibilities for Society and for Persons with Disabilities?
Session Report

Chiara Saraceno

1   The OECD Study

Policy matters, concludes the OECD report. So much so that it may be difficult to dis-entangle the impact of policies on the behaviour of people with disabilities, as well as of enterprises and other relevant social actors, from the impact of policies on the definition itself of what makes a disability a disability – at the subjective as well as social level. This is a well-known problem in comparative evaluation exercises of social policies, particularly in the case of categorical policies, which have a strong defining power, but which precisely differ, across countries, in how they define their targets, what kind of thresholds, or criteria, they use, as well as how they combine with other items in the policy package.[1] As social assistance regimes do with poverty, disability policies not only provide different resource packages, but define and assess differently disabilities and the disabled in various contexts and for various purposes. They also strike different balances within the overall social security and social assistance package (see also Mabbett's comments, and the EU study she refers to). This implies that the boundaries between people "with" and "without disabilities" not only may be set differently in the various countries, but may also shift over time within a given context. Thus, for instance in Italy until the 1984 reform the social security invalidity indemnity was de facto used as a surrogate of the unemployment indemnity, given the risible amount of the latter, as well as of the minimum social security pension for those who did not reach the minimum

contributory record.[2] Disability definitions included not only an "objective",
but a contextual, socio-economic, assessment both of "inability to work" and
of "diminished earning capacity". Consequently, the number of people receiving this kind of benefit increased, until the mid-1980s, with a high con-
centration in the South given the high unemployment rates in those regions.
The 1984 reform, aiming at reducing social security expenditure in this field,
as well as at checking a clientelistic use of the measure, excluded, much in
line with the proposal in the OECD report and counter to then contempo-
rary developments in other European countries, any context-specific evaluation of inability to work. Only "objective", medically certified total or partial inability to work was accepted as a disability for social security purposes.
But nothing was changed in the level and rules of the unemployment indemnity nor in those of old-age social security pension. Nor there existed
(and still does not exist) in Italy a minimum income provision for the poor.
Thus the need of some kind of income support for the unemployed remained.
Following this reform the number of beneficiaries of this benefit diminished
drastically. But the number of social assistance, means-tested invalidity
benefits increased, although to a lesser degree. And the overall expenditure
on disability-linked benefits (including accompanying indemnities) increased.[3] There has been a partial reshuffling of people between categories
without a clear effect neither on labour market participation nor on social
expenditure. Some commentators, including Deborah Mabbett, suggest that
this reshuffling may occur also with older workers. While early retirement
has been in some countries a way of easing the exit from the labour force of
mature workers rendered redundant and/or obsolete by changes in the labour market and in technologies, pension reforms which have reduced that
option and raised the pension age may have consequences for the demand
of disability pensions. These may be contrary to the envisaged goal of raising the labour market participation rate of older workers, in so far the context that renders them more easily redundant and "expendable" does not
change. However strongly one might advocate for "more objective" definitions of disability, they are always likely to be dependent on context- and
time-specific definitions of social policy goals and issues, which in turn shape
behaviour and expectations by all relevant actors as well as outcomes.

All this makes it difficult to develop comparative analyses of outcomes,
in so far we are comparing not only different policies in different contexts,
but also to some degree different, and shifting, populations. Analogously
to what happens with the poor in social assistance policies and regimes, dis-

ability policies not only offer national, and sometimes even sub-national specific packages, which in turn offer nationally-specific options and life course options. They also select their own public – transform individual characteristics in socially acknowledged characteristics – on the basis of often quite different criteria; thus they construct national specific groups of "people with disabilities". This specificity, which may also be articulated sub-nationally, owes as much to the design of the policies themselves as to the economic and social characteristics of a given context. It also has consequences for the outcome of the policies themselves.

The value of the OECD report lies as much in its providing the first comprehensive overview of data on policies as well as on recipients and forms of recipiency as in allowing, because of this, to understand that outcomes – in terms of employment rates in this case – are the somewhat fuzzy result of a complex interplay between policies, context, and disability itself, whatever the definition of the latter may be. The awareness of this complex interplay, thus of the inability to draw quick conclusions from comparative data on outcomes is clearly spelled out on pp. 130-131 of the report, where the authors draw conclusions from their analysis of employment outcomes in countries which cluster differently across the integration/compensation axes (see chart 6.1 and 6.2). They write in fact: "there is no aggregate correlation between policy and overall employment outcome... It would be wrong, though, to conclude that employment measures are ineffective or even irrelevant. The lack of any correlation with employment outcomes may be caused partly by the countries' compensation policies, which tend to be strong in countries with a strong integration policy, and often relatively weak in countries with a less developed integration policy. As strong as the integration focus may be, a generous and accessible benefit scheme ... may mask any employment effect. Similarly, high employment rates among disabled people can also be an indication that disabled people must work in order to have a decent standard of living".

From an analytical and research point of view I would argue that this is the major, if possibly not intended, contribution of the OECD report – which goes well beyond any specific criticisms concerning the total precision and full comprehensiveness of data for a given country (I am sure each country can find fault with some of the data, no less because often country informants themselves do not have the full view of what is available in their own country, and much depends on communication between departments and ministries). Maybe its authors will not appreciate where I put the major value of the report. But I truly believe that we need careful studies like this, based on an impressive array of quantitative data and a careful analysis of institutional and administrative features of the various policies. It is an essential starting point for future, more detailed, if less extensive, studies of what exists, how, for whom, as well as what works where, how and for whom. It is also a useful instrument for each national government to develop a more systematic overview and monitoring of their policies in the field, which often grow up – and shift – in an incremental and fragmentary way.

A second major contribution of the report concerns its symbolic, cultural impact on the policy debate. The report, and its proposals, in fact, shift the focus of the policy debate on the enabling needs and on the capabilities of the disabled, rather than on the disabled's lack, or impairment, of employment capabilities. The fact that people with disabilities may be capable of employment and often want to be enabled to obtain employment is of course no news for those people themselves. But it is important that an institution such as the OECD makes the point, with all the risks and possible ambivalent interpretations and outcomes which have been pointed out in the debate which followed the presentation of the report, including the debate at the Vienna conference itself.

From this point of view, I believe that the report's policy conclusions and recommendations should be taken not as specific indications of what should be done and how. Too many mechanisms and processes are still far from being understood and too many issues remain controversial, starting from that of what is a disability and what are the means to assess it, as it is amply demonstrated also by the Vienna conference papers and debate. Rather it should be understood and used as a provocative means to develop consciousness and debates among the relevant institutional actors, particularly governments, enterprises and trade unions, as well as within the diverse and sometimes fragmented constituency of the associations of people with disabilities and of families with persons with disabilities.

Having said this, I have both agreements and disagreements with some of the report's policy recommendations, and even more with the language they are framed in, and the images they suggest. Synthetically:

First, the report suggests the need to unbundle the disability status from disability benefit recipiency. I fully agree if this means that it should be unbundled from any a priori equation with "inability to work", thus with exclusion from work participation. But disability benefits, as the report it-

162

self acknowledges, are not limited to income (wage) replacement. They involve the acknowledgement of extra costs of care, transportation, needed machines and so forth – not only for developing one's own capabilities to work for pay, but for living and being able to fully develop one's own capabilities and to socially participate. Thus some kind of – tailored – basic income is needed in many, if not all, instances irrespective of the employment status. Amartya Sen's and Martha Nussbaum's insights might be highly useful in this perspective. Further, also within the income replacement role of disability benefits there is possibly a continuum, rather than a rigid boundary, between income support because of the inability to work, income support because one's own disability renders it more difficult to find or keep a job and income support as an integration of low earnings due either to limitations in hours or to low pay. In other words, the advocated unbundling should bring about a different packaging of income support measures (and services), rather than construct either/or categories and systems.

This does not solve the problem of the grounds for assessing disability, as Mabbett points out in her comments. I do not wish to add to the ample debate on this. I simply point out that the "social model" of disability advocated at pp. 160-161 of the report actually sounds very little "social" to me, in so far it is premised on the one hand on strict, if adjourned ("new diseases") medical assessment, which constitutes the crucial first step, on the other hand (second step) on the person's ability to work on the basis of the ascertained medical condition. In other words, the social seems restricted to the ability of the disabled person to participate in paid work, not also on the existence of labour market, work and environmental conditions which can accommodate that particular person, with his/her specific disability and skills (or ability to acquire them). Thus, although the disability status acknowledged in the first step may not hinder a priori the willingness to risk working, the socially structured inability to find a job for persons with disabilities which in turn is socially structured and not only medically acknowledgeable would remain invisible and without support.

Secondly, however desirable might appear the development of more transparent and more universalistic criteria to define disability in order to offer adequate support, while avoiding abuse, the solution offered by the report remains unsatisfactory. One might also add that possibly the redefinition of disability should not be the starting point of the process of redefining policies, in so far, as I pointed out above, they are so heavily dependent, for good as well as for bad reasons, on the way social policy issues are framed and social security and support packages are designed. A stricter definition without a rebalancing of the overall social security and support package and in a labour market which increasingly marginalises those who – for various reasons – are not fully fit and available otherwise risks worsening, rather than improving the situation for the disabled. For instance, stricter rules and more frequent recourse to re-testing in Italy periodically end with a cancellation from the disability benefit rolls not only of people who have clearly abused the system with the help of the medical profession, but also of people at the boundary, and whose disability might have become over the years more "social" than "biological" or "psychological" and who are left without resources because their age and lack of skills render them virtually unemployable in a country which still lacks a last resort minimum income guarantee.

Thirdly, however much I appreciate the focus on the right of people with disabilities to work for pay as much as they can and wish, and although I understand that the OECD report is focused on the constraints to employment imposed by many existing policies (and even more by the way work is organised and by employers' attitudes), I feel that it somewhat overdoes it. Social participation and social integration seem to be restricted only to employment participation – leaving those who cannot work either because of the severity of their disability or because of the constraints of the labour market symbolically outside any means of inclusion, as passive recipients of collective solidarity. This risk is clearly apparent in some of the wording of this report: the concept of mutual obligations (where the disabled person's obligation lies in his/her being available to work), the concept itself of participation, as spelled out in one of the otherwise most relevant and interesting policy proposals: "Each disabled person should be entitled to a 'participation package' adapted to individual needs and capacities. The package should contain rehabilitation and vocational training, work elements from a wide range of forms of employment (regular, part time, subsidised, sheltered employment) and cash or in kind benefits. It should also contain activities that are not strictly considered as work but contribute to the social integration of the disabled person" (p. 161). The latter might be said for everybody, not only for the disabled. Even non-disabled persons should not have only paid work as the means of social integration (actually, for some an exclusive focus on work, or a bad job, might hinder social integration, or produce what Paugam has called "de-qualified integration").[4] My point however is that in some cases, or for some phases of life (it is already true for old age, school age, maternity and parental leave and so forth) these activities might be and should be conceived of as fully socially integrative.

Finally, the report rightly points to the need to provide early intervention. Yet, since the focus is mainly on employment, on people who become disabled while being employed and on policies which encourage or discourage employment, almost no attention is given (and certainly no data are to be found in the report) to preventive policies such as those linked to the way schools and training agencies integrate (or exclude) children and youth with disabilities – either because they are born with some disability or because they develop it later. Across the OECD countries policies vary quite a bit concerning whether, on what conditions, with what kind of support, up to which age, children and disabled students are integrated in normal classrooms and curricula or are instead grouped in special classrooms or schools, and on which basis. The issue is controversial, both within associations of the disabled and among experts of various kinds. Yet, one might wonder why in assessing integration policies this kind of policies have not been included and whether their inclusion would have not only changed the clustering of countries, but offered some further insight in their working and outcomes. In any case, one might hypothesise that the way children and young people are integrated as students is a crucial factor not only for their individual development, but also for the overall development of a social attitude which views people with different abilities as a normal, integral part of society, whom therefore have a right to be acknowledged and integrated according to their needs as well as to their capabilities, for what they demand, as well as for what they have to give. No meaningful sense of mutual responsibilities may develop without this.

2   The Panel Theme

The panel's theme to some degree cross-cuts all the others, in so far it deals with (a) the controversial issue of who are the disabled and what makes them disabled; (b) with the full range of actors involved in "societal responsibility": government and political institutions, communities, enterprises, trade unions, self-help organisations, third-sector organisations, down to the individual citizen as a co-worker, a co-student, a teacher, a tax payer, a communication professional and so forth; (c) with the highly controversial concept of mutual obligations. This concept is increasingly popular in social policy debates. It has two different and to some degree divergent roots: a communitarian one, with its stress on the moral obligations deriving from membership; a contractual one, where individuals and society are positioned as equal partners in an exchange relationship. To point to the disabled as capable of responsibilities and obligations may appear as a means to acknowledge their full capability as human beings and as citizens, both from a communitarian and from a contractual point of view. Yet, it implies a symmetry between parties – the disabled, who are specific and concrete individuals, and "society", which is a highly articulated, often fragmented and conflicting body of institutional and individual actors – who are far from being on an equal footing. This of course is true for every individual citizen *vis-à-vis* society. It is more crucially so for the disabled, in so far disability itself is, to some degree at least, a social construct. Thus, in the mutual responsibilities/obligations nexus the disabled seem to be expected to negotiate the meaning and the conditions of a status which to a large degree depends on societal organisation and perception (or discrimination) itself. This is a well-known paradox for all "socially disabled" groups – women, racially or ethnically discriminated groups, the poor. When a physical or psychical impairment is involved, this paradox may appear even more strident.

3   The Panel Presentations and Debate

Within a general appreciation of the OECD report's focus on the need to develop more pro-active and employment-friendly policies addressing the disabled, the presentations and the debate have dealt with three main subthemes:

- The issue whether one should start from the supply or demand side or from both simultaneously in dealing with the problem of active and activation policies.

No intervention supported the idea that we should move from the supply side, although the risk that this might be the unintended outcome of the new discourse on responsibilities and obligations underlined some of the presentations and of the debate. I also have the feeling that, unavoidably, each intervention was either explicitly or implicitly rooted in the reference to specific national policy and cultural contexts. Thus concerns might differ not because of theoretical differences but because of differences in the reference contexts. Which again is an aspect to be kept in mind when proposing policy reforms: they will be received by quite diverse policy and cultural contexts and possibly put to use for different purposes.

Colin Barnes and Kenneth Apfel in their presentations made the case for the priority of the demand side. The former stressed the need to move from an individualistic and piecemeal approach to a holistic, integrated approach that calls for action on the part of the various societal actors first. The latter, in his empirically-based thoughtful reflection on the US situation, argued that mutual responsibilities may be expected, and even more so enforced, only after society, that is enterprises, local communities, local and national governments, have developed a sustained and substantial effort in providing adequate options and resources. In other words, both Apfel and Barnes, as some of the plenary debate, have raised the issue of the conditions which are necessary for developing mutual obligations, thus of the different timing in the actions which should be expected from the various actors, and particularly from the disabled people with respect to all other actors. In this view the responsibility lies first and foremost on the demand side and more generally on the societal actors, including governments. And this part of the OECD policy recommendations should be stressed first and foremost, before any change in policy.

Peter Scherer's contribution, based on the OECD policy recommendations, argued for a "both together approach". Although all his positive examples, as in the report, seem to deal with actions taken on the demand and social conditions side, rather than on changes in attitudes in the supply side. Thus, the "best practice" example of the Scandinavian countries has to do both with general high employment rates in those countries, together with a widely shared concept of citizenship based on work, which is supported and integrated by generous and universal income support measures.

Also De Jong stated explicitly that one cannot speak of low resumption rates, thus of welfare dependency firstly from the supply side. The problem lies first and foremost in the inconsistent design of policies as well as in the attitudes of employers, which explain the low work resumption rates by workers who have become disabled. He and Golinowska discussed in this perspective the reforms taking place respectively in Poland and the Netherlands. The Dutch case, if the reform at present under discussion will be fully implemented, in particular appears a test case for the OECD recommendations. De Jong's discussion of beneficial and adverse effects – for the disabled, the public budget, the administrative process, the employers – should serve as a checklist for monitoring all policy shifts of this kind.

Both Golinowska's and de Jong's presentation dealt with policies that address people who become disabled while in work which to some degree is in tune with the OECD proposals. De Jong supported this choice of focus by pointing to the fact that most impairments start during one's working life – a fact which stresses the importance of the role of employers which should create the conditions for continuing employment, as well as the role of early intervention as a key factor in preventing long-term dependency and the need to distinguish between entitlement to disability benefits and to rehabilitation (the rehabilitation package). According to de Jong's view, a consistent design for an employment-oriented policy should include the two features proposed in the Dutch reform: a disability benefit granted only to those who pass a stringent disability test, based on the full inability to work (although de Jong acknowledges all the difficulties in finding a clear-cut definition), and a rehabilitation/participation package (that includes a ben-efit) which may be applied for also by those who do not pass that test and has a time limit. It is not clear if this system envisages some additional income support linked to the additional costs incurred by those who suffer given impairments, irrespective of their working status. After the time limit (two years) has expired, and the beneficiaries are still out of work, they are treated as unemployed and may receive income support subjected to means-testing, as with everybody else (this is already happening in the Nether-lands). At the same time employers must pay sickness benefit and may dis-miss the disabled employee after two years and stop all payments only if they can demonstrate that they have made all the needed efforts to re-ha-bilitate and accommodate him/her. Thus great pressure is put on them to cooperate in rehabilitation in order to avoid long-lasting costs. Yet, analo-gously to what apparently happens with ADA (the anti-discriminatory law) in the US as pointed out by Apfel, this may incentive them to closer scrutiny of prospective employers in order to screen out those who are more likely to become disabled. Another problem which de Jong pointed out as an emerging issue is the degree to which disabled employees are expected to disclose their own health circumstances to employers: the need of the latter to be informed in order to plan their activities infringes on the rights of pri-vacy of the former.

Both Apfel and at least one of the interventions from the floor (specifi-cally from the UK experience) indicated, among the conditions necessary on the societal side, a more integrated and collaborative work by social assistance offices, employment offices and the medical profession. And involving the latter is one of the most difficult endeavours.

Little was said of obligations towards people who become disabled while out of work (e.g. as children, or as homemakers) with regard not only to benefits, but activation policies. A concern which is present in the OECD policy recommendations and in Scherer's and Apfel's presentation, although it is not fully dealt with in neither. Actually, in the policy recommendations offered as a guideline for this panel they have disappeared, in so far they only speak of "re-integration" into the labour market. Obligations towards those who are disabled outside the labour market, particularly children and the young, but also many women, of course must involve support in developing all their abilities, including the ability to work for pay. But this is conceptually and even practically different from "rehabilitation" of people who were formerly fit for work. In the case of children and the young, particularly, it involves a broader focus on education and training from the start, on considering them full citizens from the start, supporting them and their families in all phases of growing up. Early intervention is a very ambitious goal that may not be reduced simply to some job training.

- The degree of similarity of activation policies for the disabled with other activation policies, namely those for the poor or the unemployed.

This theme has been explicitly focused on by Apfel and Scherer, and in some of the debate. Scherer has explicitly linked the OECD proposal to the job strategy developed by the OECD in 1996 and more generally to the activation policies that have become popular throughout the OECD countries – in discourse, if not always in practice. Notwithstanding a critical view of many of these policies, Scherer seems to share a generally positive view of these policies, particularly if they are integrated in a social policy package where income support is provided with no time limit on receipt, even if not unconditionally with regard to the availability to work – as in most Central and North-Western European countries.

From his US observatory Apfel is less optimistic on the possibility, and opportunity to simply transpose the welfare to work reform for those receiving social assistance to those receiving disability benefits. His argument is twofold: first, in the case of the poor, the enforcement of work requirement has been prepared and accompanied by an increase in government obligations. Although direct income support for the poor has been reduced, financial support for work support programmes has vastly increased. This has not yet occurred in a comparable way in the case of the disabled. At the same time, both in the case of the poor and in the case of the disabled, employers have very little obligations. Actually the case of the US, which have a very important civil rights law banning discrimination of the disabled, indicates how legislation is not enough. As it was said in the conference, in the US the law is useful for those who become disabled while in work, but helps little those who want to enter work, particularly if they are low-skilled. Second, although the welfare reform has been modestly successful in reducing poverty (although it has substantially increased the work participation rate of those who were formerly assisted), this success is too modest, and it is accompanied by a worsening of overall conditions (e.g. in access to health care) for many. Thus, before encouraging and even enforcing the disabled person's obligations to work, more secure outcomes in terms both of income and of overall social security should be developed.

Possibly because of a resistance to easily transpose the two kinds of policies (and social groups), one of the issues raised by the OECD policy conclusions in this context has not been addressed, namely that of the opportunity to maintain the household means test in the means-tested disability schemes in a mutual obligation approach. Although in my opinion if this approach were to be implemented, together with the unbundling of income support because of the added costs from that because of – total or partial – inability to work, all means-tested disability schemes should be revised.

What rehabilitation is about, was touched only in a very marginal way. Both "disability" and "rehabilitation" were treated in a very generic way, as if skills (but also social class and education) did not matter for outcomes, both of disability and of rehabilitation.

- The twofold issue of sanctions vs. incentives: legitimacy, and target actors.

Implicit in the concept of obligations is that of sanctions. Without sanctions there are no socially and legally enforceable obligations. Actually, in the Dutch case presented by de Jong sanctions are quite clearly spelled out in regulations. This has been a highly-charged theme throughout the conference. Even if the OECD representatives have been careful not to speak of sanctions (but less careful in the report and in the policy proposals), the theme kept creeping up indicating that this is not only a highly-charged and controversial issue, but that there is a shared fear that sanctions (against the disabled) are likely to be taken up by governments and employers more readily than obligations (of governments and employers). There was a shared consensus that no discourse on sanctions for the disabled should be even initiated until the balance of constraints and resources, as well as of obligations, has changed. Barnes in his general approach and Apfel in his more detailed analysis of pitfalls and constraints from the point of view of US experience made it the centrepiece of their counter-arguments. I share particularly Apfel's conclusion that without the prior establishment of a much stronger and viable social responsibility system we would "be establishing a new paradigm: one that blames people with disabilities for the absence of work". It has already occurred for the poor.

Somebody from the floor also raised the issue of distinguishing, when speaking of possible sanctions, between people temporarily disabled and the long-term disabled, as well as between those who become disabled during their working life and those who are born such, or become such in their youth, before entering the labour market. And the relative incidence of the different age groups and populations may differ widely from one country to the next, for historical reasons as well as for reasons linked to how they are defined in policies, as it was mentioned several times in the discussion.

Interestingly, the issue of sanctions in the presentations and in the debate seems to concern only two actors: first of all the disabled themselves, if they do not comply with the rehabilitation and work requirements; second, and to a much lesser degree (and with less probability to be efficacious and enforceable), the employers. Governments and other actors appear more outside the reach of sanctions, although they are perceived as having obligations. They must provide resources and produce change. But they are not subject to sanctions if they do not comply. Which makes for an unbalanced partnership in this mutual obligation affair. Unless one interprets the obligation to pay a cash transfer to the disabled person for whom work has not be made available as sanction for society, as the OECD policy conclusions suggest. Which seems at least stretching too much the concept of sanction. Moreover, many governments as well as employers might prefer to pay this kind of sanctions rather than supporting the costs of making the overall physical and social environment more friendly for the disabled. And it is not at all demonstrated that in financial terms it will cost less to support pro-active and pro-employment attitudes. Actually Galinowska suggested that occupational rehabilitation and re-integration is very costly, and not always very efficient.

In any case, less developed than the argument against sanctions, that of incentives – for the disabled as well as for the employers – to produce a more employment-friendly approach has emerged. In the case of the disabled it emerged, particularly in Galinowska's and Apfel's interventions, in the form of incentivising choice through the offer of education, services and support and/or through making "work pay" mechanisms analogous, but not necessarily identical to those in place for the poor; in the case of employers it has emerged (e.g. in de Jong's contribution, and partly Apfel's) in terms of what is needed to make it more attractive, or less costly for employers to hire disabled people, instead of screening them, as it appears to be one of the possible unintended consequences of well-intended legislation. In my opinion, this issue has remained largely undeveloped not only in this panel, but also in the panel specifically devoted to this theme.

A theme which has been raised only by Barnes in his reply to comments by the floor, but which I believe not only provocative, but important, is that in an increasing service economy *the disabled should not be perceived mainly in terms of costs for the social budget. They play an important role in consumption, thus in the demand for goods and services.* Therefore they contribute to job creation. The disabled, in other words, should not be seen only as potential producers/workers, and their social contribution linked only to that, but also as consumers. In Barnes' words, "Disability benefits do not go in the disabled' pockets and make them wealthy ... They go back into the economy, in providing work for other people ... Traditionally society has rewarded people for hiring people, why not reward the disabled for doing so? "

4   Issues for Further Research

The OECD report, while correctly pointing out that too often the disabled are not expected to work, or are discouraged from working, puts all the blame on the policies for the disabled themselves, which disincentivise the disabled from participating into work, or put them in an either/or dilemma. It is the well-known paradigm of welfare dependency. The idea of obligations (and ensuing sanctions, even if later on) is rooted in this fear, even when it does not directly blame the disabled for their lack of effort. In the panel and the ensuing debate there was a shared consensus that the problem lies rather in the lack of policies positively supporting an employment orientation. That is, most interventions seemed not to share the idea that the problem lied with the structure of benefits themselves, but rather with the lack of options. I tend to share this overall position, although I also share the OECD concern that actually some disability benefits seem to offer impossible dilemmas to the disabled. But I do not think that the available data allow to draw a general conclusion pointing to the negative effect of policies as the main culprit. First, policies in different countries, as well as for different kinds of disabled, do not have the same either/or features. In some case they compensate for inability to work, in others they compensate for diminished earnings, or even only for impairment, irrespective of the impact on earnings. Second, the disabled populations are heterogeneous within as well as across countries, rendering it therefore difficult to disentangle possibly disincentivising effects from "original characteristics" of the disabled effects. Actually, longitudinal studies on social assistance careers have offered no proof for the well-entrenched welfare dependency paradigm.[5] Similarly careful longitudinal studies on disabled benefit recipients are necessary before drawing any conclusion concerning welfare dependency.

173

5   A Final Comment

Three themes I find undeveloped both in the report and in the debate: that of the impact of social class and skills differences among the disabled, that of prevention of disabilities in the workplace and in the labour market, that of the way of dealing with disabled children and youth. The latter is particularly striking, given the importance allocated to early intervention. If we want to give these children and youth a chance to enter the labour market, early intervention must really be "early" and involve more than incentives to work. The role of schools and education is absent in the report.

Notes

1   A comparative study on the efficacy of income support measures for the poor in different European countries among other things concluded that a large quota of the outcome may be predicted by the way the policy design selects its beneficiaries. See Saraceno, C. (ed.) (2002) *Social Assistance Dynamics in Europe*. Bristol: Policy Press.

2   In Italy there were, and still are, two kinds of disability benefits: a social security one, which is not income-tested and is paid to people who become (totally or partly) disabled while in the labour force and a social assistance one, which is income-tested and is paid to all those who are declared unable to work because of a disability.

3   A synthetic presentation of these developments until the mid-1990s may be found in Negri, N./Saraceno, C. (1996) *Le politiche contro la povertà in Italia*. Bologna: il Mulino, pp. 44-50.

4   See Paugam, S. (1997) *Integration, pécarité et risque d'exclusion des salariées*. Fondation Nationale des Sciences Politiques, CNRS, Observatoire sociologique du changement.

5   In addition to the work mentioned in note 1, see for instance Paugam, S. (1995) *La société Française et ses pauvres. L'éxperience de revenu minimum d'insertion*. Paris: PUF; Leisering, L./Leibfried, S. (1999) *Time and Poverty in Western Welfare States*. Cambridge: Cambridge University Press; Walker, R./Shaw, A. (1998) 'Escaping from Social Assistance in Great Britain', pp. 199-242 in: Leisering, L./Walker, R. (eds.) (1998), *The Dynamics of Modern Society: Poverty, Policy and Welfare*. Bristol: Policy Press.

Excursus: New Directions in Disability (Benefit) Policy: The Dutch Experience

Philip R. de Jong

1   Introduction

This paper reviews the Dutch disability benefit system and some other programmes that are part of a national policy toward persons with disabilities. It starts with a short description of the sickness and disability benefit programmes. Section 3 discusses trends in disability expenditures and beneficiaries in order to illustrate what is at stake. In section 4, I give an overview of the changes that took place in the last ten years, their efficacy, and proposals that have recently been debated. The conclusion is that Holland is moving from a wayward system to a more balanced one using elements that the OECD suggests in its new publication on disability policy.

2   The Dutch Sickness and Disability Schemes

2.1   Sick Pay

When a Dutch worker is unable to perform his/her job because of illness or injury, irrespective of its cause, he/she is entitled to sick pay. Sick pay replaces 70% of gross wage earnings but most collective bargaining agreements between employers and employees stipulate that sickness benefits are supplemented to the level of net earnings. Sick pay ends after 12 months.

As of 1996, the employer is fully responsible for financing sick pay. He may reinsure his sick pay liability with a private insurer but is not obliged to do so. Employers are mandated to contract with a private provider of occupational health services to manage absenteeism. Doctors employed by these occupational health agencies check whether the absence from work is legitimate and give a prognosis concerning work resumption.

Small firms may be unable to offer a commensurate job if an employee is afflicted by a disability that prevents him from doing his old job. In that case a reintegration service organisation should mediate towards placement in a new firm. As of 2003 employers are obliged to subscribe to the services of a private reintegration organisation to help disabled employees for whom no commensurate work is available within the firm.

2.2 Disability

Under the Dutch ruling any illness or injury entitles an insured person to a disability benefit after a mandatory waiting period of 12 months. While other OECD countries make a distinction by whether the impairment occurred on the job or elsewhere, only the *consequence* of impairment is relevant for the Dutch disability insurance programme.

Three separate benefit programmes targeting different social groups provide compensation for loss of earning capacity due to long-term or permanent disablement. The first, and by far the biggest, programme covers employees, and awards wage-related benefits. The other two address the self-employed and those handicapped from youth. These provide flat benefits at the social minimum level. Youth handicapped are entitled to a benefit from age 18 onwards. Otherwise, the design and administration of these two programmes are the same as for the wage-related programme.

The degree of disablement is assessed by consideration of the disabled worker's residual earning capacity. Capacity is defined by the earnings flowing from any job commensurate with one's residual capabilities as a percentage of earnings. The degree of disablement is the complement of the residual earning capacity and defines the benefit level. The Disability Insurance programme for employees has seven disability classes. The minimum loss of earning capacity entitling to a benefit is 15%. Wage replacement rates range from 14% of covered earnings in the 15 to 25% disablement category to 70% in the 80 to 100% category.

The other two disability schemes – for handicapped self-employed and youth – have six disability categories: they skip the first category so that entitlement starts at a degree of disability of 25%. The wage base here is the minimum wage and so the benefit at full disablement is 70% of the minimum wage.[1]

Partial benefits can be combined with labour earnings up to the level of the pre-disability wage. If recipients of a partial benefit are unable to find gainful employment they are entitled to a partial unemployment benefit. Combination of disability and unemployment benefits never replaces more than 70% of lost earnings.

Wage-related benefits are based on age and earnings. The disability benefit period is cut in two, chronologically linked parts. The first is a short-term wage-related benefit replacing 70% of before-tax earnings. The duration of this wage-related benefit depends on age at the onset of disablement. It varies from zero for those under age 33 to six years for those whose disability started at age 58 or beyond. Hence, workers aged 58 and older keep their 70% replacement rate until the statutory pension age of 65. For older workers the accrual of pension rights related to one's last job continues after entering the disability rolls. In addition, most pension plans do not require disability beneficiaries to pay pension premiums. Such contract rules discourage re-entry into the labour market by creating a gap in pension accrual rights, and make the disability system an alternative early retirement option.[2]

The second part is a so-called follow-up benefit with a lower income base and, hence, a lower replacement rate with respect to the pre-disability wage. During the follow-up period, the income base for benefit calculation is the minimum wage *plus* a supplement depending on age at onset according to the formula: 2.0% * [age at onset - 15] * [wage - minimum wage]. Age serves as a proxy for work history, or "insurance years", introducing a quasi-pension element into the disability system. Most collective bargaining agreements cover the gap between the lower replacement rates in the follow-up period and the 70% replacement rate during the first period of disablement (including the "sickness year"). The effective replacement rate when fully disabled, therefore, stays at 70% in most cases.

Disability benefits are capped by a maximum amount of covered earnings which equals about € 43,000 per annum (in 2003). This is also the maximum amount of income taxable for disability (and unemployment) insurance.

3   Trends and Issues

In May 2002 the British weekly *Economist* commented on the Dutch economy in an opinion article titled "Going Dutch". It wrote: "(...) it is the very need for consensus that has inhibited further reforms to the much-abused and excessively generous disability system, which pays out to a ludicrous one in seven Dutch people of working age." In the eyes of this commentator the Dutch disability experience is a clear illustration of the negative side of the much-praised culture of consensus and tolerance in Holland.

3.1   What Happened Really?

The data collected as part of the OECD disability policy project both confirms and refutes the stereotype of the Dutch disability system given by this quote. According to Table 2.1 of the OECD report Holland is still among the big spenders of disability benefits but it is not the biggest spending country anymore, as it was in 1990. In 1999 broad disability benefit expenditures were 4.14% of GDP, which is 28% lower than in 1991.[3]

Figure 1 shows the trend in the number of persons receiving a disability benefit as a percentage of the labour force (including disability beneficiaries),[4] and disability benefit expenditures as a percentage of GDP. Disability benefits are here defined in a narrow sense, including both benefits from contributory and non-contributory disability schemes. From a 1985 top of 4.2% of GDP disability benefit expenditures decreased to 2.6% in 2001.

At the same time, however, the relative number of beneficiaries stayed at 11% of the labour force – the level it had reached in 1981, after the disability explosion of the 1970s. In absolute terms, the number of disability beneficiaries grew continuously from 475,000 in 1976 to 921,000 in 1993.[5] Changes in the definition of disability and in the way benefits are calculated drastically reduced the number of new awards. Moreover, part of the current beneficiaries was reviewed using the new, more stringent definition. This increased the number of benefit terminations and, on balance, led to a 7% drop in the number of beneficiaries, to 855,000 in 1996. From then on the numbers started growing again, and reached 979,000 in November 2002, coming close to the politically contentious level of one million disabled.

Figure 1: DI-Benefits as a Percentage of GDP and DI-Beneficiaries as a Percentage of the Labour Force, 1974-2001

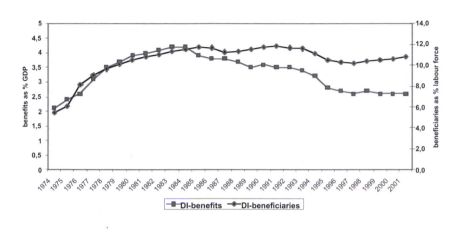

3.2 Benefit Cuts

179

Figure 1 above shows that the reduction in spending on disability benefits was not caused by a smaller number of beneficiaries. Logically, then, the average benefit must have gone down. First, over the 25 years covered by the figure cutting statutory benefits appeared to be the only policy measure to reduce the financial burden of an otherwise uncontrollable programme. In the early 1980s benefits lost 25% of their purchasing power by a series of substantial retrenchments. First, levying social insurance contributions on benefit income changed the calculation of after-tax benefit amounts. In 1982 and 1983, the after-tax DI-benefit level was reduced through the abolition of certain tax exemptions for the disabled. In 1984, the earnings base from which benefits were calculated was reduced. Moreover, all incomes under government control – transfers, civil servant salaries, and the statutory minimum wage – suffered a 3% nominal cut. Finally, in 1985, (before-tax) replacement rates were lowered from 80 to 70% of last earnings, when fully disabled. These direct cuts were accompanied by the elimination of the system of automatic indexation (adjustment) of government-controlled incomes. Benefits were cut again in August 1993, when statutory replacement rates were reduced according to age at the onset of disability. As a result benefits lost another 20% of their real value between 1985 and 1995. This loss contrasts sharply with per capita GDP, which increased by one third during the same period.

3.3 Partial Benefits

Second, after the changes of 1993 the share of partial benefits grew sharply. By these changes the notion of suitable work was eliminated from the definition of disability. Capacity is since defined by the earnings flowing from any job commensurate with one's residual capabilities as a percentage of pre-disability usual earnings. The degree of disablement is the complement of the residual earning capacity and defines the benefit level. Before 1994, only jobs that were compatible with one's training and work history could be taken into consideration in the assessment of residual capacity. This new ruling made the percentage of partials among new awards grow from 19% in 1990 to 45% in 2001.

Two thirds of partial benefit awardees work. For them, and their employers, the benefit acts as a wage subsidy. Research has shown that partial beneficiaries differ from full beneficiaries in many respects: They are older, better educated, more often male, married and main breadwinner, have a longer tenure with their current employer and work in financially healthy companies.[6] In short, Dutch partial beneficiaries are socially and economically better off. The data suggest that partial benefits often are used to offer older employees easier work conditions and act as a partial early retirement scheme.

3.4 The Average Beneficiary Has Changed

Over the past three decades the typical new disability beneficiary changed from an older male industry worker with a long work record in physically strenuous work into a younger female employee in the service industry with a relatively short labour market record. As 57% of Dutch women work part-time their wages and their D.I.-benefits are lower.[7] An increasing proportion of women among D.I.-entrants, therefore, implies lower benefits, other things equal.

Figure 2 displays the disability beneficiary incidence rate for men and women. Women had lower rates until 1985, and have higher ones ever since. More importantly, the gap between the two incidence rates increased continuously from 1983, when the female rate was 15% lower than that of men, till 1998 when women had a 80% higher chance of becoming dependent on disability benefits. It stayed at that level since.

In absolute terms the total number of disability beneficiaries grew 6% between 1991 and 2001. While the male beneficiary volume decreased by 13%, its female counterpart increased by 43%.

Figure 2: **New Beneficiaries as a Percentage of the Labour Force by Gender, 1971-2001**

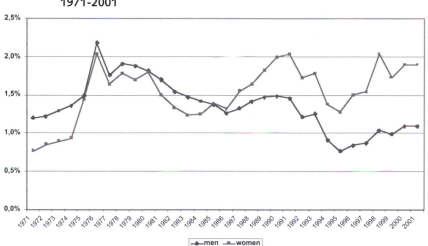

The sharp increase in female disability was matched by an equally strong growth of the labour force participation of mothers. Traditionally, Holland had very low labour force participation rates of married women. In the 1970s three out of four women stopped working after the birth of the first child. Twenty years later only one third stops. In other words, the traditional single-earner model has been replaced by that where husbands work full-time and wives have part-time jobs. This social change has been accommodated by the disability scheme. Disability benefits allowed to let market production be replaced by home production without a sharp drop in household income. The feminisation of disability benefit dependency illustrates how an income-oriented disability policy invites to put the strains of dual earnership in medical terms.

4   New Policies: Privatisation and Reintegration

In the early 1990s Dutch policy-makers turned to defining the disability issue in terms of "moral hazard". They concluded that the system lacked appropriate incentives for the three parties directly involved: employees, employers and system administrators.

4.1   Enhanced Incentives for Employees

Employees were hit by benefit cuts in 1993, when the "two-phases" system was introduced – a wage-replacement phase followed by a phase with a lower, age-dependent, replacement rate (see above). Although collective bargaining agreements correct the gap between the lower rate in the second phase and that in the first phase for most employees these supplements came in the place of supplements on the standard 70% replacement rate up to 100% of the net wage. All in all, the effective rate went down for most employees.

As part of the 1993 amendments the definition of disability under the Disability Insurance Act became stricter. The loss of earning capacity used to be assessed against work that was considered suitable with respect to someone's education and achieved level of functioning. If a disability would prevent employment in suitable work one was considered fully disabled. As of August 1993, the extent of disablement is assessed by considering the complete labour market, instead of the parts that are suitable. This is one of the reasons why the share of partial benefits increased sharply. Moreover, the disability status of all beneficiaries younger than 45 was reviewed according to the new standards. These reviews led to a surge in benefit reductions and terminations.

The 1993 amendments also affected the incidence of new disability awards (see Figure 2). The decrease in awards may well be the combined result of increased stringency of the gatekeeper and lower application rates because disability benefits lost part of their financial appeal due to lower benefits and stricter eligibility requirements. But the benefit cuts, together with a booming economy and an increasingly tight labour market during the last six years, also changed the face of disability. Better paid workers with long careers tried to avoid becoming fully dependent on disability benefits as they had better opportunities in the labour market. Secondary breadwinners and low-wage workers lose less when going on disability and are therefore strongly over-represented among the current disability entrants.

A smaller number of awards and a steep increase of benefit terminations resulted in a 7% decrease of the disability beneficiary population over the three years between 1994-1996. So far these were the only years in which the number of beneficiaries declined since the introduction of the comprehensive disability insurance scheme in 1967.

4.2 ... and for employers

SICKNESS BENEFITS WERE PRIVATISED

In March 1996, the Sickness Benefit Act was abolished. Under this Act sick pay was collectively financed through sector-specific insurance funds. These funds were administrated by public agencies. By abolishing this Act employers became responsible for coverage of sick pay during the first 12 months of sickness, after which Disability Insurance takes over. Under the Civil Code, firms are obliged to continue payment of 70% of earnings during sickness. They may choose freely whether they want to bear their sick pay risk themselves or have (part of) it covered by a private insurer.

This is a remarkable change. A fully regulated monopoly market to which private insurers had no access has been transformed into a deregulated one on which private insurers freely bid for contracts with firms that seek to insure their sick pay liabilities. Firms are legally mandated to contract with a private occupational health agency and buy a package of services including sickness prevention and management of sickness claims. These new mandates seek to reduce absenteeism and inflow into the disability benefit programme by confronting firms with its full cost. Investment in prevention and reduction of sickness is profitable as it reduces avoidable costs of absenteeism.

Sickness absence rates dropped from 8% in 1990 to 6% in 2000 – a 25% drop.[8] Both these years represent a cyclical top and comparison between these, therefore, controls for the influence of the business cycle on absenteeism. This large drop, then, can be ascribed to privatisation, and its associated incentives. This favourable result is obtained despite the fact that about 80% of all firms took up some form of private insurance to cover their sickness liabilities.

There appears to be a strong negative relationship between firm size and insurance coverage: while firms with less than 20 employees have a coverage rate of about 83%, only 25% of those with 100 or more workers buy insurance. Larger firms also choose a larger co-insurance period or buy a stop-loss arrangement.[9]

To avoid adverse selection insurance companies stipulate that no employee be excluded from coverage under a sick pay policy which the employer buys. Insurers also demand that firms contract occupational health agencies, and stipulate which set of services is to be contracted.

A parliamentary majority expected that privatisation of sickness benefits would make the labour market less accessible for people with disabilities because employers would check the health status of job applicants more strictly. To counter that problem an Act banning medical examinations as part of an application procedure was introduced. Survey data show that selection on health risks has not increased due to privatisation: in 1999 about one third of firms report that they scrutinise applicants sharply on health. The same share did so around 1990. To what extent this result is due to the Act on medical examinations is unclear.[10]

Surprisingly enough privatisation did not induce a surge in conflicts between workers who claim to be sick, and employers refusing to continue payment of their wages. This may also be the result of the fact that the privatisation was enacted in a boom period. The current recession may be used to test to what extent private financing of sickness benefits is "weatherproof".

DISABILITY CONTRIBUTION RATES ARE EXPERIENCE-RATED
Since 1998 experience rating of firms is gradually phased into the disability insurance scheme. Pre-1998 benefits are still funded by the existing uniform pay-as-you-go contribution rates but as of 1998 the first five years of disability benefit recipiency of new beneficiaries is paid out of premiums that are levied according to the "polluter pays principle". If an employee is awarded a disability benefit, the firm will face a higher contribution rate, and vice versa if a firm employs a disability beneficiary. Moreover, firms are allowed to opt out of the public insurance system, but only with respect to the coverage of the first five years of benefit recipiency.

The disability insurance scheme for employees is now financed by levying two separate premium rates, both paid by the employer. The first is a uniform pay-as-you-go rate covering the benefits of those that were already on the rolls before 1998. Five years after its start – i.e. from 2003 – the pay-as-you-go rate also covers benefits that started after 1997 and last more than five years. Over the past five years this rate has gone down from 7.55% to 5.05% of taxable wage (up to € 43,000 per year).

The second rate covers the first five years of benefit recipiency and is differentiated according to the firm-specific disability risk. To calculate the risk in year t the total expenditures on disability benefits of the firm's disabled employees in year t-2 is taken and expressed as a percentage of the average wage-bill over the past five-year period. This firm-specific risk determines the differentiated rate. The average risk rate has increased from 0.30% in 1998 to 2.38% in 2003. As of 2003 only firms with a wage-bill of more than € 600,000 pay differentiated rates. These rates are limited by a lower and an upper bound. The upper bound increased from 1.12% in 1998 to 8.52% in 2003.

Five years after the inception of experience rating the system can be considered mature. The uniform pay-as-you-go rate is expected to stay at about the current level of 5% of taxable wages. What the average risk rate will do strongly depends on how the inflow rates develop.

At the end of 2001 only 0.9% of Dutch firms had opted out of this public financing scheme and had chosen to self-insure the risk of paying the first five years of disability benefit payment (first six years if one includes the sickness benefit year). These firms account for 5.6% of total wages because, naturally, "large" employers (with a wage-bill larger than € 600,000) are over-represented among the self-insured. In the public pay-as-you-go division of disability insurance only 12% are large firms. Among the self-insured 25% are large.

Whether experience rating has reduced the inflow rates is yet unknown. The phase-in stage of differentiated premiums has just ended, and the period since those rates are "biting" is still short.

4.3   ... but not for the gatekeepers of the programme

In the debate on disability policy the focus gradually shifted from the programme itself toward the programme administrators. In 1993, a multi-party parliamentary committee investigated the operations of the then-existing Insurance Agencies that were organised by sector of industry and held a legally protected monopoly with regard to the administration of sickness, disability and unemployment insurance benefits. The committee devoted special attention to the administration of the disability insurance scheme. The committee publicly interrogated a vast number of current and former administrators, civil servants, and politicians. The picture that emerged from the nightly televised summaries was devastating for the image of the Insurance Agencies. What most suspected, and what had already been shown by research, was now publicly confirmed. The committee's report created broad political support for drastic changes regarding, in particular, the dominant, and autonomous, position of the trade unions and employers' representatives in the management of social insurance.

In 1995, as a result of the committee's recommendations, an independent supervisory body was set up. It publishes annual reports on the efficiency and legality of the administration of the social insurance programmes. In

1997, the public Insurance Agencies that were run by the social partners were privatised, and regrouped themselves into five organisations. Next to their traditional tasks in administering public (unemployment and disability) insurance programmes, they set up a range of private activities, offering medical and vocational rehabilitation, and occupational health and employment services.

The original plan was to create a competitive market on which these five agencies, as well as new entrants to this market, would compete for contracts with companies or groups of companies to administer wage-replacing unemployment and disability insurance. The trend was towards offering "full-service packages" that would cover the legally mandated social insurance liabilities as well as pensions, health insurance and outplacement of redundant employees.

The public debate on this model of private delivery of social insurance disclosed several problems. A competitive insurance market for mandatory coverage of disability risks could be viable, and efficient, if private insurers would be allowed to control all the links in the "insurance chain": running from drafting policies, calculating premiums, administering indemnities, controlling damages and managing claims. Insurers could offer firms tailor-made packages by varying elements such as the extent of co-insurance and the intensity of damage control through prevention, swift rehabilitation and monitoring activities. One crucial element in this chain is the assessment of the degree of disablement. A political majority was unwilling to subject disability assessment to the business interest of private insurers. As a consequence, a hybrid model was proposed in which the whole chain was privatised except disability assessment, which was to be done by a separate public (medical) agency.

Second, while disability is a privately insurable risk, unemployment is not. Privatisation of unemployment insurance would obtain socially neither acceptable nor efficient outcomes. Apart from the insurmountable problem of risk dependency, employers would only be interested in the cheapest unemployment insurance administration contract because they would not profit from investment in quick re-employment of workers after they became redundant. Putting disability and unemployment risks in one basket, therefore, would result in a (socially) sub-optimal outcome.

Third, private agencies that cover the mandatory (public) insurances are likely to offer additional, related, insurance services, such as health insurance and pensions. To the extent that the portability of such employee benefit packages is limited, employees are locked into the firm. Likewise, firms may find it difficult to change providers of employee benefits.

And, finally, private agencies that get data on covered workers because they run public schemes may abuse those for other commercial activities. Similarly, they may use moneys from mandatory, public, insurances for their private business. Auditing such hybrid organisations is complex, controversial, and expensive.

For such reasons a political majority pulled the plug on this privatisation plan in the summer of 1999. In 2002 the Social Insurance Institute was established to run the disability and unemployment insurance schemes as a so-called quango (quasi-autonomous non-governmental organisation) under contract with the Ministry of Social Affairs and Employment. Only rehabilitation (reintegration into paid work) is contracted out to private firms. This could offer an opportunity for the existing occupational health service companies that now do the management of sickness benefit claims to broaden their scope.

187

4.4   Reintegration

REA-PROVISIONS
In contrast to countries with a similarly broad social welfare system the Dutch disability programme used to lack effective mandates regarding vocational rehabilitation and a rehabilitation infrastructure to support such mandates. This was increasingly felt as system failure. In July 1998 the Act on Reintegration of Work Handicapped Persons (REA) introduced a new target group. Under this Act the set of provisions in kind and subsidies that previously were scattered over a number of schemes were added together and made consistent.

Work-handicapped persons are all those that meet one or more of the following qualifications:

- having a disability that reduces one's productive capacity,
- being entitled to a disability benefit, or having lost one's entitlement less than five years ago;
- being entitled to an in-kind provision or subsidy to maintain or restore one's productivity, or having lost one's entitlement to such provision less than five years ago;

- belonging to the group targeted by the Sheltered Work Provision Act;
- not belonging to any of the before-mentioned groups but having been assessed (through medical examination at a social insurance agency) as work-handicapped.

The status of work-handicapped is allowed for five years after which it has to be re-established. REA excludes all those work-handicapped persons that have an employment contract, unless they have reached the 12-months sickness limit, with or without a disability insurance award, and those that have not reached this limit but are unable to go back to their current employer.

In 2000 about 1.2 million persons (12% of the working age [18-64] population) were counted as work-handicapped. Of those 79% are benefit recipients; 34% of the work-handicapped population are employed. Work-handicapped are older than the average employee: 61% are older than 45 against 28% of all employees.

As of 2002 REA covers the following types of provisions:

1. Work-handicapped employees may be entitled to schooling, training, mobility provisions, trial placement and personal assistance and certain therapies (like stress and RSI training) to maintain or restore their productivity.

2. Companies pay a lower disability insurance rate and are exempt from experience rating for handicapped workers. The sickness benefits of handicapped workers are covered collectively so that their employers do not bear the financial risk of continued wage payment if they would turn sick.

3. Companies are entitled to subsidies that cover the cost of accommodation of the workplace.

In 2001 57,000 REA-provisions were awarded to employees, and about 50,000 to employers. As employees, or their employers, often get more than one provision the number of employees that get a provision is much less than the total number of provisions given in 2001 (107,000). But even if this sum would be the number of workers getting a REA-provision it is small compared with a target group of 800,000 non-working handicapped.

Moreover, survey data on cohorts of those that reached the disability insurance waiting period of 12 months sickness in 2001 show that the instruments are used selectively in a sense that suggests a certain extent of deadweight loss: REA helps those that are in a relatively favourable position more often than others. The group that gets a relatively large amount of support from REA is very similar to those that get partial disability benefits: they are better schooled, they have longer tenure, they are more often breadwinners, and work in large, financially healthy, firms.[11] The report on this survey concludes that the introduction of REA has not (yet?) led to a significant improvement of the reintegration process.

REINTEGRATION PLANS

This conclusion is based on a study of workers who are on long-term sickness but still have an employment contract with their current employer. In that case, the employer and his occupational health agency do the application for a REA-provision. Concerning disability beneficiaries REA-provisions are usually part of a reintegration (back-to-work) plan drafted by vocational experts of the Social Insurance Institute. These plans may be compared with the "individual participation packages" proposed by the OECD. On the one hand beneficiaries can influence the design of the plan by stating their preferences for certain REA provisions and lines of work. On the other hand, beneficiaries are legally mandated to take all steps necessary to restore their productive capacities. Therefore, those that are offered a plan cannot refuse to cooperate, unless they can prove that they already are on the road back to work.

The Social Insurance Institute contracts private reintegration service organisations to execute reintegration plans. This is done by parcelling out groups (plots) of beneficiaries to organisations with the best offer in terms of price, successful placement record and professionalism. These plans are financed out of the REA budget, and cover both the reintegration instruments and the effort of the reintegration service. In 2001 about 50,000 reintegration plans were contracted for the work-handicapped. About half of these concern disability beneficiaries; the others are unemployed jobseekers (with or without an unemployment transfer income). In other words, plans were made for about 2.5% of the disability beneficiary population. According to contract 35% (17,500 of 50,000 plans) should result in successful placements (employment for at least six months).

REINTEGRATION REPORTS

As of April 2002, the responsibilities of the sick employee, his/her employer, and the occupational health service are legally specified, and mandate a structured approach to early intervention in cases of sickness. After a maximum of six weeks of absence the occupational (health service) doctor has to make a first assessment of medical cause, functional limitations and give a

189

prognosis regarding work resumption. On the basis of these data employer and employee together draft a vocational rehabilitation plan in which they specify an aim (resumption of current/other job under current/accommodated conditions) and the steps needed to reach that aim. They appoint a case-manager, and fix dates at which the plan should be evaluated, and modified if necessary. The rehabilitation plan should be ready in the eighth week of sickness. It is binding for both parties, and one party may summon the other when considered negligent.

After 35 weeks of sickness the Social Insurance Institute sends a Disability Insurance application form to the sick employee. Disability Insurance claims have to be delivered before the 40th week of sickness. Claims are only considered admissible if they are accompanied by a rehabilitation report, containing the original rehabilitation plan, and an assessment as to why the plan has not (yet) resulted in work resumption. If the report is delayed, incomplete, or proves that the reintegration efforts were insufficient the claim is not processed and the employer is obliged to continue paying sickness benefits even after 12 months.

This is a serious step in the direction of mutuality of rights and responsibilities both in the relationship between employer and employee, and of both parties in their relationship with the state, represented by the Social Insurance Institute. Employees who consistently refuse to cooperate with their employer to execute the plan can be dismissed. To that end the labour law was changed, because until now an absolute dismissal ban was in force for the first two years following the onset of a disability.[12] Employers can be sanctioned by a one-year extension of the payment period of sickness benefits if proven at fault. And employees may be penalised by cutting their disability insurance benefit.

4.5   The Donner Report

In May 2001 a National Advisory Commission on Disability proposed to drastically revise the current scheme. It is called the Donner Commission, after its chairman. The proposal takes the mutual responsibility of employer and employee to promote work resumption and prevent benefit dependency as a starting point. The employer is obliged to take care of the necessary accommodation of the current job, or to offer another job, inside or outside his firm. The employee has to provide the medical information necessary to adapt employment conditions, and has to accept any job offer earning at least 70% of his previous wage.

The sufficiency of the return to work efforts of employer and employee are to be judged by the Social Insurance Institute. Insufficiency will be sanctioned. If the employer is held liable he will have to continue payment of sickness benefit, until he has taken the steps judged necessary by the Institute. If the employee proves unwilling to collaborate with reasonable plans and job offers the employer may dismiss him/her. The latter rules have already been introduced in April 2002, except that the Donner committee proposed to make the waiting period before a benefit claim can be filed to be more flexible, with a minimum period of three months.

This system of mutual obligations to promote swift work resumption is underscored by a new risk definition under Disability Insurance. People are only awarded a disability benefit if they can be considered permanently and severely disabled. Partial disability is not covered anymore by the public Disability Insurance programme. Expectations are that this alone will reduce the inflow rate by two thirds. Only if the inflow rate declines significantly the benefit under this new system can go back to its pre-1993 level of 70% of earnings.

Disabled workers who, under this strict regime, are not eligible for disability benefit and who, despite reasonable efforts of their employer and themselves, are unable to find commensurate work can claim unemployment benefit.

One of the main goals of this blueprint is to emphasise that sick workers should do everything reasonable to go back to work as soon as possible. To that end they can appeal on broad support from their employers. Employers who remain negligent have to continue paying sickness benefit for an unlimited duration. This sanction should replace experience rating of the firm-specific disability risk. Those that are eligible for disability benefit are presumably left without any residual earning work capacity, and are therefore not subject to rehabilitation mandates.

4.6   The SER Proposals

The Donner proposals met with fierce opposition. Although the central recommendation to restrict the Disability Insurance programme to the permanently and fully disabled and to privatise partial disability was broadly accepted, the fact that many of those who are now entitled to disability benefit may become unemployed and end on social assistance was equally broadly considered unacceptable. Others noted that doing away with experience rating, together with the possibility of eventually higher replacement rates, would bring the system back to its pre-1993 state and would reinstate all the wrong incentives the system got rid of over the past years. A third form of criticism concerned the concept, definition and implementation of full and permanent disablement. The gatekeepers of the programme would never be able to apply such a strict standard, especially under the pressure of disabled workers claiming a benefit, which would soon turn to be higher than any other transfer income.

The Donner proposals were send to the Social-Economic Council (SER) – the advisory body the government has to consult in matters of social and labour market policy. This Council consists of trade unions' and employers' representatives and independent Crown Members. These three parties have equal shares in the Council.

The SER accepted major parts of the Donner report but modified two crucial elements:

1. Benefits were to compensate 75% of lost earnings. The trade unions demanded this as a *quid-pro-quo* for the employers' bonus: elimination of experience rating.

2. Partial disability would be eliminated from Disability Insurance but a new system was proposed in which two classes of partial disability would remain: those who are not fully disabled but suffer a loss of capacity of more than 35% and those that have a limitation which reduces capacity by less than 35%.

The first group would get a supplement on their wage if they were employed. Firms would be legally obliged to take out private insurance to cover these supplements. In case of unemployment they would be entitled to a benefit which eventually would go down to the level of the social minimum but which would remain (until age 65) an insurance entitlement without means tests. The second group (with a capacity loss of less than 35%) would be entitled to support from their employer to stay in employment. In case of unemployment they would be treated as regular unemployed who eventually end on means-tested welfare.

Government considered this mollification of the Donner proposals as undue. It argued that the mandatory private insurance system for those in the 35-100 disability class would work adversely. At least two of the three parties involved in this game (employers and private insurers) were expected to prefer unemployment over claiming a wage supplement – damages which could be avoided by making the employee redundant. And compared to a partial disability benefit under the current system the unemployment option was in many cases an improvement, too.

4.7 Government Proposals

Government takes a stand close to the Donner proposals. Four new amendments are currently being prepared:

1. A Bill is drafted in which the mandatory waiting period is extended from one to two years. This extends the sickness benefit payment period for employers but reduces the burden of experience rating correspondingly.

2. The definition and operationalisation of the disability criterion proposed by Donner is under serious study both by physicians and lawyers.

3. An element, which is neither part of the Donner nor the SER proposals, is the introduction of an employment record requirement before one is covered by Disability Insurance. The current coalition is in favour of the introduction of such an additional requirement.[13]

4. If one were to choose a Donner-type criterion, the ILO treaty 121 ratified by the Dutch government requires that those that would get partially disabled due to a work-related accident or occupational disease are covered by social insurance. Government has drafted a Bill to cover work-related risks by mandating employers to contract private insurers. The need to do so would only be enhanced by the introduction of a contribution record requirement.

All in all, "Donner" would bring the Dutch disability benefit system in many respects back into the international mainstream. But in other respects it remains unique: it keeps its heavy employer mandates and reinforces elements of mutuality.

Notes

1 In 2003 the minimum wage equals € 16.189,63 per year.
2 Dutch early retirement programmes have no statutory basis; they emerged as an element of collective bargaining agreements between trade unions and employers in 1975. The tremendous growth of early retirement plans since, the expected fiscal pressure of an ageing workforce, and benefits being paid out of pay-as-you-go funds, called for changes in these actuarially unbalanced programmes. An increasing number of these – collectively bargained – plans are now being transformed into capital-funded flexible pension schemes with a much closer link between contributions and pension rights. These changes are likely to boost the interest in the disability benefit option.
3 "Broad" includes disability benefits, sick pay and work injury benefits.
4 The labour force is measured in full-time equivalents (i.e. corrected for part-timers); disability beneficiaries are measured in full benefit equivalents (i.e. corrected for partial benefits).
5 In 1976 the disability scheme was broadened. From then on it also included those handicapped in youth and the self-employed. The absolute numbers quoted are not corrected for partial benefits.
6 Philip de Jong and Vincent Thio, "Donner versus Veldkamp", APE report 53, October 2002 (in Dutch).
7 *OECD Employment Outlook*, Paris, 2002, p. 69.
8 T.J. Veerman en J.J.M. Besseling, *Prikkels en privatisering*, The Hague: EBI, 2001, p. 60.
9 T.J. Veerman, E.I.L.M Schellekens, J.F.L.M.M. Dagevos, J.A. Duvekot, F. Marcelissen. P.G.M. Molenaar-Cox, *Werkgevers over ziekteverzuim, Arbo en reïntegratie*, The Hague, EBI, 2001, pp. 22-27.
10 E.L. de Vos, M. Westerveld, A.M. Kremer, M. Aerts and F. Andries, *Evaluatie wet op de medische keuringen*, Zorgonderzoek Nederland, The Hague, 2001.
11 G.J.M. Jehoel-Gijsbers and C.G.L. van Deursen, *Reïntegratie bij arbeidsongeschiktheid*, Amsterdam: UWV (Social Insurance Institute), 2003.
12 A comparison among 10 European welfare states, the United States and Japan, shows that the Dutch system of job protection during sickness (still) is much stronger than in any of the 12 countries (H. Bakkum and S. Desczka, *De Nederlandse WAO in internationaal perspectief*, The Hague, Ministry of Social Affairs and Employment, Werkdocument no. 241, 2002, pp. 15-16).
13 An element, which makes the Dutch disability programme more accessible than those elsewhere, is the absence of a required contribution period before a worker is fully covered. Such absence is natural under a Work Injury scheme, because a construction worker, who falls from a scaffold on the first day on the job, has to be covered. But general disability benefit programmes in other countries all require a certain contribution payment period, which may run up to 5 years, before full coverage is obtained. See Bakkum and Desczka, 2002, op.cit., pp. 33-36.

Who Needs Activation, How and When?

Key Issues

1. Expenditure on activation programmes for disabled people is on the rise but is still very low as a proportion of total expenditure on disability-related programmes.
2. Vocational rehabilitation and training is often used too little and initiated too late. Average costs for such interventions are low compared to average costs of a disability benefit.
3. While segregation of disabled people in special forms of employment is increasingly seen as inappropriate and in need of being replaced by initiatives aimed at integration into the open labour market, empirically the protected sector remains as important as ever. Tailored and individualised programmes spread only slowly – often due to a lack of qualified personnel. Average public costs of usually permanent jobs in special, sheltered employment often exceed those of an average disability benefit.
4. There is a striking age bias in all types of integration programmes. This is especially true for vocational rehabilitation and training programmes for which people seem to be selected primarily on the basis of age.
5. Several countries use different eligibility criteria for access to different types of integration programmes, and lack coherent administration and coordination of those services.

OECD Policy Conclusions

- Each disabled person should be entitled to an "individual participation package", depending on needs and capacities. This package could contain various work and rehabilitation elements, and also cash and in kind benefits.
- Tailoring integration packages will only be possible with small-scale, focussed programmes. More permanent on-the-job support, such as individual job coaches or personal help for work-related and social activities, appears to have strong potential.
- This individual approach will place a wide range of new demands on disability gatekeepers. Case workers will need extensive knowledge of the range of available instruments. Doctors must be enabled to fulfil their role as medical assessors. A one-stop philosophy can promote equality of access to all programmes for all people, and would help gatekeepers to manage the full menu of available interventions.
- The timing of activation plays an important role. The longer a disabled person stays out of work, the lower the chances of reintegration will be. An effective measure against long-term benefit dependence appears to be a focus on early intervention. In many countries the period of sickness absence is "lost", because vocational intervention starts only when a person is potentially entitled to or already paid a disability benefit.
- As all these measures are potentially expensive, adequate longer-term evaluation of new programmes will be required.

Who Needs Activation, How and When? Introductory Comments

Hedva Sarfati

Yesterday's discussions focused on what "being disabled" meant and what were the rights and responsibilities of the different actors – the state, society, the employers and the disabled. Discussions pointed to various ways of addressing the complex issue of disability, among which activation was acknowledged as one of the major instruments for social integration. A number of obstacles were identified and discussed at some length. So I hope that our panel's discussion today will end on a more positive assessment of activation's potential.

In opening this panel on who needs activation, how and when, I would wish to add a fourth question – why? Why are we interested in activation? I would note two main reasons. First, because disability is associated with social, economic and cultural exclusion and poverty for large numbers of the disabled. Second, more materialistic perhaps, but still important, because it creates a burden on the welfare systems at a time where there are heavy constraints on public budgets and expenditures, across the OECD region but more particularly in the EU under the stringent obligations stemming from the Growth and Stability Pact. Activation seems to offer a policy-mix that is likely to improve the situation on both counts. But this option encounters a number of obstacles for its implementation. Indeed, as the OECD report notes, while "segregation of the disabled people in special forms of employment is increasingly seen as inappropriate and in need of being replaced by initiatives aimed at integration into the open labour market", the protected sector remains as important as ever". Moreover, while the report highlights the crucial importance of employment for determining personal income, the employment rates of working-age disabled persons are rather low.

The OECD report provides a quite comprehensive cross-country over-view of policy-mixes, priorities, current and forthcoming reforms and trends for integrating people with disabilities into the labour market. It recalls the high and rising prevalence of disability in the working age population (14% on average) and the relatively high incidence of severe disability (a third). It explains some of the shortcomings and perverse or undesirable effects of existing policies, which are in a nutshell: *too little, too late, too costly and lacking coordination and coherence.* This sounds rather ominous! So, to set the framework of our discussions on activation – I would highlight, among the different challenges, the following nine:

1. Although rising, *activation* measures represent a very low proportion in total expenditure for disability-related programmes.

2. While *vocational rehabilitation and training* measures have the most promising potential and their per capita cost is much lower compared to disability benefits, they still get relatively low priority and limited resources and take place too late, which may partly explain their limited outcomes.

3. *Special employment programmes* change very slowly and differ widely among countries. Sheltered employment measures are still prevalent although their cost may exceed average disability benefits.

4. *Individualized tailor-made programmes* – which were identified yesterday by many among you as the most effective measures – are rather costly and require qualified staff which is often unavailable. Such programmes therefore spread only slowly.

5. Some countries focus their activation approach on *anti-discrimination legislation,* about which we heard speakers yesterday, but there still is a striking *age bias* in all types of integration programmes in all countries in favour of the younger age groups, which not surprisingly also have a better record of integration. This "creaming effect" is also evident in activation programmes in the open labour market targeting non-disabled people. Interestingly, on the whole, the report finds that countries with strong anti-discrimination legislation are doing relatively badly in terms of relative employment rates.

6. Of particular concern is the OECD finding that, while legislative approaches to employment promotion differ (rights-based, obligations-

based, incentives-based) all tend to *benefit people already in employment* much more than those who are out of work and looking for a job. The report suggests that enforcement and sanctions on employers are the best means for an effective implementation. I would argue for the persuasion and incentives approach, which seem to be effective. Indeed, in Denmark, for example, financial incentives are granted to municipalities via higher cost reimbursement for providing vocational rehabilitation and training to the disabled rather than disability benefit. Another example from the UK provides payment to contracted job brokers according to agreed outcomes. My concern and emphasis here is on outcomes. The last example I wish to mention is that of the Netherlands, where the focus is on employer-targeted incentives. These are incentives for the recruitment or re-integration of disabled persons, consisting of major reductions in employers' social contributions to both invalidity and unemployment insurance. In addition, subsidies are provided towards extra costs of such recruitment, for example, employers have the option to recruit a disabled person for a six-month period with the salary being met by the local authorities. So clearly the focus is not only on sanctions.

7. Given current demographic trends, one should note the *age-related* gradual increase in the prevalence of disability – there are 25% of disabled in the age group 50-64, two and a half times more than among the 20-49 age group where it is 10%. Moreover, as noted yesterday it is *negatively correlated with low educational attainment.* Though this correlation is less pronounced than in the case of age, there are 19% disabled people among lower-educated vs. 11% among the better-educated. Arguably, there is a mutual causal relationship between low educational attainment and disability (that is, lower educational attainment can result in disability, for example through greater frequency of work accidents, while disability, particularly from birth or in early childhood may impair learning capacities). And yet, despite the policy implications of these two correlations, few countries participating in the OECD project considered training for persons over age 45, as is the case in the "open" labour market as well. What is more worrying here is the actual use of disability benefit systems to get non-disabled middle-aged people out of the labour market. On this, the OECD report warns that, "disability programmes *cannot* be expected to solve the broader problems in the labour market, particularly the high levels of unemploy-

199

ment and low demand for older workers in general". Arguably, in an unfavourable labour market situation, work capacity assessments may become less stringent for income replacement benefits. However, the report notes somewhat surprisingly that there is "no evidence on programme interchangeability between early retirement and disability benefits". I wonder how the OECD arrived at this conclusion, since there is evidence of such interchangeability and several governments who may have encouraged it are now trying to reverse it.

8.   The recent new emphasis on activation, aiming at bringing disability policies closer to the philosophy of unemployment programmes, requires greater attention to the *labour demand side* whereas until recently the main focus has been on the labour supply aspect. Indeed, the demand aspect is a major determinant for jobs creation. Agencies dealing with service delivery should involve employers in the formulation and assessment of activation measures and in providing assistance to employers on workplace and work practice accommodation. On the other hand, they should try to reduce the gap between expectations of the disabled people and the jobs on offer. As regards good corporate practices in adapting the work situation to the needs of the disabled, I wish to draw your attention to the ILO code of practice entitled "Managing Disability in the Workplace", published in 2002.

9.   Lastly, the OECD and other recent EU reports on labour market policies and issues related to people with disabilities – one from the Dublin Foundation, two from the EU Commission and one from the French Senate – all share one common finding, namely that there is a *dearth of cost-benefit analysis and of assessments of the effectiveness of existing labour market re-integration measures*. When I refer to cost-benefit analysis it is in relation to the outcome and effectiveness of policies, the absence of which bodes ill for the responsiveness of costly measures to the acknowledged needs. This would suggest the usefulness of further cross-national research or exchanges on such issues as:

  • how to harmonize definitions of the target population; arguably, arriving at common definitions is very difficult as shown in previous discussions here, but some common ground must be found to improve policy outcomes;

- how to link and better coordinate transitions between disability benefit assessment and entitlements, on the one hand, and job placement and work incentives on the other. Indeed, various speakers already mentioned the lack of cooperation or coordination between employment offices and welfare agencies;
- developing a more appropriate methodology for assessing and comparing the effectiveness of activation measures;
- lastly, as developments in the general labour market, including activation, also strongly impact on the integration of disabled people, it may be worth drawing some lessons regarding positive factors in job uptake of people with reduced work capacity. A useful contribution in this respect is ISSA's brochure *Who returns to work and why? – Evidence and policy implications from the new disability and work reintegration study,* published in 2002. Although this project focuses on a small number of countries (six countries) and on one, but major, source of disability – namely, back problems –, it provides useful insights to the broader policy implications for improved targeting, timing and modus operandi of measures to facilitate and accelerate work resumption.

In spite of the important limitations of activation policies, on the whole it is encouraging that the OECD report concludes that, with one exception, *no country with a significant focus on employment programmes for disabled people has below average employment rates, and many have relatively high rates!*

201

Building New Pathways to Work

Rebecca Endean

The Background to Change

Since 1997 the UK Government has helped deliver a strong and stable economy and created the Department for Work and Pensions, Jobcentre Plus, the New Deals (for the unemployed, lone parents and people with disabilities) and given better in-work support through tax credits. The significant reductions in the numbers of unemployed and lone parents on benefit, and the fact that well over 1 million more people are now in work, are a testimony to the success of this strategy.

However there are currently 2.7 million people of working age receiving incapacity benefits because of a health condition or disability. This is 7.5% of the working age population (rising to 15% in the most affected local authority areas in the North West and South Wales). This number has more than trebled since the 1970s, despite improvements in most objective measures of health since that time, and has continued to increase (albeit at a slower rate) since the mid-1990s.

People do not have to be incapable of all forms of work in order to get an incapacity benefit. Instead entitlement is based on whether a person has a level of incapacity at which it is felt unreasonable *to require* them to seek work. It is not set at a level of incapacity at which doing any form of work is impossible. The clear evidence is that the vast majority of people who start a claim to an incapacity benefit expect to get back to work and that, for most, a return should be a real possibility if the right help is offered at the right time. For example:

- Around three quarters of new claimants have more manageable medical conditions such as back pain, depression and mild circulatory disorders rather than a severe disability such as Parkinson's disease, schizophrenia or severe learning difficulties.
- Best medical evidence suggests that for the main conditions reported by claimants, a return to normal activity including work is likely to enhance well-being and improve long-term recovery.[1] The outlook for a return to work should also be positive.
- Surprisingly high numbers (up to 40%) of claimants in the early stage of their claim do not see their health as a key obstacle to them finding work at all.
- People coming onto incapacity benefits do report a wide range of obstacles to work that are unrelated to health. These include low confidence about finding a job, poor skills, little or no financial incentive to get a job, employer discrimination and a belief that they cannot work with their health condition.

204

Yet the longer claimants remain on incapacity benefits the more likely that they will find it difficult to make a successful return to work. So later work-focused interventions risk being less effective because of declining health, compounded by a declining attachment to labour, and worsening skills. Out of every 100 people claiming an incapacity benefit, over 40 will still be there one year later. By this point their prospects for getting back to work are very poor, whatever condition they report. *Once people have been on incapacity benefits for a year, the average duration of their claim will be eight years.*

So What Should We Do?

In order for the government to achieve its overall welfare to work objectives it is imperative that we attempt to find an integrated package or measures that helps people remain in contact with the labour market and move back into work. However, hard evaluation evidence on "what works" in terms of an integrated package, both in the UK and across the world, is limited. Therefore the UK is proposing to pilot a package of measures for people coming onto incapacity benefits much in roughly 8% of the country. *The pilots will be subject to an extensive programme of evaluation and it will be the findings from this that will determine what should be rolled out nationally.*

Detailed Proposals Offered in the Recent UK Green Paper

1. *Providing a Better Framework of Support*

We intend to engage individuals and provide effective support through:
- Ensuring new incapacity benefits claimants maintain contact with skilled personal advisers throughout the crucial early stages of a claim through a series of mandatory work-focused interviews.
- Ensuring new claimants draw up an action plan with their personal advisers to help them focus on their long-term goals and set out the steps they are willing to take to prepare for a return to work.
- Developing a new team of specialist personal advisers equipped with a much broader set of skills.
- Close linking of the incapacity benefit medical assessment process and the new work-focused interviews.

2. *Direct Access to a Wider Range of Help*

People claiming incapacity benefits can already access a range of disability and mainstream employment programmes such as the New Deal for Disabled People, Work-Based Learning for Adults and basic skills provision. In addition the Paper recommends filling a critical gap in the provision of services at present through:
- The establishment of new joint programmes combining support to find jobs delivered by Jobcentre Plus personal advisers with health-focused rehabilitation delivered in collaboration with the NHS.

3. *Offering Improved, Visible Financial Incentives*

The Working Tax Credit will, from April 2003, improve incentives for many claimants. However there is still room to improve incentives further – many of those currently out of work would be worse off in work if they took a job of 16 hours a week paying the national minimum wage. To encourage people to look for jobs and improve the certainty that they will be better off moving into work the Paper recommends:
- a simple Return to Work credit, paid through Jobcentre Plus, to help all those moving off an incapacity benefit back to employment. It will

be paid at £40 a week for 52 weeks where personal income in work will be less than £15,000 a year. This will significantly improve financial incentives for those returning to work.

• Provide more financial support to enable claimants to compete effectively in the job markets by enabling advisers to make discretionary awards of up to £300 to spend on anything that will help their client obtain a job (for example new clothes for an interview or work equipment) through widening access to the Advisers' Discretion Fund.

By offering this support we will have created a "Choices Package" for incapacity benefit claimants – balancing improved opportunities with greater responsibilities to actively consider a return to work.

The full and summary versions of the Green Paper are on the DWP website at: www.dwp.gov.uk/consultations/consult/2002/pathways

Note

1 Waddell, G./Burton, A.K. *Occupational Health Guidelines for the Management of Low Back Pain – Evidence Review*. London: Faculty of Occupational Medicine; Jones, D./West, R. *Cardiac Rehabilitation*. BMJ Publishing Group; Acheson, D. (Chairman) (1998) *Report. Independent Inquiry into Inequalities in Health*. London: TSO.

Activation Through Sheltered Work?
Not *If* but *How*

Erik Samoy

Sheltered work became an important instrument of rehabilitation policy some 50 years ago. From the start it had a double role to play. It had to provide a temporary solution for disabled people who were not yet ready to enter or re-enter the regular labour market but it was also a permanent resort for those who were unable to get or hold a regular job. Over the years the latter function became dominant, and because few people left the workshops the total number of sheltered workers kept on growing. Once in a while there have been attempts to remind the workshops of their role as a transition institution but the outflow to regular jobs remained low. The largest transition numbers occurred in periods when the economy was going well, probably because at such times workshop employees had faith in their chances to make more money or find more interesting jobs on the regular market. Paradoxically, in the same periods there was a large growth in the number of workers in sheltered employment. This is explained by the fact that when the economy is at a high, regular firms have a lot of sub-contracting work that is tendered to sheltered workshops.

A Large and Diverse Sector in the Economy

Over the years sheltered workshops have become an important business. In a study for the Council of Europe, in the mid-1990s, we found that they employed nearly 500,000 workers in 17 European countries.[1] The federation "Workability International" states on its web site (www.workability-international.org) that more than a million people are employed by work-shops in 28 countries all over the world. Table 5.3 of the OECD-report *Transforming Disability into Ability* illustrates how countries attach a different importance to sheltered employment within their employment programmes for the disabled. The table compares the number of people per 1000 of the population, in subsidised, supported or sheltered employment. The range for the total number of people in all three types of programmes together goes from 0.2 (Portugal) to 16.2 (Sweden). The range for sheltered employment goes from 0.1 (Portugal) to 10.1 (Poland). The top five countries for all employment programmes are: Sweden (16.2), Poland (12.1), France (9.5), the Netherlands (9.2) and Norway (7.2). The top five for sheltered employment are: Poland (10.1), the Netherlands (9.2), Switzerland (5.6), Sweden (5.2) and Germany (3.3). Three countries, Poland, Sweden and the Netherlands appear in both lists, which means that in these three countries, which all have a high overall number of disabled people in employment programmes, sheltered employment plays a very important role. But there are also other countries, such as Belgium, where sheltered employment has a large share, although the overall number of people in programmes is not that high.

A recent study compares sheltered work in Australia, Austria, Denmark, Great Britain, Sweden and the Netherlands.[2] In all those countries sheltered workshops face the challenge of how to reconcile an economic target with a social target while having to stimulate transition to open employment. Some of these countries have gone a long way in reducing the number of people in traditional sheltered workshops (Australia, Great Britain). Some never had many people in workshops (Denmark, Austria), but others keep a large number occupied in the traditional collective workshops (Sweden, the Netherlands). Although the Netherlands has the largest number of people in sheltered employment (in proportion to the workforce), this is somewhat misleading because some 10% of the employees are in fact working in a regular environment (alone or in small groups) with little or no supervision by workshop staff, but they remain under contract with the workshop. Some other countries have similar schemes, but for smaller numbers. The scheme may constitute an intermediate stage between traditional sheltered work and supported employment (whereby the employee has a contract with an ordinary employer). As in the Netherlands, it may also be a permanent situation. Although it is preferable that the employee has a regular contract with an employer on the open market, it is not always easy to make that happen. To the employer it's more comfortable when the sheltered work agency remains the official employer and he buys the services from that agency. It is a flexible arrangement and he has no responsibility towards the disabled employees when it comes to the termination of the contract. But the disabled employees themselves may also prefer such an arrangement because being employed by a sheltered employment agency gives them more job security. One can easily see how an intermediate arrangement, which is in the interest of both parties becomes a permanent state of affairs. One way of preventing that people get stuck in the intermediate stage is that the sheltered work agency itself becomes a supported employment agency and moves people from one situation to the other, but even that is not always easy to do.

The diversity between sheltered workshops is so great that it's very hazardous to talk about sheltered employment in general. What they have in common is that they all create special employment conditions to activate people with disabilities, and sometimes also other target groups. But the type of activities, the status of the employees and the position of the workshops in the economy and in the field of services for the disabled differ a lot. It also matters who the disabled people are. In some countries (e.g. France, Germany) the overall majority of the employees are people with a mental disability, whereas in other countries they make up less than half of the workforce (e.g. Great Britain).

Activation Needed?

It should be clear from what has been said that the question is not *if* sheltered employment contributes to the activation of people with disabilities but *how*. One is inclined to think that no explanation is required: people in sheltered employment are at work and are being paid for it, so they are no longer inactive and dependent on benefits. There is no doubt about them being at work, although the pace and intensity differs, but they are not always regular workers with a normal wage. In some countries the workshop employees' income is an income from work much below a minimum-wage level, but topped up with allowances and benefits. There are other countries where the wages paid in sheltered employment compare favourably with open-market wages. The difference in pay-levels somehow reflects the productivity of the workers, but also the amount of state subsidies for sheltered employment.

Activation is not always exclusively activation through what we normally consider as work. There are workshops (or parts of workshops) where people spend some of their time on occupational activities and social skills training. These workshops resemble some day centres where occupational activities and social skills training are dominant, but part of the time is spent on productive work. Another important activity in some workshops is vocational training. The aim of the training is primarily to produce better workers for the workshop itself, but it may also benefit the person to find a regular job. When people enter a workshop there may be an assessment and training period that is meant to find out which employment option is suitable for the person (regular work or permanent sheltered work or referral to a day centre). In some countries vocational training and sheltered work are intensely interwoven whereas in other countries they are institutionally quite separated.

Abolish or Develop?

Although in many cases the sheltered work environment provides good opportunities for the activation of people with disabilities, many people want to see it abolished on the grounds that it is a segregated form of employment which does not really lead to integration in the labour market in the sense of not only having a paid job but also of being at work amongst non-disabled people. A new type of programme, called supported employment, is preferred. Supported employment contains the same elements as sheltered work (a wage subsidy / adaptations to the workplace / personal support on the workplace), but it realises these elements in a regular work environment, where disabled people are working with non-disabled people. Many countries do not have such programmes yet. In others they are still relatively small, compared to the workshops. Sometimes supported work programmes mainly exist for people – often with a mental disability – who are performing unpaid work.

The challenge for the future is to find a model of sheltered work (some people will prefer to use the term "adapted work") that fits the needs of every single person. We are dealing with a set of components that piled onto each other will produce a continuum of employment supports. The basic form of intervention is subsidised employment, which may be limited to a wage subsidy, but material or immaterial adaptations to the workplace may be added. When there is also personal support we end up with what nowadays is called supported employment. And when all this is organised in a collective way, we have the traditional model of a sheltered workshop.

We have defined supported employment as a form of employment with personal support which may come from a job coach who is employed by the supported employment agency, but it may also be natural support such as from colleagues, or and preferably, it may be both. In the literature, supported employment is often defined in a wider sense. It is not limited to the end product of a supported workplace but all the previous stages of assessment, job-finding, job-analysis, matching, coaching and training, are regarded as part of the supported employment model or method. All these stages are in fact very important because once a person is put in a specific situation it's proven to be very difficult to make a move to another (less protected) situation. There are always many interests (of the agencies or the person) that hamper transition. It seems that no country yet has found the solution to a system of assessment and allocation that puts most people in the right place from the start. Therefore in one country you will find people with the same type of work capacities in different environments and when comparing countries one sees that, what is thought to be the same type of agency, in fact serves different target groups. This makes cross-country comparison of sheltered employment notoriously difficult.

To offer tailor-made solutions to people we may need to break barriers between organisations, administrations and regulations. And we will need these tailor-made solutions to adapt to changes in the economy. The traditional workshop model was conceived in the industrial age of the 1940s and 1950s. Therefore most workshops are like factories and what happens inside is organized in the same way. In fact it was and often still is a copy of work that is no longer done in ordinary factories, but is contracted out to a sheltered workshop, for various reasons. As the amount of "factory work" in our economy diminishes and is replaced by service-type of work, the sheltered workshops have to adapt to that. Many jobs that could be done by disabled people, with some support, cannot be brought to a workshop, but have to be performed on the spot. Therefore the support must also be moved to where the work is done. And that requires tailor-made solutions. Although there is still room for sheltered workshops in the traditional sense, the days of expansion are probably over. It's time that management looks for new ways to support disabled people in the open economy. In some countries we see this happening, but it's only a start and there remains a lot of resistance to overcome.

Notes

1   Samoy, E./Waterplas, L. (1997) *Sheltered Employment in Five Member States of the Council of Europe: Austria, Finland, Norway, Sweden and Switzerland.* Strasbourg: Council of Europe.

2   van Genabeek, J./Hazelzet, A.M./Zwinkels, W.S. (2003) *Werkgelegenheidsvoorzieningen voor de Wsw-doelgroep: buitenlandse ervaringen.* Raad voor Werk en Inkomen (RWI) – TNO-Arbeid.

Not Only Samhall
A Swedish Report*

Jan Rydh

Samhall – the Swedish System for Sheltered Employment

After my report on the Swedish Health Insurance System, I was appointed
to lead another investigation on "Samhall", the Swedish system for sheltered employment. Sheltered employment was introduced in Sweden in a
variety of forms during the 1960s. The responsibility was local and shared
by a large number of agencies. In 1980 a central state-controlled foundation
was created. This foundation was later transformed into a state-owned company: Samhall AB.

213

    During 2002, the number of employees with occupational disabilities
was 24,386. The workforce has contracted in recent years, and the company
now faces structural profitability problems and further cutbacks. The task
of the commission was to look for alternatives or complements to today's
system of rehabilitation of people with occupational disabilities. My experiences from my work on the Swedish Health Insurance System led me to
the conclusion that there also was a need for a more general change of the
rehabilitation process. The system of today is very much a system based on
ad hoc solutions. In the report, I proposed that the government should introduce a more firm system consisting of three phases.

    The Assessment phase will involve the employment office working
closely with the individual to agree on the support measure(s) or
programme(s) relevant to his or her needs.

---

*   English summary of "The Report of the Committee on the Control and Activities of
Samhall AB", Stockholm 2003. Swedish original: Inte bara Samhall, Statens Offentliga
Utredningar, SOU 2003:56.

Temporary placement phase. After this introduction, the individual and the employment office should look for a job at the open market. If needed the individual could be supported by a wage grant. If employment supported by a wage grant is not judged an appropriate option for an individual, the employment office can offer him/her employment with Samhall AB or some other employer for a maximum of two years. This limited period of employment should include substantial elements of rehabilitation, training and education, and have the aim of enabling the individual to get a job or education at the "open" market.

Secure employment phase. Individuals whose needs could not be met through the programmes offered by the first two phases, should be offered ongoing employment with Samhall AB or other employers who have declared their willingness to provide appropriate work in what is called a *secure employment phase.*

During all phases, the employer receives a wage grant and is refunded for the costs according to the individual plan and the agreement with the employment office.

If the government and parliament accept this report, new opportunities will be open for people with occupational disabilities in Sweden. I am convinced that this type of system also will be more cost-effective than the present system based on a state monopoly. This is an English summary of the report "Inte bara Samhall".

The Committee Proposes:

- that a new labour market policy measure to be known as General Sheltered Employment (ASA) be introduced with effect from 1 January 2005, replacing the existing scheme Sheltered Employment at Samhall;
- that the General Sheltered Employment scheme should be open to other providers besides Samhall AB;
- that a new, three-phase approach should be introduced: assessment, temporary placement and secure employment. The temporary placement and secure employment phases will take the place of the present measure Sheltered Employment at Samhall. The first phase – the assessment phase – is intended to form a common "gateway" to the whole range of labour market policy measures for people with occupational disabilities. This phase should be opened up as soon as possible to

occupationally disabled individuals currently supported by short- or long-term sickness benefit from social insurance offices or social assistance from local authorities;

- that Samhall AB should ensure that individuals currently employed at Samhall who wish to do so are given the opportunity to begin the assessment phase as soon as possible;
- that the current restriction which prevents labour market policy programmes and measures being combined with sheltered employment at Samhall should be lifted;
- that the National Labour Market Administration should be responsible for the assessment programme. The Government should, without delay, commission the Administration to draw up proposals concerning the development of an organizational framework for assessment. This should be seen as a further development on the assignment previously entrusted by the Government to the National Labour Market Administration and the National Social Insurance Board (N2003/459/A);
- that the county labour board concerned should revoke the placement of an employee with an occupational disability if the purpose for which it was made can no longer be pursued. Such a decision may be taken on the initiative of the county labour board or at the request of the employee, if there is an objective basis for it;
- that individuals placed in sheltered employment should continue to be excluded from the provisions of the Employment Protection Act;
- that the existing arrangements for funding should be replaced by a new system, linked to the proposals put forward by the Committee in chapter 4;
- that the new funding system should consist of individual *wage grants* to compensate for the employee's reduced capacity to work and *reimbursement of the costs* of development measures undertaken by Samhall AB and other providers to implement the individual development programmes established by the National Labour Market Administration;
- that possible arrangements for a *bonus for progression into open employment* should be evaluated on the basis of a trial scheme;
- that the new funding system should take effect on 1 January 2005;
- that the Government should channel the funding and control of all activities for people with occupational disabilities through the National Labour Market Administration. The General Sheltered Employment scheme should be financed under Expenditure Area 13 Labour Mar-

215

ket, Appropriation 22:4 *Special measures for people with occupational disabilities;*

- that, for a transitional period of five years, placements with Samhall made prior to 1 January 2005 should be financed under Expenditure Area 13 Labour Market, Appropriation 22:9 *Grant to Samball AB*. Placements after 1 January 2005 should be financed under Expenditure Area 13 Labour Market, Appropriation 22:4 *Special measures for people with occupational disabilities;*
- that the goals and requirements regarding employment, progression and recruitment which currently apply to Samhall AB should – in conjunction with the introduction of the General Sheltered Employment scheme – instead apply to the National Labour Market Administration;
- that the National Labour Market Administration should assume full responsibility for monitoring implementation of the labour market policy measure Sheltered Employment at Samhall and subsequently of the General Sheltered Employment scheme;
- that the Institute for Labour Market Policy Evaluation (IFAU) should remain responsible for evaluating the Sheltered Employment at Samhall scheme and subsequently the General Sheltered Employment scheme.

The terms of reference of the Committee have been to review the control and activities of Samhall AB (Terms of reference 2002:34). The problems to be addressed are clearly described in the terms of reference.

To begin with, the Committee emphasizes that the main purpose of the new labour market policy measure General Sheltered Employment (ASA) will be to promote the rehabilitation and development of people with occupational disabilities. The Committee also believes that individuals with occupational disabilities should primarily have access to employment in the open labour market. However, there will continue to be a need for what is commonly referred to as sheltered employment. The Committee's main finding is that the existing labour market policy and social objectives of this type of employment cannot be achieved by the state relying on a single company, Samhall AB. The present arrangements for sheltered employment at Samhall need to be reformed and opened up to other potential providers. The Committee proposes a new system to fund the General Sheltered Employment scheme, whereby employers will be reimbursed on the basis of the rehabilitation measures they undertake. This funding system will also apply to rehabilitation within Samhall AB. The existing state grant to Samhall AB should be phased out over a period of five years.

Facts about Samhall

In chapter 1 of its report, the Committee describes the origins and development of Samhall. Sheltered employment was introduced in a variety of forms during the 1960s, with responsibility for it shared among a large number of agencies. What is now Samhall has its origins in a central foundation created on 1 January 1980, Stiftelsen Samhällsföretag, and 24 regional foundations which were responsible for day-to-day operations. As early as 1992, however, these foundations were reconstituted as regional limited companies (see chapter 9), linked by a parent company, Samhall AB. According to Samhall AB's present articles of association, the purpose of its activities is to produce goods and services that are in demand and thereby to provide occupationally disabled individuals with meaningful employment which promotes their development, wherever the need arises. Since becoming a company in 1992, the enterprise has changed its organizational structure with appreciable frequency. At the end of 2002, the number of employees with occupational disabilities was 24,386. The workforce has contracted in recent years, and the company now faces structural profitability problems and further cutbacks. In addition, a shift is taking place in the work carried out, from the industrial sector to the services sector. Chapter 1 also includes an account of earlier inquiries and the current arrangements for central government control of Samhall AB. Like several previous studies and inquiries, the Committee identifies a clear conflict of goals between the profitability requirement and the requirement to offer individuals with occupational disabilities meaningful employment which promotes their development, wherever the need arises.

An International Comparison

According to chapter 2, the trend internationally is to move away from an exclusive employment sector towards an inclusive one. A shift is occurring, from a selective, segregated approach, based on special measures for people with occupational disabilities, to a more general, integrative approach. The key concepts in the European discussion are *mainstreaming, social inclusion* and *empowerment,* although in practice many countries still rely largely on targeted measures and specially tailored solutions.

Points of Departure and Reflections

In chapter 3 the special expert chairing the Committee outlines the points of departure and reflections that have guided its work.

A Reformed, Three-phase System of Sheltered Employment

The Committee proposes a reformed system of sheltered employment, consisting of three phases:

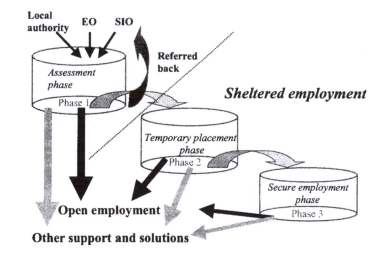

Assessment Phase, Phase 1

The assessment programme, *Phase 1*, will involve the employment office (EO) working closely with the individual to agree on the support measure(s) or programme(s) relevant to his/her needs and abilities. The assessment carried out should be precise enough to result in a clear individual plan for the foreseeable future. The individual's own ability to assume responsibility should be enhanced. In this regard, the Committee wishes to highlight the need for a change of perspective. The Committee believes that in the future system official action should – to a far greater extent than in the past – take account of and mobilize the wishes and capabilities of the individual. The assessment programme should extend over a *maximum of eight weeks*.

The assessment programme could have applications over a broader range of areas than labour market policy alone. The Committee proposes that, once the programme has been implemented and developed for the existing target groups of employment offices, it should also be made available to people receiving benefits from a social insurance office (SIO) or social assistance from a local authority.

Temporary Placement Phase, Phase 2

If employment supported by a wage grant is not judged to be an appropriate option for an individual, the employment office can offer him/her employment with Samhall AB or some other employer for a *maximum of two years*. This limited period of employment should include substantial elements of guidance, work assessment/work training, rehabilitation, training and education, and have the aim of enabling the individual to progress to open employment or mainstream training and education during or at the end of the two-year period.

219

Secure Employment Phase, Phase 3

Individuals whose needs could not be met through the programmes offered after the assessment or temporary placement phase should, in the absence of any special reasons to the contrary, be offered ongoing employment with Samhall AB or other employers who have declared their willingness to provide work in the *secure employment phase*.

All employers who accept individuals with occupational disabilities in the framework of the General Sheltered Employment scheme will of course be expected to demonstrate that they operate in accordance with satisfactory procedures with regard to quality and results.

The Government should guide the scale and priorities of the General Sheltered Employment scheme through its appropriation directions to the National Labour Market Administration. These directions should also set out the Government's requirements regarding progression into open employment.

The Committee notes that significant underemployment currently exists within Samhall. It is important to give present employees of Samhall the opportunity, if they so wish, to undergo an individual assessment to establish whether they can be offered better alternatives.

The Committee proposes that the National Labour Market Administration should be given responsibility for the assessment programme. Its recommendations emphasize the responsibilities of employment offices. The Committee wishes to stress that significant further development of the structure and quality of the Labour Market Administration's services and programmes is needed. The Committee assumes that the development process embarked on within the Administration will produce the intended results.

New Funding and Control Arrangements

In chapter 5, arrangements for funding are considered. The existing arrangements are based on the concept of "additional costs". However, this concept is not defined. The overall assessment of the Committee is that the present system of funding is unsatisfactory. This is particularly true in situations where the market is changing rapidly and Samhall AB has to undergo major structural changes.

220

In summary, the Committee concludes that the traceability of existing reimbursement payments for additional costs to the costs concerned is poor. Nor do Samhall AB's budget estimates link requests for such payments to specific costs. The company's owner – the state – does not determine the level of additional cost reimbursement, nor does it monitor how the state grant is used in relation to additional costs incurred. Equally, Samhall AB's internal allocation of cost reimbursements received is not based on any assessment of the costs in question. The additional cost reimbursement system is not structured – either in the framework of state control of the company or internally within Samhall AB – in such a way as to ensure traceability.

The Committee's conclusion is that the additional costs concept is too imprecise and vague to provide a basis for determining the level of state funding. It should be abandoned in favour of a system which as far as possible reimburses actual costs and is linked to the activities/services provided and the results achieved.

Transition from the Present System to General Sheltered Employment

Chapter 6 deals with the transition from the present system to the General Sheltered Employment scheme. The Committee considers there to be a strong case for putting the proposed scheme into effect as soon as possible. However, it is reasonable to give Samhall AB some advance warning of the changes to come, and also to give the National Labour Market Administration an acceptable basis for planning. For Samhall AB, the proposals represent a substantial change.

The Committee proposes transitional rules that will progressively reduce Samhall AB's current state grant over a period of five years.

Competition and State Aid Issues

Chapter 7 deals with the competition and state aid rules that are relevant to Samhall's activities. Samhall's operations could have competition-distorting effects and the financial support given to Samhall AB could be in conflict with EC legislation.

In summary, the Committee concludes, first, that the new system of funding which it proposes will eliminate the present uncertainty regarding competition neutrality and, second, that it will not constitute state aid.

Needs, Alternatives and Complements

Samhall AB's capacity to offer employment to people with occupational disabilities is decreasing by the year. Its "volume of hours of work" has fallen by a fifth since the mid-1990s, from 34.7 million hours in 1995 to 27.3 million in 2003.

Chapter 8 describes current needs and the alternative and complementary programmes that have emerged in recent years. The Committee's study of what needs exist makes it clear that alternative initiatives are required. The Committee presents various data as a basis for its appraisal of actual needs in terms of places of work providing occupationally disabled people with meaningful employment that promotes their development. According to the assessments made, at least 25,000-30,000 people may be assumed to be in need of a *"secure place of work"*.

The size of the target group for the *temporary placement phase* of the General Sheltered Employment scheme is more difficult to assess. However, in the Committee's view it is reasonable to assume that 10,000 people could benefit from this phase at any one time.

It is important to develop alternative and complementary arrangements. Above all, there is an urgent need to build up programmes that enjoy strong local support. Such programmes may assume many different forms: they could for example involve private companies, incorporated associations, cooperatives or local authorities, working on the basis of the needs existing in local labour markets.

Samhall's Form of Association

Chapter 9 discusses Samhall's form of association. Samhall AB is a limited company. The Committee's terms of reference included an evaluation of Samhall's form of association and an assessment of whether the conclusions set out in Committee Report SOU 1991:67 and Government Bill 1991/92:91 (which formed the basis for its conversion into a company) remain valid.

The Committee finds that those conclusions are by and large still valid and that there is no reason to change Samhall AB's form of association.

Samhall AB's Performance in Relation to its Mission

In chapter 10 the Committee points out that Samhall AB has a wide-ranging, complex and composite mission, and that the expectations placed on it vary according to whether the emphasis is on creating employment, individual development/rehabilitation, regional policy or redistribution/social policy.

The company's business operations are an *essential precondition* for its role in terms of labour market and social policy. At the same time, it is here that the *contradiction* in its mission lies. For commercial reasons, Samhall's activities have gradually become more specialized, focusing on the needs of major customers and on larger-scale and more concentrated production. In the Committee's assessment, the consequences in terms of effectiveness have changed (deteriorated) as Samhall AB has – at least in part – increasingly become a company like any other. It has become more and more difficult to reconcile commercial operations with the company's labour market and social objectives. In its report, the Committee draws attention to several areas where significant tensions exist between the company's business operations and these objectives.

The Committee's overall assessment is that, *given the basic conditions prevailing,* Samhall AB is fulfilling its mission in an acceptable manner. At the same time, the Committee believes that substantial change and development are needed with regard to the company's performance of its labour market policy role as a whole and of each of the specific tasks laid down for it: to provide meaningful employment, to provide employment that promotes the development of the employee, to offer employment wherever the need arises, and finally to provide employment for those with the greatest needs.

Goals and Results of Samhall AB's Current Activities

In chapter 11 the Committee notes that, under the existing arrangements for funding and control, reimbursement payments to the company are linked to an agreement between it and the state. This agreement sets out the goals and requirements which central government expects the company's activities to meet. Employment, recruitment and progression into open employment are currently priority objectives which are quantified in the agreement. Since becoming a company, Samhall AB has basically achieved all of the priority goals for its activities, but there is cause to question both the effectiveness of those goals and the quality of the data reported.

The Committee notes for example that the employment target has been adjusted downwards in the light of what the company has been expected to achieve. The working hours of individuals who are underemployed are included in the volume of hours of work which Samhall AB reports to the Government. The Committee suggests that the Government should consider setting an employment goal expressed in net terms (excluding underemployment), i.e. referring only to productive working hours that promote the development of employees.

The Committee also notes that Samhall AB has formally met its target for progression into open employment (currently 5%), but considers this target to be an extremely low one. There are appreciably more people working within Samhall who could reasonably be expected to progress to jobs on the open labour market. The Committee has made a particular study of

223

women and progression, and is of the opinion that substantial efforts must be made to ensure that women make up a larger share of those moving into open employment.

The recruitment requirement exists in order to ensure that occupationally disabled individuals facing the greatest difficulties have access to the labour market policy measure Sheltered Employment at Samhall. The Committee agrees with the National Audit Office that the National Labour Market Board's application of existing regulations does not provide sufficient control and guidance for officials responsible for referring individuals to sheltered employment with Samball. The Committee also considers that priority groups are not sufficiently clearly defined, creating scope for differing assessments by individual employment office staff. With the existing definition of priority groups, it is not possible to measure and monitor progress towards this goal. The present goal should therefore be reformulated.

224

Monitoring and Evaluation

Chapter 12 deals with monitoring and evaluation issues. In the view of the Committee, it is at present unclear who is responsible for monitoring and evaluating the activities of Samhall AB. What is more, there is a lack of relevant information that would allow the owner – the state – to control the company's activities in an effective manner.

Impact Analyses

In chapter 13 the Committee presents analyses of the impacts of its proposals.

Who Needs Supported Employment and How?*

Charlotte Strümpel

What is Supported Employment?

Supported Employment is a perspective that involves supporting people with a severe disability to find and maintain a job on the ordinary labour market. It offers individual, tailor-made support in the job-finding phase and on-the-job with the help of job coaches.

For Whom Is Supported Employment?

The key idea of Supported Employment is to support people with a substantial disability that otherwise would not work in an ordinary work setting. It was conceived for a target group that was traditionally non-employed or employed only in sheltered work settings.

Supported Employment thus challenges a phrase which is often heard in discussions on employment of people with a disability: "those people not able to work on the ordinary labour market". There are many examples of people not regarded by their environment as able to work on the ordinary labour market but that through Supported Employment have succeeded in finding and maintaining such a job.

However, policy in many countries has been about defining the success of Supported Employment through the number of placements made. This can lead to an effect known as "creaming", where Supported Employment providers choose people with less severe disabilities as clients in order to more easily fulfil quantitative placement criteria. Especially in cases where the overall labour market situation is difficult, this may lead to excluding those from Supported Employment services that they are actually meant for.

Recommendation 1: Supported Employment must maintain its aims to cater to people in need of a vast amount of support to work on the ordinary labour market.

What Is the Relationship between Supported Employment and Sheltered Work?

The relationship between Sheltered Work and Supported Employment is much discussed and is also subject of other statements at this conference. In his contribution, Erik Samoy states that Supported Employment and Sheltered Work form a continuum and that very much the same elements are involved in both these provisions, such as wage subsidies, adaptation to the workplace and personal support. Many people active in Supported Employment would not see this as a continuum, but rather regard Sheltered Work as a symbol for a segregated work setting and a job on the ordinary labour market as a symbol of an integrated work setting.

The objective of Supported Employment is to find a job on the ordinary labour market which fulfils certain criteria. These are: a valid contract of employment, adequate wages and a stable job. This also means a job that matches the employee's skills and abilities including a positive atmosphere at the workplace, a satisfied employer as well as a good relationship with and support from co-workers (see also www.quip.at).

Erik Samoy mentions large differences between sheltered workshops in terms of wages, working conditions, amount of support offered and level of segregation. Thus it is hard to make overall judgements on sheltered work. However, the ultimate aim of all activation measures – no matter what they are called – should be full employment in work settings that fulfil the above-mentioned criteria. It should be about offering high-quality jobs for people with a disability. However, in reality, people with a disability – whether in sheltered or integrated settings – are still mainly found in low-paying, low-status, odd jobs that are not permanent.

Sheltered work settings should continue to develop in such a way that they fulfil aspects of the „ordinary labour market" and the so-called „ordinary labour market" should continue to develop in such a way as to accommodate and offer support to people with different needs. This is the idea which underlies the discussion on mainstreaming. In the whole mainstreaming debate there is of course the issue that targeted support can be missing for people with vast support needs.

> "I would like to find a real and interesting job" (Job seeker, Austria)
> "I want to find the job I want to do, and not just any old one" (Job seeker, UK)

Recommendation 2: When designing activation measures to support the integration of people with disabilities into the labour market, the main focus should be on the characteristics and the quality of the job.

What Makes Supported Employment Work?

227

Tailor-made Approach

The key to the success of Supported Employment lies in the tailor-made individual approach. This involves individual planning, individual support for job seekers, supported employees and employers, as well as flexible help when needed. The methods used in Supported Employment can be an impulse for other activation measures.

> "I like that you are not only a number" (Job seeker, Austria)
> "As SE is an individual approach, the problem is never the same" (Job coach, Norway)
> "They always come when we need them" (Employer, Spain)

Recommendation 3: Activation measures should take into account Supported Employment's tailor-made, flexible approach that encompasses the needs of the individual person with a disability and those of the employer.

Including Stakeholders as Partners

A further key issue with respect to activation measures like Supported Employment, is how to involve the many actors in the provision of the service.

While traditionally, job seekers or employees with a disability, employers as well as policy-makers are seen as customers, that are offered a service by the SE provider, in the future a stronger focus should be put on involving these stakeholders as partners and co-producers and not as passive recipients of a service.

A crucial role is that of the *job seeker/supported employee* with a disability. One of the main objectives of Supported Employment is to actively involve job seekers in the Supported Employment process, support them to make their own decisions and generally support their empowerment. However, this is an aspect which is not yet systematically implemented in practice. Here social service attitudes, where things are done for and not by the job seekers or supported employees with a disability, are still predominant in practice. There are also big differences between various countries in self-advocacy and user involvement in service provision. There is a large scope for improvement in this field.

228

"It is based on clients' expectations and abilities, on dialogue with the client" (Policy-maker, Czech Republic)
"We (my job coach and I) are a good team, we work together as equals" (Job seeker, UK)

Recommendation 4: Supported employees and job seekers should be actively involved at all levels of the Supported Employment process and user involvement in service provision should be encouraged.

The role of the *employers and co-workers* in Supported Employment is one of the most difficult issues as is also in general the case when looking at the employment of people with a disability. It is a challenge to actively involve employers in promoting the employment of people with a disability. Another issue is involving and informing co-workers and supporting them to support employees with a disability. This is also a field where improvements are necessary.

"The job coach was here, but we preferred to use a colleague to teach the employee the work" (Employer, Norway)
"There were no troubles with the colleagues, on the contrary they facilitated his integration" (Employer, Spain)

Recommendation 5: Employers should be regarded more as co-producers and be encouraged to actively contribute to the success of Supported Employment.

The Job Coaches

The job coach plays a pivotal role in Supported Employment. The job coach is a broker and a go-between between all other stakeholders in the SE process. The job is characterized by very high expectations towards the job coach and a wide variety of key skills that the job coach is said to need. Within many Supported Employment organisations there is a high turnover among job coaches, which is especially problematic because of the importance of the personal relationship between job coach and supported employee, and job coach and employers. One reason for this may be the difficulty in negotiating and moving in the "two worlds" of social service logic and business logic. Also in most countries there is no systematic training for job coaches and people from many different backgrounds work as job coaches.

229

"It is the variation and diversity of competence that counts in SE work" (Job coach, Norway)
"Job coaches need fearlessness in dealing with employers" (Job seeker, Czech Republic)

Recommendation 6: Working conditions, as well as training of job coaches need to be reviewed and improved.

One Service of Many

Another crucial point that is also mentioned in the OECD report *Transforming Disability into Ability* is how Supported Employment relates to other services. It has to closely work together with other services to be able to refer people who need different kinds of support. Networking and referral between the vast variety of services to promote the integration of people with a disability needs to be improved. This is connected with the question of how people are referred to different activation services. It is still the case that access to Supported Employment is based on chance encounters or referrals rather than being the result of a systematic approach.

"Developing the process of learning from each other between different providers of services for people with a disability" (Employer, Hungary)

"I don't like agency tennis: being hit from side to side" (Job seeker, UK)

Recommendation 7: There is a need to improve cooperation between labour market services, social services and providers of SE.

Which Role Should Policy Have?

In many countries we find that employment and disability policies actively promote Supported Employment measures. In some countries there is a clear legal background for Supported Employment, in others there is not. As mentioned above, there is a strong focus on quantitative placement measures to determine the success of Supported Employment providers by policy-makers. This can lead to forgetting important aspects of Supported Employment like the quality of the job, opportunities for career development, targeting those people that need the service most or long-term job retention and may jeopardize the main aims as well as the quality of Supported Employment.

Recommendation 8: Supported Employment needs to be firmly embedded in national employment policies for people with a disability. Criteria for success should not only focus on quantitative placement measures but on providing good, long-term jobs for people with a disability.

Note

*   This statement is based on the project "QUIP – Quality in Practice: Stakeholders' View of Supported Employment" which was carried out in the framework of the European Commission's LEONARDO-programme 2001-2002. It was coordinated by the European Centre for Social Welfare Policy and Research and involved partners from Austria, the Czech Republic, Hungary, Norway, Spain and the UK. For more information see: www.quip.at

Comments on the Policy Conclusions

Vappu Taipale

In Finland, the Act on Services and Support for Persons with Disabilities was created nearly 20 years ago. Since then we have got used to think of disability as a relationship, a relationship between an individual and his/her environment. The more enabling the environment is, the less disabilities are barriers to independent living.

The OECD report *Transforming Disability into Ability. Policies to Promote Work and Income Security for Disabled People* promises a profound change of paradigm. The elements of this change are unbundling disability and benefits, mutual obligations, individual packages for people with disabilities, employer involvement and reforming programme administration.

Who needs activation? This is a very relevant question, since decision-making structures, local decision-makers and personnel providing services are also in need of activation. For instance, the high-level negotiations within the World Trade Organisation, where the point of view of persons with disabilities might be highly relevant, may one day end in a free trade of pensions and services and globally change the opportunities and the living environments of all people, not only those of people with disabilities. From this point of view the question also arises to what extent persons with disabilities and their organizations have been given the opportunity to participate in the preparation of this OECD report.

The Agreed International Standard of Non-discrimination and Inclusion of People with Disabilities

The United Nation's Standard Rules as well as the premises of current European legal frameworks imply that people who have disabilities should not be discriminated and that each individual sector is responsible for managing disability issues in an inclusive manner. As regards the labour market, there is also the new ILO Code of Practice with the same effect.

Societal Challenges

There are many societal phenomena and challenges in the OECD countries that have to be faced when speaking about transforming disability into ability.

The Development of Information Societies

All the OECD countries will face the rapid societal development into information societies. The sudden leap into the information society is a most intrinsic process in all our societies. The significance of the information society is measured by the relevance of the contents it is producing through its means. Information is a commodity whose importance grows when it is being distributed. Education is a means for producing well-being and control of life. The development opportunities are tremendous. The societies can implement the idea of life-long learning – nobody is too young, too disabled or too old to learn. Technologies are available which allow us to overcome the obstacles of distance, time and disability. Through satellite connections, the most remote health centre in the midst of mountains or rain forests can get the most modern information on treatment. There exist technologies that allow people with grave disabilities to live with autonomy and dignity. The technological innovations primarily made to serve warlike conditions can be converted to be used in everyday life.

But, the challenges are even greater: to make an information society a society for all. In an information society, learning and skills become a major asset, and people with learning disorders and poor learning environments will easily face marginalisation and exclusion. The hectic working life produces more and more stress-related problems and disorders. The more there are mental problems and the more persons with disabilities are mentally incapable or ill, the more difficulties the caretaking systems will face.

The Need for Integrated Policies

Social policy programmes are the best way to enhance social protection and to reduce vulnerability. The present economic, environmental and social situation in the world challenges national policies; international cooperation is needed. Within national social policies a stage has been reached where there is a growing need to replace vertical policy-making by horizontal activities and connections. The various policy sectors have become more interdependent: agricultural policy bears on health, equality policies influence competitive capabilities, transport policies influence industrial policies, employment policies affect pension schemes, and regional policies involve socio-political responsibilities. The issues of disability and ability should be consistently tackled by multi-sectoral, integrated policies. However, policy-making has become very sectorised, and responsibilities are difficult to share. Sectors also develop independently of each other, not knowing the philosophy or the practicalities of other sectors. The real future challenges are coordination of efforts and managing of networks.

233

The Importance of the Civil Society

Social capital is based on inclusion, participation and promotion of an enabling environment. There are studies to show that the existence of a civil society is not only the precursor and guarantor of good governance, but also the key to sustained socio-economic development. Social capital brings into daylight the networks between people, the confidence people feel in their transactions, and the stability and reliability of functioning in municipalities and localities. The concept addresses the economy from the social point of view and shows that important pre-conditions of economic life are social. But, the civil society needs to be strengthened everywhere. The challenges of empowering people are the same whether the societies are rich or poor, developing or developed. NGOs of people with disabilities are most important in the societal dialogue. However, they are not strong enough and there are countries where NGOs are not considered as important partners in societal discussions. Especially the NGOs of mentally ill people are weak. I do hope that you know organisations such as Hearing the Voices, Relatives and Parents of Schizophrenics, Victims and Survivors of Psychiatry etc. There are also such most successful activities under way as the Fountain House organisation with Club House enterprises supporting the move into the open labour market.

The Ageing of the Population

Ageing is a natural phenomenon, but it often brings with it multiple minor disabilities. All OECD countries are being faced with demographic, structural, social and technological changes of major importance. The ageing process will not only change the population structure of countries profoundly. The process will be inter-sectoral, part of everything. It will cover all policy areas. We have to develop a perspective that enables all societies to see the population changes as positive opportunities for societies and economies. The opportunity lies in innovative social, organisational and technological responses to the rising challenges.

From Disability to Ability

The Current Magnitude of the Issue

Internationally, the magnitude of the issue of disability is remarkable, and the world is still rather producing disabilities than preventing their emergence. Poverty, hunger, malnutrition, wars and conflicts, infectious diseases, traffic and work accidents cause traumas, disabilities, and disease that could be prevented.

It also has to be kept in mind that neither people with disabilities nor older people are a homogeneous group, a grey mass of people. They differ greatly from each other: hard of hearing people need different policies and aids than mentally ill people, a child with CP has different needs from an adult with diabetes.

In the Finnish context we are speaking about a population of five million people. There is no single source of valid and reliable statistics on the labour force status of people with disabilities. According to the registers of the Ministry of Labour, there are 85,000 people with disabilities in the open labour market in Finland. Out of these, 67,000 are unemployed and 16,000 employed. Additionally, there are 11,000 people with disabilities engaged in sheltered jobs. If we assume that people with disabilities account for about 5% of the labour force, half – or rather two thirds – of all people with disabilities are not recorded in employment statistics and are thus without employment. Hence, the challenge is enormous. However, this issue cannot be solved by sheltered jobs, either.

Policy Conclusions

Solutions need to be sought primarily at the open labour market, but the challenge is huge. Thus, in respect of the policy conclusions, the following issues arise:

1. Due to the magnitude of the issue, to "roll out" or expand the idea of individual participation packages is realistic only if integrated with the basic rehabilitation process of each individual with disabilities. This is not yet standard practice due to sector boundaries. There is a need for *designing a cross-sectoral and integrated concept of seamless services and a system of rehabilitation services.* In the field of technology, there are concepts like "mass-individualisation" . The concept of seamless services has greatly been enhanced also by the development of telemedicine and telematic services.

2. Similarly, individual case-by-case coaching is difficult to expand. Rather, a "resource centre" type of *job accommodation services in collaboration with e.g. the organisations of people with disabilities* may be more feasible.

3. There is a serious challenge in raising the *awareness* of gatekeepers, and intense interventions are needed both in the basic *training and retraining* of staff involved in gate-keeping. At the end of the day all services are face-to-face contacts.

4. As of early intervention, there is a need *to review legislation* to allow flexibility between benefit eligibility and work-related income.

5. Systematic *evaluations of the impact of alternative interventions* are indeed scarce and should be baked into any new programme. Policies always have both intended and unintended consequences.

235

Some Additional Points of View

COMMUNITY BASED REHABILITATION

It is obvious that no significant increase in the inclusion of people with disabilities in the open labour market will be possible by focusing on activating only people with disabilities or excluded people themselves. Experiments should be initiated to try out the ideas known as Community Based Rehabilitation (CBR) to activate and involve the community's private and public actors to take part in the rehabilitation and inclusion of its members with disabilities. This would foster shared responsibility and ownership by the community of the outcome of inclusion efforts.

DESIGN FOR ALL

There is also a need to elicit demand for the productive potential of people with disabilities. This implies changes in both the policies and in the knowledge, attitudes and practices of all stakeholders: employers, legislators and organizations of people with disabilities. The "Design for All" principle needs to be internalized and applied at all levels.

CORPORATE SOCIAL RESPONSIBILITY

Inclusion is a public good that does not seem to be catered for properly by the market. There is a case for stronger public intervention to ensure that businesses need to bear their social responsibilities to promote the cohesion of their communities and society as a whole. Corporate Social Responsibility refers to manifold activities of enterprises and allows innovative ways to meet the needs of people with disabilities.

Empowerment! Evidence!

Furthermore, there is a need to reorient disability-related services and social security from the traditional safety-net approach towards becoming empowering "springboards" aiming clearly at inclusion and active participation rather than serving as a disempowering harbour for those already excluded.

Evidence-based medicine, with all its limitations, has grown in importance in the last ten years. Could we call for evidence-based policies? There are too little research and studies about different national systems for people with disabilities. What we need is long-term studies and evaluations of the efficacy of systems, not merely of their cost-effectiveness.

Who Needs Activation, How and When? Session Report

Hedva Sarvati

Highlights of the Discussion on Theme 3

The discussion focused on the following issues: the role of wage subsidies; the relationship between sheltered work, sheltered employment and other activation measures; job retention; the need to balance the activation efforts between those in and out of work; and the need of voice for the disabled and partnerships.

Role of Wage Subsidies

There was a long discussion on the role of wage subsidies in activation measures. While they were seen as being important by most of those who mentioned this topic, questions were raised as to whether wage subsidies should be a long-term provision or only short-term support to "get started". The provision differs greatly between countries.

In Belgium, wage subsidies are an important element in the participation package and functionally equivalent to a partial benefit. The view is that if the state has to pay anyhow, it is preferable to pay a wage subsidy, because it meant that there was a job behind it, even if some benefits had to be maintained. And yet, there was a strong political resistance to them, especially to the long-term subsidies. The OECD stressed that it was strongly in favour of wage subsidies for disabled employees in certain circumstances. But a problem in Belgium and in other countries, including France, was that there were far too many regulations, far too detailed and difficult to understand, with the result that people do not know of their existence or trust that they can use these wage subsidies. If they were simplified and focused, the OECD is in favour of wage subsidies that help to make work pay. In the UK, there are no massive wage subsidies in terms of giving the employer a subsidy, but rather a system which pays disability benefits in and out of work. Benefits include both a non means-tested disability living allowance that tends to meet extra costs and an income-related disability in work benefit. But there is a problem that actually more help is provided to the long-term unemployed than to the long-term sick and disabled. Sweden also has high and long-term wage subsidies. There is evidence that once people are on wage subsidies they tend to stay on all their working life. But it is hard to reduce the subsidy; even when conditions improved, people tended to stay in low-paid jobs.

Some participants pointed out to an "ideological" dimension, raising the question of whether some employees who receive wage subsidies are really employed on equal terms. Moreover, the usual objection to it was that it maintained job segregation. It was also found necessary to combine the two debates about wage subsidies and the "benefit traps" in the area of disability and how to tackle the issue of the working poor, for example through a negative income tax. This could improve transparency, even in an increasingly market-driven society and facing liberalisation efforts of the WTO.

Relationship Sheltered Work / Sheltered Employment to Other Activation Measures

There was an interesting exchange on the functioning of sheltered workshops. One participant suggested that these workshops could be moved more towards competitive sectors and products as sub-contractors, and there are successful examples of such practices. This was countered with the argument that too many people in sheltered workshops have a mental disability, and therefore need simple manual work to do. It was not by attracting new high-tech activities that the challenge resides for future employment policies for the mentally disabled people. The limits of this niche approach were illustrated by the example of a Belgian sheltered workshop employing a few hundred employees, nearly all mentally disabled, for packaging all Duracell batteries for distribution throughout Europe. If this workshop were to be replaced by a highly sophisticated packaging system – there would be little chance that the disabled employees would keep their jobs. It came out clearly that there are different "communities" involved in different activation measures (such as sheltered employment and supported work) and that these communities were quite tightly knit and usually work in "their worlds". There is a need to bring together experts in different areas of activation – also for different target groups, not only for people with disabilities – to exchange views and expertise. This is especially important with respect to the discussions on mainstreaming going on everywhere.

Measures for Those In or Out of Employment?

The basic question here was whether activation measures for the employment of people with a disability focused on those in or out of employment. The OECD report found that most measures targeted people in employment. This was true for measures like quota schemes or special protection against dismissal that usually benefit those in employment and pose barriers for those seeking employment. However, activation measures usually focus only on those seeking a job. In developing activation measures as well as other measures, there should be a focus on balancing the benefits of measures for both groups of people and avoid going into one extreme.

239

Early Intervention, Anti-discrimination Legislation

The representative of the European Disability Forum, an umbrella organisation of associations of disabled persons, commented from the perspective of his organisation urging caution on the issue of *early intervention*, especially associated with sanctions, which were mentioned in the OECD report. Early prompting of work resumption shortly after a serious work or car accident, resulting, for example, in paralysis or loss of sight, would be inappropriate. With reference to age discrimination, it was necessary to keep in mind the heterogeneity of the situation. Consider young disabled persons graduating from school or university – efforts should be made to bring them into the labour market as soon as possible. Compare this situation to that of a person that after 30 years of work in a hard industrial work environment has become disabled as a result of such work. Should the same effort of work entry or re-entry be undertaken in both cases? Or should one rather ask, in the latter situation, if the person is keen to return to work. Mention was also made of the low employment rates of people with disabilities in countries with anti-discrimination legislation. Here too, caution is needed in the analysis. Anti-discrimination legislation has a huge impact on the way society considers people with disabilities. It has an important mid-term effect on education and will eventually result in employment. The European Disability Forum strongly believes that it is necessary to have a combination of legislation outlawing discrimination, which sends a strong message to society that it is unlawful to discriminate against disabled people. But this needs to be accompanied by a positive action of comprehensive measures, such as incentives to employers and wage subsidies.

In the area of early intervention, a recent ISSA study on work integration was briefly discussed. This study is a kind of snapshot of the interventions. It involved six countries, and interviews with about 2,500 people who were out of work for more than three months due to lower back pain. The patients were followed for two years with the objective of finding out how to improve the return to work of people with work incapacity, whether the various interventions – medical, vocational and institutional – made a difference as to work resumption patterns and, if so, what were the best interventions. The results were quite striking. Intervention made a difference, but there were huge inter-country variations. After two years, Germany had a resumption rate of 35%, Denmark – 40%, Israel – 60%, the US – 62%, Sweden – 63% and the Netherlands – 72% . This huge gap between the lowest and the highest performers was partly due to the difficulty in having homogeneous country cohort samples, but the main explanation resided in the interventions, in labour legislation, in institutions, etc.[1]

The ISSA study found that most interventions occurred during the first year. Very few work resumptions (between 5-19%) took place after the first year. In fact, three countries – Denmark, Israel and Sweden – had improved the resumption rate during the second year, while the three others saw a slight decrease of resumption rates. By contrast, there was no evidence of linkage between medical intervention and work resumption. Only in one country was surgery for lower back pain significantly connected to work resumption. And, interestingly enough, Sweden, which boasted high work resumption rates, had the lowest frequency of surgery. The third comment concerned wage subsidy. While none of the six countries in the study seemed to have wage subsidies, there were huge differences between countries that had job protection legislation and those who did not. The Netherlands and Sweden, who came on top with work resumption, both had such legislation, while the lowest performers did not. Moreover, while Denmark and the Netherlands had quite similar patterns and interventions and a close philosophy of work resumption, they had very different outcomes. What

240

made the difference was the job protection legislation in the Netherlands and its absence in Denmark. As a result of these findings, the Danish partner in the study had taken up the matter in an effort to improve outcomes.

The Role of Health Intervention

A representative of the British Society of Rehabilitation Medicine stressed that the kind of conditions that were leading people to ask for incapacity benefits were amenable to health interventions given a proper working environment and a supportive employer. Therefore the health issue, which he felt was rather played down in the OECD report was very counterproductive. As a health professional trying to influence politicians he took the view that it was a lot cheaper to keep people in work. Therefore strategies aiming at job retention are probably the most likely to be helpful in the short term. The health provision links with employers' attitudes, because often, being a good employer was seen as being tolerant of sickness according to the medical assessment of work capacity. Yet, all the evidence suggests this is wrong, and that there needed to be a partnership between the health provider and the employer for a phased return to work.

241

The OECD acknowledged that more work needed to do done on the health aspect. The report was ambitious in its current scope, but the interaction between health service and employment was missing . The same error characterised many national administrations and there clearly was need to look more closely in future at this interaction. The OECD had just started work on the tendency of health care systems to rely on waiting times to manage their surgery rights. An issue that arose in this context was that the conditions that determine these waiting times were precisely those that kept people out of work. And these were not the considerations that entered in the decision criteria of the health care systems, that look at the efficiency of their hospitals. There seemed to be a social externality here that was still absent from the way in which health services governed themselves.

Voice and Partnerships

A participant from the Italian Ministry of Labour and Social Policy underlined the need for cooperation among all parts of society and the role of the trade unions and the social partners. and the need to give a voice to the organizations representing the disabled. One way to achieve it was by enabling these associations representing the disabled to participate in all the deliberative bodies dealing with disability issues at national, regional (EU) and international levels.

Conclusions

Given my work on activation policies and social protection systems related to the "open" labour market, I found the OECD report and the discussions at the conference stimulating and thought-provoking, both in terms of policy shortcomings or obstacles and in the pathways to potentially improved outcomes in the areas of activation for people with disabilities. This included the better horizontal and vertical linkages mentioned by some speakers and participants, between administrators and service delivery agencies, and between these institutions and the users – individuals who want to return to the labour market and their potential employers.

What both the OECD report and the discussions seem to indicate is that there still are a number of issues that need to be addressed, among which I would note the following:

- The need for developing appropriate training packages for the very demanding job of staff of the often-mentioned one-stop shop and the individual case managers.

- The urgency of developing criteria and a methodology for *assessing the broad cost-benefit analysis and effectiveness of the activation measures*, evaluating the outcomes in the light of the policy objectives and of the means put at their disposal. Such evaluation and assessments require comparisons with control groups, which seem to be missing at present in national contexts.

- The *health dimension* was not adequately taken into account, and there would be room for further objective evaluations of contributions of long-term wage subsidies and tax credits to the success of activation policies

- The discussion on *wage subsidies* indicated that the issue raises various objections particularly when it is granted on a long-term basis, and these objections appear to be somewhat "extraneous" ("ideological" arguments as some have put it) to the objective of ensuring social or economic integration of the disabled. These arguments reflect concerns of "unfair" competitive advantage (raised by the WTO) or "discrimination" due to unequal pay for similar jobs. The former argument seems marginally true for those countries that may massively subsidize sheltered workshops or jobs. But is it as frequent as to create real problems? As regards the second argument – wage subsidies are certainly facilitating job entry to people with disabilities, who are likely to be more costly to employ because of the necessary work organization and workplace accommodation and have lower productivity than their non-disabled co-workers. So there is a need to provide fiscal incentives to the employer. On the other hand, fiscal incentives are also necessary to "make work pay" for the disabled people. Such subsidies seem justified both socially and economically as, on the whole, they contribute to achieving both the social objective of integration and the economic objective of reducing the welfare burden, because they are less costly than keeping disabled people only on disability benefits. Interestingly, the discussions only raised objections to (and arguments in favour of) "wage subisidies", but not to tax credits.

- The impact of the stage of the *business cycle* needs to be looked at. While accelerated growth is expected to "lift all boats" – as it did for youth unemployment in the US in the late 1990s to an extent and pace unparalleled by all the activation measures – it did not happen for the disabled people. In the European context it was seen that, while growth contributed to the exit of disabled workers from sheltered workshops into "regular" employment, it has also increased flows into sheltered workshops due to increased outsourcing from "regular" firms. **243**

- Turning to the overwhelming issue of an ageing society, there was little if any consideration of the *extent to which exclusion coincided with age* and how it could be addressed through life-long training. The OECD report clearly indicated the increased prevalence of disability among the aged and among people with lower educational attainment. This links to my earlier comment on the inadequacy of evaluation and the need for further development of activation programmes which leads me to suggest three questions:
  - (i) To what extent does evaluation include disaggregating by age. In other words, what works for specific ages or age groups?
  - (ii) To what extent is this linked to the concept of life-long learning and retraining?
  - (iii) To what extent are changes in knowledge, attitudes and practices of the various stakeholders documented in evaluation efforts, again disaggregated by age groups of the target populations?

- Lastly, I would like to concur with comments of a number of speakers and participants about the vital importance of participation of all the stakeholders in the formulation, implementation and evaluation of activation policies. Employers and trade unions have here a major role to play in raising awareness of the issues related to integrating disabled people in society and at developing and negotiating innovative modalities to achieve it. Given my ILO background, I was somewhat surprised to note the quasi absence of trade unions in the meeting, and in particular that the two trade union panellists, scheduled in the programme to deal with barriers to participation, did not show up. Was it an indication of the low priority they grant to the topic? There was however an interesting contribution on the role of employers and of temporary work agencies in facilitating labour market entry of people with disabilities. So, to conclude on a more positive note, where there's a will, there is a way – and this applies to all stakeholders.

244

Note

1   Bloch, F.S./Prins, R. (Eds.) (2000) *Who Returns to Work and Why? A Six-country Study on Work Incapacity and Reintegration*, ISSA, International Social Seucrity Series Vol. 5. New Brunswick and London: Transaction Publishers. A brochure summarising the findings was published in 2002 and is available from ISSA.

How Should Disability Benefits Be Structured?

Key Issues

1. Different disabilities lead to different degrees of work capacity. Half of the countries offer at least some type of benefit for partial disability, and one in four have partial disability benefits at several gradations. In the latter group, one in three awards is for partial disability.

2. At the same time, partial benefits may become an easy bridge into benefit dependence, because outflow from such benefits is also low. Paradoxically, some countries aim to introduce or broaden the scale of partial benefits while others are in the process of abolishing them.

3. Many disability benefit schemes take the applicant's age and/or the length of the insurance record into account to determine the benefit level. This may systematically discriminate against certain groups of disabled people.

4. Flat-rate disability benefits avoid such discrimination but will often fail to secure a disabled person's current standard of living. And household means-testing of disability benefits, that is targeting of available resources, can also be problematic.

5. Often, disability benefit schemes provide little incentives to work.

OECD Policy Conclusions

- Disability cash benefits should be available with sufficient flexibility to take account of both different cases of remaining work capacity and of the evolution of an individual's disability and work status over time.
- Many disability schemes are centred on income-replacing benefits and tie other benefits and services to eligibility for such cash transfers, thereby discouraging disabled persons from trying to return to work. Such systems need to be dismantled so that benefits and services can be awarded independently.
- Benefit entitlements should be designed in a way that the disabled person is not penalised for taking up work. After-tax income including all transfers should be higher in work than the income the person received while out of work.
- Take-up of work may need to be encouraged through financial incentives. In-work top-up payments are likely to be most effective. Such top-up payments would be strictly work-related for compensation of low pay or reduced working hours.
- Wage subsidies paid to the employers would play a less important role under this new approach, since beneficiaries would receive direct in-work benefits. There may, however, be a case for compensating the employers for the extra costs of workplace accommodation.

How Should Disability Benefits Be Structured? Session Report

Dennis J. Snower

Response to the OECD Report

The OECD has compiled an impressive report, one that makes a significant contribution to our understanding of the determinants of disability as well as the formulation of policy guidelines to mitigate the social welfare losses from this problem.

The OECD case for making disability policy consistent with unemployment policy is strong and deserves serious consideration in all member states. The main reason is that the personal incomes of disabled people are heavily dependent on whether the people find work. Employment turns out to be an extraordinarily effective avenue out of poverty, since the average incomes of disabled people are nearly as high as those of the non-disabled. In addition, there is ample evidence that just as the move from employment into long-term unemployment is often accompanied by psychological and other health problems, the move in the opposite direction often has symmetrically salutary effects. This consideration is particularly important since psychological problems account for between a quarter and a third of disability benefit receipt levels in the OECD.

Along these lines, considerations of equity – viz., the equitable distribution of income, wealth and, more generally, well-being – suggest that employment policy should play an important role in providing for disabled people. In fact, divorcing employment policy from disability policy is tantamount to excluding disabled people from playing a productive part in modern economies, thus compounding the problem that disability policy is meant to help overcome.

Inequities in the provision of disability benefits are significant. In the OECD, nearly 20% of the disabled of working age receives no income from either work or benefits. On the other hand, approximately a third of the disability recipients do not classify themselves as disabled.

Beyond that, considerations of economic efficiency – the avoidance of waste in the allocation of resources, in the production of goods and services, and in their distribution among households – reinforce the need to integrate disability and employment policies. Integrating the disabled in the workforce would be a wasteful policy if the disabled were a largely homogeneous group, with severe congenital disabilities that prevented them from generating revenue from the production of goods and services in excess of their subsistence income. But this is not the case. Only a third of the disabled have severe disabilities, and a much smaller proportion of these disabilities are congenital. The existing evidence provides ample reasons to believe that the majority of the currently disabled populations in OECD countries could be integrated into the workforce, in various forms, provided that the policy framework is appropriate.

It is thus striking that all OECD countries appear to be far removed from this goal. The disabled people of working age have relatively low employment rates. Disabled people over the age of 50 and those with relatively low educational attainment have far lower employment rates. The resulting waste of human resources is substantial, since disability prevalence in the OECD, as percentage of the working-age population, averages to around 14%. In most OECD countries, a significantly larger share of the working-age population receives disability benefits than unemployment benefits.

It is also striking that most disability policies in the OECD appear to be quite ineffective in helping people into work. Special employment programmes, for example, play only a minor role in raising employment rates. Across OECD countries, there appears to be no significant relation between benefit recipiency rates and employment rates.

The origins of this policy problem are not clear, although the following factors deserve serious consideration. Since disability awards fall disproportionately on people over 50, this group needs special policy attention. At present, these people get offered little vocational rehabilitation and training. Often these people move from unemployment to disability benefit recipiency to retirement with little incentive to re-enter the workforce.

Another factor is that job loss by disabled people is often reversible if it can be identified early and if sufficient work incentives can be provided.

A common problem appears to be that government measures to re-integrate the disabled in the workforce are often put into effect only once remaining out of work has become a way of life for the disabled.

A final, and particularly important, factor is that the successful implementation of disability measures must rest on the exploitation of central policy complementarities. It is pointless to offer disabled people employment incentives if employers do not make provision for them at the workplace; it is equally pointless to require employers to give disabled people access to their facilities if the disabled have no incentive to accept work. In short, it is important to exploit complementarities among three groups of policies: (i) employment incentives to disabled people (coupled with benefit sanctions when these incentives are not taken up, even though the nature of the disability is not an obstacle), (ii) regulation of employers to ensure that disabled people are not discriminated against at the workplace, and (iii) policy reform by the government that aims at early intervention, simple administration of benefits, and emphasis on active labour market policies.

The main gaps in our knowledge appear to be centred on the nature of these complementarities. More empirical work needs to be done to assess which policies work best with one another and what institutional environment is appropriate to the exploitation of these complementarities.

Overview of the Thematic Session

The key conclusions of this session may be summarized as follows:

- One important aim of disability policy should be employment creation for people with disabilities. Thus disability policy becomes part and parcel of employment policy. Naturally, however, disability as a policy challenge involves special issues not present in mainstream employment policy, such as medical expertise in screening. Thus employment policy for disabled people requires a thorough rethinking of policy design.
- Employment incentives should be created through a variety of policy instruments, since people with disabilities are a very heterogeneous group. Active labour market policies (ALMPs) provide an important set of policy instruments, since they can be designed to enable people with disabilities to find jobs. Various ALMPs are potentially useful in this regard: wage subsidies, in-work top-up payments, insurance-re-

lated schemes, etc. However, passive policies, such as cash assistance, have a role to play as well, for without such policies there would be a danger that the freedom of choice and personal autonomy of people with disabilities could be undesirably restricted.

- Disability policy should be based on the principle of mutual obligations. The responsibility for the integration of people with disabilities into the workplace must be shared by the disabled, their employers and the government. In the words of Jan Ryhd, we need to be concerned not just with the rehabilitation of people, but also of the workplace. Employers and employees must cooperate in this regard, because it is pointless for disabled employees to be rehabilitated if their workplace cannot accommodate them, and it is pointless to restructure the workplaces if disabled people are disinclined to accept work. Although it is recognized that large numbers of people with disabilities wish to work, the government nevertheless bears the responsibility to provide the incentives necessary to induce employees and employers to integrate disabled people in the world of work.

- Disability policies should be formulated conjointly with other welfare policies, and especially in conjunction with measures to promote education and training, to reduce unemployment, and promote health. In short, the entire welfare system needs to be "activated".

- Institutions play a crucial role in enabling the integration of disabled people in society and especially in the world of work. The institutional framework helps determine the social mores and cultural values that identify people as disabled and in need of support. Although there exists a hard core of people who are objectively recognizable as severely disabled, wider definitions of disability are highly subjective, and institutions are important in setting the relevant objective standards.

- The politics of disability policy needs explicit attention. This aspect is important for a variety of reasons. First, as Kenneth Apfel pointed out, if the mutual obligations inherent in disability policy fall too heavily on employers and disabled employees, then governments are likely to assume less responsibility for providing adequate facilities and incentives to integrate the disabled in the workplace. Second, the more emphasis is put on passive policies, e.g. cash benefits, to support the disabled, the more people who are not genuinely disabled will apply for disability benefits, possibly as a substitute for unemployment benefits or early retirement. Third, the political process determines what disability policies are feasible in the sense of being supportable through the electoral process. In order to gain broad-based support for disability policies, some form of conditionality may well be necessary, at least for milder forms of disablement, specifying that disability benefits be granted in return for a demonstrated willingness to work on the part of the recipients. Such conditionality is widely accepted in the area of employment policy, and the panel was in favour of treating disability policy in close conjunction with employment policy. Finally, the political process is required to establish employment as a right, not merely a desideratum, for the broad majority of the disabled. This right commits society to devoting substantial resources towards the social integration of disabled people.

Emily Andrews indicated that the above approach to disability differs markedly from the traditional concepts of assistance, according to which people with disabilities were assisted outside their communities. Ms. Andrews stressed that since the above approach is meant to be empowering and inclusive, it is natural that disability policy should encourage labour force participation. In this context it is important to keep in mind that work disabilities come in many guises: occupational illness, injury on the job, disabilities stemming from childhood, and so on. On this account, it is unreasonable to expect that there can be a "one size fits all" disability policy. Different disability measures – flat-rate benefits, means-tested benefits, income-related social insurance, universal benefits, public provision, private sector insurance, etc. – have a role to play in dealing with different disability problems.

David Kalisch stressed that it is not just the design of disability measures that is important, but the implementation – and, in particular, the administration of disability benefits that is critical for the success of disability policy. The disbursement of benefits needs to be based on accurate assessments of claims, regular reviews of conditions, in a consistent fashion. The emphasis should be on facilitating access to assistance to those who make the transition into the labour market. The administration needs to focus on people's work capacities and on ways to modify existing jobs to suit these capacities. This requirement is an important aspect of the mutual obligations theme. Early intervention is important, because once disabled people have banished work from their aspirations, it is difficult and costly to induce them to return to the labour market. On the other hand, of course, early intervention is also associated with relatively large deadweight costs (viz., the cost of benefits to people who would have re-entered the labour market without them). Mr. Kalisch also stressed the need to design disability measures in conjunction with unemployment, education and training measures.

Jan Ryhd provided an overview of the Swedish system of disability support and its implications for the future of disability policy elsewhere. Sweden provides an important case-study for the design of disability measures because of the generosity of its benefits and the associated danger of disbursing these benefits to those who are not genuinely disabled. Mr. Ryhd indicated that over the past five years, the number of Swedes on sick leave has doubled. It now corresponds to about 14% of the working-age population. Women account for two thirds of this increase, although there is no medical explanation for this development. Moreover, there is also no medical explanation for why the proportion of people on sick leave should differ widely across municipal and council employees, central government employees, and government employees, or why the rate of sick leave should rise with company size. Mr. Ryhd presented the policy proposals of the Commission of Official Inquiry into the Swedish Insurance System. The highlights of these proposals included extending the period over which employers pay for sick leave, the need for employers to adapt working conditions to enable people with disabilities to work and a corresponding obligation of the employees to return to work. Medical advice is important in this context, since doctors would need to certify what type of work could be done during given periods of illness. Finally, benchmarking could play a promising role, as noted in the recommendation that companies and other organizations present figures on sick leave in their annual reports.

Raymond Wagener outlined the new benefit strategy that is being implemented in Luxembourg. The new law on work disability is meant to make the provision of benefits more generous while at the same time increasing incentives for disabled people to participate in the labour force. For this purpose, the new strategy introduced redeployment measures (that would enable people to continue work, even if they are unable to do the work they did prior to their disability or the work of their non-disabled counterparts) together with a compensatory allowance (for those who have suffered drops in their wage earnings) and a waiting allowance (for those who are no longer entitled to their unemployment benefit but have not yet been redeployed to a new job). This interaction between passive and active support is meant to achieve the government's equity and efficiency objectives.

Finally, *Harold Wilensky* emphasized the need for governments to provide the appropriate infrastructure for rehabilitation and integration of the disabled at the workplace. This infrastructure is largely missing in most OECD countries, Mr. Wilensky explained. In its absence, the insistence on mutual obligations is not meaningful. An analogous problem exists with regard to active labour market policies in many countries. Mr. Wilensky also stressed the importance of formulating disability, employment and welfare policies conjointly. On this account, a "one-stop" service coordination agency would be desirable. Mr. Wilensky emphasized that there are instructive cross-country variations in disability policy: the Netherlands until the mid-1990s, he argued, was an example of what not to do (loose definitions of disability, indulgent administration, emphasis on passive support); Sweden was on the opposite side of the spectrum, and Germany occupied an intermediate position.

How Should Disability Benefits Be Structured? A World Bank View

Emily S. Andrews

The ideal structure of disability benefits depends upon society's core values with regard to the position of persons with disabilities in the society. Over the past 100 years, these values have been changing. A key ingredient for modern disability policy in the 21st century is the concept of inclusion, with the objective of independent living and fulfilling one's potential. Disability policies based on inclusion may be quite different from those based on older concepts of assistance, which often contained an implicit assumption that persons with disabilities could only be assisted outside the community, either for their "own good" or because society was embarrassed by their presence (for undoubtedly a long list of cultural reasons beyond our purview today). I still remember my work in Bosnia when representatives of disabled veteran's associations kept repeating that they were not "social cases", suggesting that other persons with disabilities were or should be.

Income support programmes, such as social insurance, can still be consistent with the concept of inclusion, as are programmes focused on poverty alleviation, particularly for persons without work history and those disabled from childhood. However, these benefits should be a safety net that hopefully is provided to a small proportion of the disabled population. Above and beyond cash benefits, one of the best ways to develop inclusion is through labour force participation, as work challenges individuals and provides independence.

But, I should start off by defining the term "persons with disabilities". I am using disability to mean *work* disability (or activity disability) not medical condition or impairment; that is, the effect of impairment on one's ability to do tasks related to daily living, study or work. We should also remember that to some extent, we are all disabled, as none of us can do all the jobs that are available because of lack of strength, agility, or mental ability. Further, the likelihood is strong that any one of us may become disabled as we age. So disability is an issue that affects us all personally and directly.

The onset of disability may come at different times during a lifetime, and, as such may require different types of interventions to promote inclusion, independence, and the full use of abilities. Some persons with disabilities are disabled from childhood, with assistance needed in the area of education, possibly supplemented by other interventions throughout adult life. In this case, education, care-giving, and even income support may be important. Second, and more frequently, individuals may become disabled during their working lives. Here disability benefits, physical, psychological and vocational rehabilitation are appropriate interventions. Others may become disabled through an occupational illness or injury. Many countries provide separate occupational insurance, in part, as a means to improve working conditions, particularly if payroll tax rates reflect firm-specific incidence of injury or disease. Occupational insurance is also useful to restrict litigation on the part of employees, replacing individual lawsuits with a system of insurance. Other adults may become disabled before they have a job record, either because they are young or because they have worked at home raising a family. These individuals also need rehabilitation opportunities and, if necessary, cash assistance.

No one programme is suitable for each type of disability or for each and every country. One size cannot fit all. Age, age at onset, type of disabling condition are all part of the set of individual characteristics that require individual solutions – or at least, solutions that are sensitive to the different circumstances of the individuals affected. Similarly, different countries may select different options either because of a tradition of benefit design or other cultural differences. For example, cash benefits come in a variety of colours – flat benefits, income-related social insurance, means-tested benefits, low benefits, high replacement rates, universal public benefits, private sector insurance or some combination of the above. There is no one good solution.

Programme parameters for cash benefit programmes also vary widely in both OECD and transition economies. Some countries provide benefits for full disability only, while in others cash benefits are provided for partial disability as well. Partial disability pensions can help workers with disabilities enter into the workplace, or provide serious disincentives for work, depending upon the country and the level of benefits provided. Each case needs to be evaluated independently.

The disability determination process can also influence whether a disability programme will be successful or not. Certainly, the disability determination process should be designed to be consistent with international standards. Further, the process should be efficient and impartial. However, we do not necessarily know what the best mix of professionals should be. Probably, a panel of physicians, as is seen in a number of transition economies, is too many. Probably consideration should be given to physical, psychological and rehabilitation criteria. But what to do in a country such as Russia where there is a current undersupply of vocational and occupational experts, which hinders the implementation of forward-looking legislation?

In terms of impartiality, disability determination personnel should be independent. This means that decisions should not be left to the applicant's own doctor – as moral hazard could be great. Disability determination panels should be paid appropriately so that doctors do not look for bribes and can refuse those that are offered. In Hungary, many thought that doctors were bribed to certify persons as disabled who did not meet disability criteria. However, it could also have been the case that doctors accepted bribes to make a disability determination that was correct, just as medical services often require additional payments! Some OECD countries have experienced yet another problem. While the disability determination process is not subject to bribes, it may be subject to political demands. For example, in the Netherlands and the United States, disability determination decisions have been more or less strict, depending upon the political climate of the day

While it would be ideal if every country could establish an extensive system of proven policies to assist all categories of disabled persons with individual assistance that ensures inclusion and independence, the financial resources to do so must also be considered. This is yet another area in which programmes must be designed to meet the possibilities of the country in question. For example, payroll tax rates in both the Netherlands and Poland have been higher than in many other countries. But the Netherlands is better able to sustain such a strain on its resources than is Poland, where economic growth is essential, particularly as an upcoming member of the EU. Thus, inefficiency and overprotection in the Netherlands can better be afforded than in Poland. Too often disability programmes are designed with little or no concern for budgetary constraints. Programmes that promise more

257

than they can deliver are probably worse than limited programmes as they can only operate in a climate of favouritism and will not serve the population well. One of my favourite examples of an unfunded mandate is the promise in more than one transition economy of personal transportation (cars) for persons who are 100% disabled, a promise that is primarily honoured in the breech.

Independent living may be highly dependent on finding work, which provides the resources for financial self-sufficiency. One method that does not appear to work is the imposition of quotas on employers to hire the disabled. Employers tend to prefer to pay taxes than to tax their workforces with individuals they do not want to hire. The use of sheltered workshops also has serious problems either for financial abuse or because persons with disabilities are placed outside the community. Poland is one of the most problematic cases as sheltered workshops have basically sheltered employers from competition. But, sheltered workshops may be helpful in some cases, even for persons without serious mental retardation – the disability most often suggested for this type of programme. For example, in countries in which transportation is poor, a community of persons with disabilities at a workplace may lead to greater independence than other alternatives. This argument was made to me in one case in Bosnia, and I cannot say it was wrong.

Another lesson I have learned by talking to persons with disabilities in Poland and Bosnia is that policies other than cash benefits are as important, and even more important than money. For example, access is crucial – access to buildings, access to transportation, and access to the workplace. Similarly, access to personal assistance devices, such as wheelchairs (comfortable ones), hearing aids, seeing-eye dogs, and many other aids that are not necessarily expensive but vital to independent living is also needed. I believe that we have far to go to determine what public funding is necessary and efficient to promote access. Similarly, we need to think outside the box in other areas. For example, a caregiver's allowance could be a better use of public funds if it allows a person to work, than poverty benefits that do not provide work incentives.

In all countries, the public still needs more education to understand that inclusion, independent living, and the development of abilities should be the goals of public policy. Persons with disabilities, themselves, may also need the same public information. I was amazed in Bosnia to find a stark difference in attitude between disabled persons who had become acquainted with examples of independent living in the United States and disabled war veterans who thought that work was not necessary but benefit eligibility was. What a waste of a young man who is not interested in achieving as much as he can. Attitudes can change through public information, through educational systems that are as inclusive, and through anti-discrimination laws such as the Americans with Disability Act in the United States.

While there is no "ideal" disability policy, better methods of programme evaluation are needed in the future to determine how effective programmes are with regard to the underlying goals of disability policy. For example, a system with a high social insurance replacement rate, such as those in place in transition economies at the beginning of the 1990s, could not be considered successful measured against modern criteria of inclusion, independence, and the development of abilities. Pre-transition policies warehoused people in institutions and sheltered workshops, removed them from the labour force and/or provided meaningless jobs within an enterprise. We should consider setting millennium development goals in the area of disability policy to promote inclusion, independent living and the maximization of abilities. Labour force participation could be one measure. The development of others should be our challenge for the future.

How Should Disability Benefits Be Structured? The Australian Experience

David Kalisch*

The Australian Benefits System

The Australian income support system differs from those of most other developed countries: payments are funded from general revenue rather than from direct contributions by individuals; are generally not time limited; and benefits provide a basic flat-rate income support payment. Payments in Australia are made under specific social security legislation, which can be subject to change depending on support from both the community and Parliament.

Disability Payments

Some form of disability pension has existed in Australia for around 100 years, the same time as our Age Pension. The Disability Support Pension (DSP) is a non-contributory, means-tested (except for blind applicants) income support payment equivalent to 25% of male average weekly earnings for single people and is non-taxable income. It is funded by the Federal Government and administered by Centrelink. Non-cash benefits and concessions are also available.

Current eligibility criteria for DSP is as follows:

- Applicants must be aged over 16 and under Age Pension age.
- Applicants must have a medical impairment that attracts at least 20 points under the DSP impairment tables (this does not necessarily

---

* The views in this paper are not necessarily shared by the Australian Government or the Department of Family and Community Services

correspond with a 20% impairment) and a continuing inability to work 30 hours or more per week at award wages, or inability to be re-trained (through mainstream training) for such work, within two years. For those over 55, the availability of work in the local labour market can be considered.

- Special eligibility provisions apply for blind applicants who only need demonstrate that they meet required medical tests for permanent blindness.

Sickness Benefits and Workers' Compensation

Disability pensions are complemented by other arrangements for sickness benefits and workers' compensation:

- Sickness benefits in Australia are provided largely by employers. People who are not covered by their employers or private insurance (such as casual employees), those who have exhausted their private cover, or those seeking employment, may be eligible for income assistance from the Commonwealth Government.

- Assistance to people injured or killed as a result of workplace accidents is a responsibility of State/Territory Governments. The Commonwealth Government manages workers' compensation arrangements only for its own employees. People who are not covered by any of these options may be eligible for a safety net Commonwealth Government income support payment.

Some of the Recent Trends in Australian Disability Benefits

THE NUMBER RECEIVING DSP HAS BEEN GROWING STRONGLY, AND FEW LEAVE FOR WORK

Australia has witnessed considerable growth in the number of people on disability pensions. The number of people receiving DSP has been doubled over the last decade, and is still growing at an average rate of around 4% per annum over the past four years. Just under 40% of new entrants to DSP transfer from unemployment payments, suggesting that a significant proportion have experienced long-term labour market disadvantage. Almost half of all people granted DSP are aged 50 years or over, providing an early retirement option for many recipients. Around 1 in 19 people of workforce age in Australia are now receiving DSP, in total more than are in receipt of unemployment benefits.

Few DSP recipients have any contact with the labour market, despite relatively generous (by Australian standards) means-testing provisions and a significant part-time employment sector that could accommodate those unable to work full-time. There has been a gradual increase in the percentage of DSP customers with earnings since the DSP reforms in 1991, from 6% in 1992 to the current level of 9.7%. The majority of those who exit DSP payments do so because they have transferred to Age Pension on reaching the qualifying age or have died.

HETEROGENEITY EXISTS BUT CERTAIN CONDITIONS DOMINATE
The heterogeneity of people with a disability presents a particular challenge: not only the severity of disability, but the extent to which the disability affects the capacity to work and the attitudes of people with a disability towards working vary considerably.

The most common medical conditions among DSP customers are musculoskeletal and connective tissue conditions (also the case for the last decade), representing approximately 33% of the total DSP population. Psychological/psychiatric conditions represent 24% and intellectual learning disabilities represent 10%. Younger DSP customers are more likely to have an intellectual or learning disability, and have more earnings from employment. Older DSP customers are more likely to have musculoskeletal conditions and less likely to have earnings.

Some Key Issues for Design and Administration of Disability Benefits

ADMINISTRATION MAKES A DIFFERENCE
Design of disability benefits can be either undermined or supported by tight, consistent, appropriate administration. The practices of benefit delivery agencies can influence rates of claim for disability benefits and they play a critical role in accurately assessing claims, undertaking regular reviews of conditions, and facilitating access to assistance that can help people undertake or expand participation in work. Where medical impairment is part of the qualifying test for a disability pension, expert review is important.

EARLY INTERVENTION AND GREATER FOCUS ON WORK CAPACITY
   HOLDS PROSPECTS FOR IMPROVEMENT

In Australia, too many people come onto DSP long after their condition has deteriorated, either while they have been unemployed, sick, or receiving workers' compensation from State/Territory based schemes.

New arrangements in Australia now have a greater focus on the assessment of work capacity, to establish what people applying for DSP can do in relation to workforce participation and to identify what services and supports may help people back into work or to continue to work. These changes are part of efforts to build an integrated and responsive social support system that effectively combines income support and services for people with disabilities. We are encouraging workers' compensation schemes to expand efforts on early rehabilitation, rather than the lower cost approach (for these schemes) of simply providing cash support. We are looking to mainstream employment services to assist more people with disabilities, and desirably achieve better outcomes for them.

264

Among the DSP population, there is a wide range of work capacities yet too few DSP customers work. Some with very extreme medical impairments desperately want to work, yet others with milder conditions just want to be left alone now that they have achieved the goal of receiving a disability pension. The system needs to take a balanced approach towards enabling and encouraging people to fulfil their potential, especially if flexible employment such as part-time work is more readily available.

THE AGEING OF THE POPULATION PRESENTS ADDITIONAL CHALLENGES

In Australia, around half of the inflow to disability benefits over the past decade has been people aged over 50 years. This could increase further over coming years, as our baby boom generation (born between 1945 and 1960) moves through the critical "pre-retirement" years. Relevant issues here include the extent to which early retirement is desired by the workforce, the extent to which older people are treated more generously in claims for disability benefits, and the broader dimension of the extent to which there are successful complementary policies and programmes that assist older workers to stay within and re-enter the labour market.

CONSIDER INTERPLAY BETWEEN DISABILITY AND OTHER BENEFITS:
   MAY NEED A SYSTEM SOLUTION

Given the heterogeneity of the population with a disability together with understandings of the incidence of disability among other benefit recipients, it is sensible to consider disability benefits within the context of the entire income support system.

The OECD perspective of introducing greater consistency between unemployment and disability benefits, in terms of benefit packages, conditions of receipt and work incentives, could be viewed as a minimalist approach. A more radical approach would entail complete redesign of the entire benefit system, which is what we are contemplating in Australia.

Recent experience suggests that more effective solutions may lie in broadly based reform of income support across the working age population rather than more limited reform of disability pensions. The Australian government is currently engaged in a community consultation on the future structure of income support payments for people of working age. Many issues affecting people with disabilities will be considered as part of this process, including eligibility and coverage, structure of assistance, income tests and incentives for paid work and participation requirements. The consultation paper is available at: www.facs.gov.au/welfare_reform

Responding to the costs of disability as a component of the system has considerable potential, particularly if we are to move to a situation where the core features of unemployment and disability income support are more similar. There is a choice between seeking to cover the additional costs of living, the additional costs of participation or both. Designing such an arrangement responding to the costs of disability that is fair and relatively simple to administer is not easy, given that costs vary enormously between people with a disability.

Mutual obligations warrant further consideration, and could be a feature of successful reform. We already have a form of mutual obligation in the current arrangements – government generally provides modest but increasing support; and benefit recipients have some limited notification and medical review requirements.

If we are serious about the potential benefits of early intervention and rehabilitation, vocational training or other labour market assistance, then mandating participation in activities that could be worthwhile for the individual could be considered. Our evaluation evidence suggests that voluntary participation leads to far too few people participating in positive intervention programmes. This does presuppose the presence of sufficient suitable rehabilitation and active programme interventions funded by government. In the community and Parliamentary environment within Australia, any changes that vary obligations are likely to be skewed more towards considerable expenditure by government with modest, if any, requirements on individuals.

IMPORTANCE OF COMMUNITY SUPPORT

Any reform of the benefit system is challenging. Community attitudes and expectations of benefits vary considerably and changes to the benefit system for people with a disability are often controversial, even if they are packaged with positive elements. In the Australian Commonwealth Government's 2002-03 Budget, new measures to change the qualification criteria for DSP were announced. These changes would have limited DSP to people with more restricted work capacity (not able to work more than 15 hours at award wages), allowed a broader range of interventions to be taken into account in assessing the possibility of moving back into the workforce within two years, and those aged 55 years and over would no longer have their local labour market conditions taken into account. These measures to reform DSP eligibility were not well received at the time of their release and to date have not successfully progressed through the Australian Parliament.

Effective engagement of people with a disability is critical to the design of better policies and programmes. However, this is no magic solution as our experience is that there is a wide diversity of views of people with a disability towards benefit eligibility and participation requirements, covering all potential views across the spectrum of possibilities.

In conclusion, benefit design is important but is still only part of the picture. It needs to be complemented by better access to education and training, early rehabilitation, action to address access barriers and reduce the level of discrimination faced by people with disabilities.

A Programme for Better Health in Working Life in Sweden

Jan Rydh

Background

During the last five years, Sweden has seen an incredible increase in people on sick leave. The increase has been more than 20% per year meaning that the figures have doubled in less than five years. With very few exceptions, all people working in Sweden are insured through the Swedish general sickness insurance scheme, financed by the state budget. For 2003, the total cost for the state (disability pensions and sickness compensation) is calculated to be about 125 billion Swedish Crowns (about 13 billions Euros). This sum represents more than 15% of the total state budget and is more than twice the cost of the Swedish defence system or three times the cost of the Swedish educational system. In November 1999, I was appointed by the Swedish government to lead an Official Inquiry into the Swedish Insurance System in order to analyse this development and, based on that analysis, recommend proper actions. The report was delivered to the government in January 2002. This paper is mainly based on the facts and recommendations of that report. I include also comments of the Swedish debate during the 18 months after the presentation of the report as well as comments of the changes in legislation that have passed the Parliament in spring 2003.

Basic Facts of the Report

At present (June 2003), some 130,000 people have been on sick leave for a period exceeding one year. About a third of them have been on sick leave for more than two years.

Total sickness absence, including short- and long-term absence, corresponds to 400,000 person years and the number of people receiving a disability pension adds up to another 400,000 person years. Absence from work due to ill health corresponds to some 800,000 person years or *14% of the working-age population.*

The short-term absence has not increased – today there are not more persons on short-term sick leave than five years ago.

Women count for two thirds of the increase. However, there is no medical explanation to this overrepresentation in sick absence of women.

The most important findings of the report were that *the proportion of people on sick leave differs* between various sectors of the labour market. Those differences between sectors were much bigger than expected even after considering variations of the staff (age, education, gender, social factors etc). Illness-related absence is extremely high among municipal and county council employees, while central government employees are at the average and the private sector employees about 20% lower than the average. In towns and cities and at county councils responsible for health care in Sweden the majority of the employees are women. There are also surprising differences in relative sick leave figures between towns and cities, which cannot be explained by demographic factors such as age or other factors as education etc. Also between similar organisational units within a town or a city, there are differences in sick absence. These differences cannot be explained by individual differences in health status of the people employed.

Looking into the private sector you will find the same kind of distribution. The 25% of companies (working places) with the lowest sick absence have an absence rate of only 1.72% compared to the 25% at the top with an absence rate of 9.2% on average.

Another remarkable finding was that the *rate of sick leave absence increased with the size of a company.* Small and medium-sized companies had a much lower rate compared to big companies and organisations.

Conclusions and Suggestions

The most important conclusion of the study is that there is no significant support for the generally accepted assumption that the increase in sick leave absence is mainly due to differences in individuals employed – may it be medical, psychological, social or "moral" factors. With "moral" factor I mean for example willingness to work or, its opposite, willingness to "cheat" the system. Nor has there been any change during the period studied in the compensation level. To clarify, Sweden does not have a more favourable compensation system than other European countries with much lower figures of people on sick leave.

The Commission presented its final report in January 2002 with a number of proposals to the Swedish government. On a more general level, the Commission suggested that the *insurance system* should be changed and based on more *market-oriented principles.* The period during which the employer pays the sick pay should be extended to 60 days. The health insurance charge (financed as a social "tax" paid by the employers) should be reduced corresponding to the increase of sick pay costs. This suggestion created a big debate and was opposed by both employers' organisations and trade unions. However, the government, especially the Ministry of Finance, has not turned down the idea of giving the employer a more direct financial responsibility. The government considers even "harder" alternatives. In a paper presented by the Ministry of Finance, it was argued that neither the current nor the proposed system provided sufficient economic incentives. The ministry proposed in January 2003 that all employers starting with the public sector should pay a considerable part (about 25%) of the sick pay up to one year. This suggestion created even a bigger resistance and the government abolished the suggestion accordingly and quickly.

The Commission further recommended that *administrative changes* should be made, stressing the importance of the employer taking the first action in order to give the employee possibilities to go back to work as soon as possible. It is extremely important that the employer adapts the working conditions in such a way that the employee could work even if he/she cannot work effectively for a shorter or longer period. The employee should of course have an appropriate medical and/or social rehabilitation but there is always a possibility to *"rehabilitate" the working place*, the tasks and the organisation. If the employer does what is needed there is of course *a corresponding obligation for the employee* to go back to work. For companies and authorities this would in the end be a "cheaper" solution compared to the current system, which creates abnormal sick leave figures and a corresponding high social tax level. For the state budget, such a system would take away a substantial burden.

The doctor plays an important role when meeting his client. The doctor certifies that his client needs to rest from work. It is a widespread assumption among the public, doctors as well as their clients, that an illness or disease certified by a doctor should be accompanied by a sick-pay period. However, current regulation says that the doctor should rather certify what type of work could be done during a shorter or longer period of illness. Studies in Sweden show that a long passive sick leave period in the majority of cases rather prolongs the illness and makes it even more difficult to go back to work. The Commission recommended that the education of doctors should include those findings and that more regular use of part-time sick leave is a better way of rehabilitation. However, it is important that this change in attitudes and routines should be accompanied by a better accommodation of the working place.

It was also recommended that all authorities, companies or organisations should present their relative figures on sick absence in their annual reports. The Swedish Parliament has already adopted this proposal and a new law will take effect from 1 July 2003. Accordingly, in 2004, media will publish comparisons, listing for example the sick leave figures of the top 10 companies noted on The Stockholm Stock Exchange, or the top 10 big cities etc. This benchmarking is expected to provide interesting incentives to employers with high figures to do better in the coming years.

Governmental Bill in April 2003

After more than a year of debate and discussions, in April 2003 the government presented a bill to the parliament. In the bill, the government proposed a number of changes in legislation and work routines. Most important is that the employer has to present a plan for rehabilitation after 28 days of sick leave. In this plan the employer is supposed to show what could be done at the workplace in order to make it possible for the employee to go back to work on a full- or part-time basis.

The government also proposed that the sick pay period should be prolonged from two to three weeks. Even this very small change was firmly opposed by both employer's organisations and the trade unions. I am convinced, however, that very soon a more substantial reform must come in order to give more economic incentives to the employer. Such a reform must include a longer sick pay period and include a more market-oriented insurance system. In such a system, an employer with low sick leave figures should pay a lower insurance fee and accordingly an employer with high figures pay a higher fee.

In order to save money for the state budget the bill also included a minor reduction of the compensation scheme for individuals. The bill was adopted by parliament and is in effect as of July 2003.

Final Comments

I am quite convinced that Sweden has to strengthen the emphasis on work-oriented rehabilitation. Sick benefits and disability pensions should not be regarded to be part of the benefit system. As there are remarkable differences between sectors and employers in Sweden, it is obvious that those differences also must be cured at the level of the workplace. The fee, paid by the employer, should be calculated on market principles – companies with a high level of sick leave should pay a higher fee and companies with a low level a lower fee.

Personally, I agree with the policy conclusion presented for Theme 5: "Existing employer-employee relationships should be utilised as much as possible, both through positive incentives and through mandated obligations." The figures on sick leave in Sweden could serve as a warning. It will take some hard years for Sweden to return to a 50% lower level – a goal set by the Swedish Government.

Data Annex

Figure 1:   Number of People Sick-listed for Longer than 30 Days at the End of the Period 1976–2001

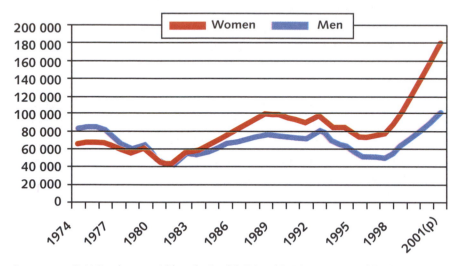

Source: HpH. Based on material from the Swedish National Social Insurance Board (RFV).

Figure 2:   Proportion of People Sick-listed for Longer than 30 Days at the End of the Period 1976–2001 by Percentage of Population (16–64 years old)

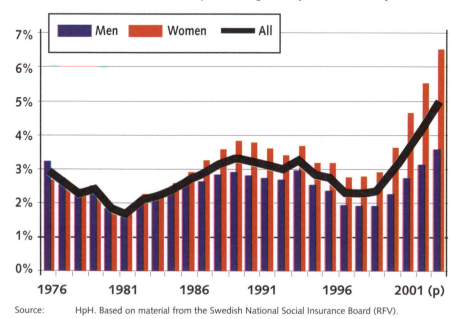

Source: HpH. Based on material from the Swedish National Social Insurance Board (RFV).

Figure 3: Number of People Sick-listed for Longer than 365 Days at the End of the Period 1992–2001

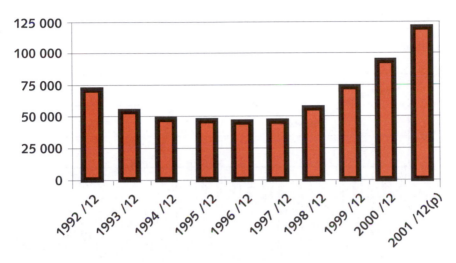

Figure 4: Total Number of People Sick-listed for Longer than 30 Days and Disability Pensioners at the End of the Period 1993–2001 (forecast) by Proportion of Population (16–64 years old)

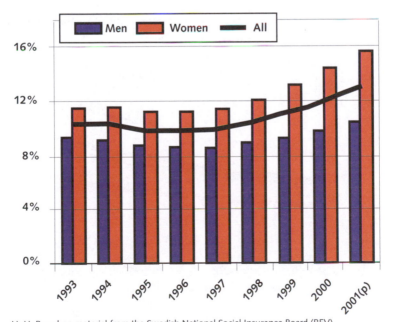

Source: HpH. Based on material from the Swedish National Social Insurance Board (RFV).

Figure 5: **Days with Replacement Payment by Health Insurance, Days of Sickness Payment 1976–2001 (prognosis). Days of Partial Replacement Rate Are Counted as Full Days**

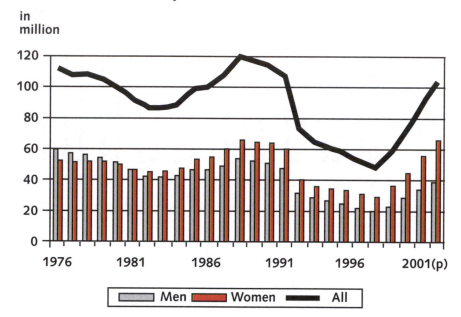

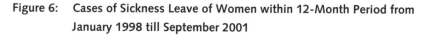

Source: HpH. Based on material from the Swedish National Social Insurance Board (RFV).

Figure 6: **Cases of Sickness Leave of Women within 12-Month Period from January 1998 till September 2001**

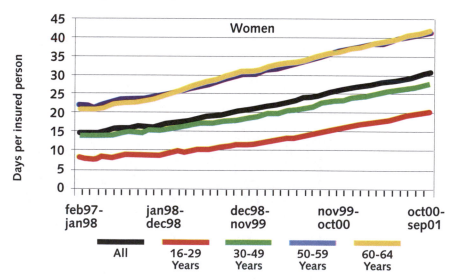

Source: HpH. Based on material from the Swedish National Social Insurance Board (RFV).

Figure 7: Cases of Sickness Leave of Men within 12-Month Period from January 1998 till September 2001

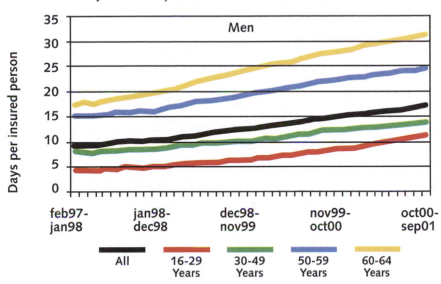

Source: HpH. Based on material from the Swedish National Social Insurance Board (RFV).

Figure 8: Monthly Change of Increase in Cases of Sickness Leave of Women and Men in Various Age Groups, within Overlapping 12-Month Periods from January 1999 till September 2001

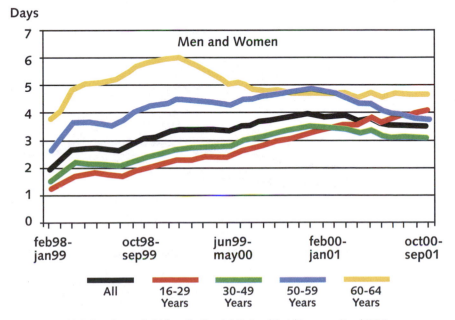

Source: HpH. Based on material from the Swedish National Social Insurance Board (RFV).

Figure 9: Monthly Change of Increase in Cases of Sickness Leave of Women in Various Age Groups, within Overlapping 12-Month Periods from January 1999 till September 2001

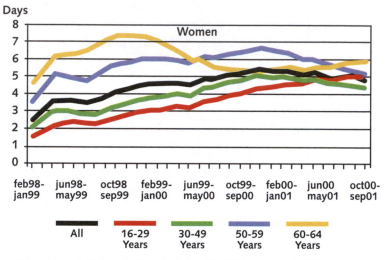

Source: HpH. Based on material from the Swedish National Social Insurance Board (RFV).

Figure 10: Monthly Change of Increase in Cases of Sickness Leave of Men in Various Age Groups, within Overlapping 12-Month Periods from January 1999 till September 2001

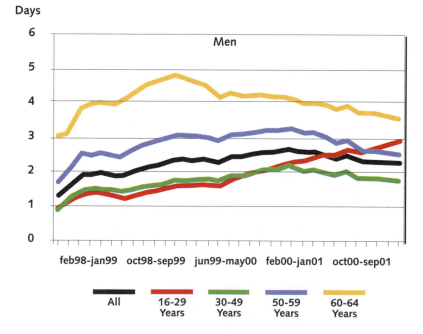

Source: HpH. Based on material from the Swedish National Social Insurance Board (RFV).

Figure 11: **Estimated Days of Sickness Leave throughout All Age Groups, Differentiated by Leave of Absence, Sickness Leave of 2–14 Days as well as Sickness Leave of 15–60 Days, Year 2000**

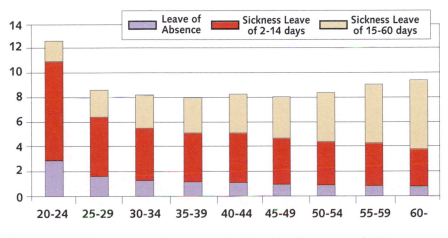

Source: HpH. Based on material from the Swedish National Social Insurance Board (RFV).

Figure 12: **Sick Leave for Male and Female Employees at Workplaces of Various Sizes in Individual Sectors, 3rd Quarter 2001, Percentage of Employees**

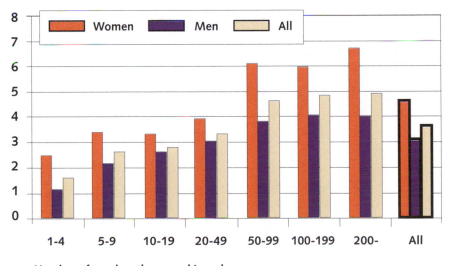

Number of employed per working place

Source: HpH. Based on short-term employment statistics of Statistics Sweden (SCB).

Figure 13: Sickness Leave in Workplaces with more than 100 Employees, Private Sector, Second Quarter of 2001. Sickness Rate = Share of Sickness Leave in Per Cent of Employees

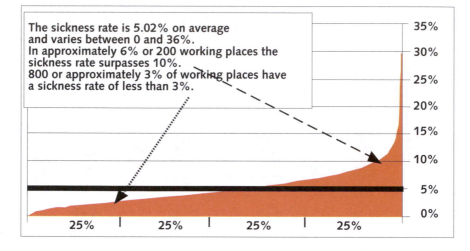

> The sickness rate is 5.02% on average and varies between 0 and 36%.
> In approximately 6% or 200 working places the sickness rate surpasses 10%.
> 800 or approximately 3% of working places have a sickness rate of less than 3%.

Source: HpH. Based on short-term employment statistics of Statistics Sweden (SCB).

Figure 14: Sick Leave at Workplaces with over 100 Employees, Private Sector, Second Quarter of 2001. Proportion of Sick-listed Individuals by Per Cent of Employees. The Workplaces Are Ranked by Total Amount of Sick Leave among Female, Male and Total Employees, and Divided into Four Equal Groups, for which the Average Values Have Been Calculated

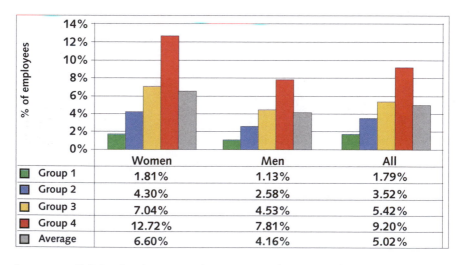

	Women	Men	All
Group 1	1.81%	1.13%	1.79%
Group 2	4.30%	2.58%	3.52%
Group 3	7.04%	4.53%	5.42%
Group 4	12.72%	7.81%	9.20%
Average	6.60%	4.16%	5.02%

Source: HpH. Based on short-term employment statistics of Statistics Sweden (SCB).

Figure 15: Number of People on Actual Full-year Sick Leave and Disability
Pension in 2000, Distributed by Employment Sector in 1999,
Compared to Expected Figures (100 means that the actual figures
equal the expected figures)

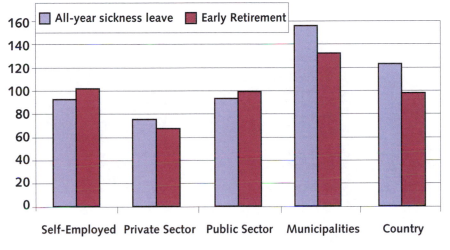

279

Source: HpH research programme SOU 2002:5, appendix 2:4.

Figure 16: All-year Sick Leave in 2000, Separated by Municipalities and Countries. Deviations from the Expected Value in Per Cent. Figures Indicate the Values for Municipalities with the Lowest and Highest Sickness Rate, respectively. Negative Figures Indicate that Actual Sickness Leave Is Lower than Expected. Accordingly, 45 Means 45% of Expected Sickness Leave.

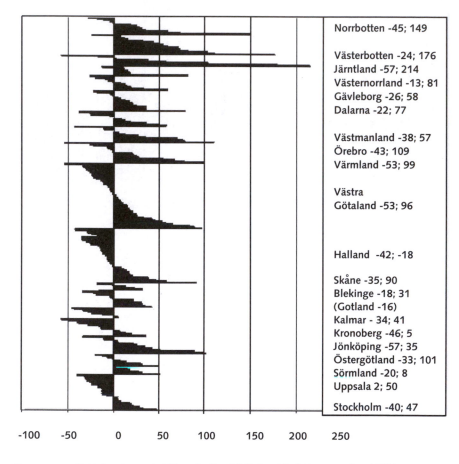

Norrbotten -45; 149

Västerbotten -24; 176
Järntland -57; 214
Västernorrland -13; 81
Gävleborg -26; 58
Dalarna -22; 77

Västmanland -38; 57
Örebro -43; 109
Värmland -53; 99

Västra
Götaland -53; 96

Halland -42; -18

Skåne -35; 90
Blekinge -18; 31
(Gotland -16)
Kalmar - 34; 41
Kronoberg -46; 5
Jönköping -57; 35
Östergötland -33; 101
Sörmland -20; 8
Uppsala 2; 50

Stockholm -40; 47

-100   -50   0   50   100   150   200   250

Source: HpH. Based on material from the Swedish National Social Insurance Board (RFV).

The New Benefit Strategy Being Implemented in Luxembourg

Raymond Wagener

Why a Reform?

In 1987 Luxembourg pension legislation covering blue- and white-collar wage-salaried and self-employed workers was unified in a General Pension Scheme. Only civil servants and employees assimilated to civil servants belong to other pension schemes. The reform introduced the following definition of a disabled person:

> "An insured person who, as a result of prolonged sickness or disability, has lost the ability to work to such a degree that he or she is unable to carry on the occupation of the last post, or another occupation suited to his/her capacity."

In the first few years following the 1987 unification law the definition of disability was interpreted broadly as follows. Workers unable to keep their last job because of a prolonged sickness or a disability were entitled to a disability benefit, regardless of the global situation on the labour market. As a consequence the number of beneficiaries of a disability pension increased substantially. But several court rulings during the period to 1996 determined firmly that disability must be defined by simultaneously taking into account the two criteria stated in the law: Is the person concerned unable to continue working in his/her last job and is he/she able to work at another job? Due to these rulings the number of new beneficiaries of a disability pension decreased considerably, but at the same time some persons became exposed to the risk of falling out of the social security safety net. These were workers: who were no longer able to return to their last job; who lost the right to sickness benefit (which is limited to a maximum of one year); who were unable to find a new job; or who managed only to find a poorly-remunerated occupation compared to their previous employment.

Initially the government proposed to introduce a two-level disability pension system with a general disability pension benefit and a professional disability pension benefit reduced to 50% of the general disability benefit. But the main trade unions categorically refused this proposal, because they were afraid that such a two-level disability benefit system would not avoid the poverty trap for workers entitled only to a professional disability pension benefit. Hence, the government abandoned its proposal and in 1999 convened a tripartite working group of representatives of the Ministries of Labour and Social Security, the trade unions and the employers. The group developed a new proposal, introducing a reinsertion grant instead of the professional disability pension benefit, combined with rehabilitation and reinsertion procedures. Although the working group did not reach consensus amongst its members, the government developed a new proposal based on the discussions of the working group. This was finally approved by Parliament in 2002 and has been in force since October of that year.

Description of the Procedure

The purpose of the new law on employment disability and professional reintegration is meant to improve the social protection of workers who can no longer work in their last job but are nevertheless not entitled to a disability pension, because they are not disabled according to the disability definition of 1987 which defines disability with respect to the entire labour market. The reform introduced two complementary measures to improve the social welfare of these workers:

- *Redeployment measures* within the firm, or on the general labour market so that these workers may continue participating in the labour market.
- A *compensatory allowance* in cases where the new salary is lower than the former one, and a *waiting allowance* for workers who are no longer entitled to unemployment benefit and have not been redeployed to a new job.

It is of course important to start the redeployment procedure as soon as possible and not to wait until the end of the period of sickness leave. Therefore every worker on prolonged sickness leave is examined within the first four months of the leave to determine if he/she is still unable to work because of his/her illness. If the worker is found able to return to work, sickness benefit payments are stopped (and administrative procedures in case of contest are accelerated). If the examination shows that the illness is likely to continue, another examination is scheduled at a later date. If the worker applies for a disability pension benefit, a medical examination will determine if he/she is disabled according to the 1987 definition. If this is the case, the work contract is dissolved and the worker is entitled to a disability pension benefit. If this is not the case, the occupational medical service will determine if he/she is able to continue working at the same job. The redeployment procedure begins if the occupational medicine examination concludes that the worker is no longer able to keep his/her job.

The redeployment of a worker may be:

- *Internal redeployment* within the same firm but to a different job or on different terms of employment, or
- *External redeployment* in the general labour market.

The decision to redeploy a worker is taken by the *Joint Commission* composed of representatives of the insured persons, the employers, the Medical Control of Social Security, the Occupational Medicine Department of the Health Ministry, the Labour and Employment Ministry and the Employment Administration.

Internal redeployment of a worker is compulsory for companies with more than 25 workers which have not yet fulfilled the legal measures concerning the employment of disabled persons. The employer is entitled to special support as well as special tax deductions. On the other hand sanctions (half of the social minimum wage during a maximum period of 24 months) may be imposed on employers who fail to comply with their obligation to internally reclassify their disabled workers. If the salary of the new occupation is less than the former one, the Employment Fund pays a *compensatory allowance* to make up for the difference (up to five times the social minimum wage). In addition, the redeployed worker enjoys special protection from dismissal for one year.

If the internal redeployment of a worker is not possible, he/she is registered as a job seeker with the Employment Administration's new Department for Workers with Reduced Work Capacity. If this department can find a suitable job, disabled workers and their employers are entitled to the same benefits as in the case of internally reclassified workers. Compensatory benefits are calculated according to the previous salary and regardless of the level of unemployment benefit the worker received in the interim.

A worker who could not be redeployed to an alternative employment during the legal duration of unemployment benefit payments is entitled to a waiting allowance, which corresponds to the level of a disability pension. The disabled worker, however, has to remain available for any job placement attempts and the waiting allowance will be stopped once a suitable occupation is found. The waiting allowance is not paid by the Labour Fund, but by the pension insurance scheme.

What Will Determine Success or Failure of the Reform?

The implementation of the reform on occupational disability and professional reintegration started only in October 2002, so that it is far too early to make an evaluation of its success or failure. Nevertheless from the description of the redeployment procedure it seems obvious that it is an ambitious reform, which depends on the active collaboration of the concerned workers, the employers and various administrations. Some of the conditions of the success of the reform are described below:

- The role of the Joint Commission is crucial in organising rehabilitation and reintegration measures and in ensuring successful redeployment of workers to new jobs suited to their skills and experience.
- Of course jobs have to be available and adapted to the capacities of the concerned workers: this is only possible if it is an important social concern of the employers to foster the employment of disabled persons.
- Redeployment of workers to new jobs needs an efficient system of rehabilitation, retraining and reintegration measures.
- Occupational medical services and the Employment Administration have to play an important role in helping disabled workers to find a suitable workplace.
- And of course nothing is possible without the active commitment of the workers themselves to find a suitable job, and to prepare for it through active participation in a process of rehabilitation and reintegration.

Reflections on Disability Based on a Comparison of 19 Rich Democracies*

Harold L. Wilensky

1   Work-oriented Rehabilitation vs. Passive Income Replacements (Treating the Disabled as if They Are Unable to Work)

Passive benefits are a bad idea not only for disability policies but for unemployment insurance (vs. an active labour market policy [ALMP]) and public assistance (vs. a universal family policy including child care, parental leave, housing and transportation help and earned-income supplements). Heavy means-testing in all these programmes creates political resistance to funding them at an adequate level. The distinction between divisive means-testing and simple, quiet income testing is important. By "means-testing" I mean (1) non-categorical benefits targeted to the poor via a stiff income- and/or assets-test, (2) applied by welfare administrators with substantial discretion, (3) with a high probability of stigma. "Income testing" is the opposite. It is categorical as a social right with co-payments graded by income bracket and, because it is private and invisible, has no stigma. Although the disabled are certainly not as unpopular as the non-working, non-disabled, non-aged poor, the principle holds: Highly visible, highly targeted benefits for any handicapped population will be less adequately funded than either universal benefits or quietly income-tested work-oriented benefits. The political effects of means-testing (tax-welfare backlash) are reinforced if the visible benefits are seen as lavish or result in too many inequities as is the case for some of the disabled.

---

*   These reflections are based on Wilensky, H.L. (2002) *Rich Democracies: Political Economy, Public Policy, and Performance.* Berkeley: University of California Press.

2   The Need to Recognise the Interdependence of Separate Clusters of Social and Economic Policies

A central theme in my analysis of public policies and effects (Wilensky, 2002, pp. 550-558, 101-108) is the *need to recognise the interdependence of separate clusters of social and economic policies.* Consider the problem of reintegration in the labour force and workplace, *applying sanctions without forcing the disabled into inappropriate work or into poverty. Solving this problem of the right to cash and services vs. the obligation to work highlights the interdependence of separate clusters of public policies.* Success in that balance for the disabled, as for other vulnerable populations, depends on the existence of serious support for ALMP, including job creation; and a wage structure that does not impoverish low-paid workers (e.g. ensuring a high minimum wage via laws, executive enforcement, collective bargaining, and subsidies to low-paid or short-hours workers); and fiscal and especially monetary policies that are pro-growth. Finally, without universally effective schools on which to build, no programme designed to rehabilitate, train, and place the disadvantaged in a modern economy – the chronically unemployed, the disabled – will be very effective. Policy linkages directly affecting the disabled can best be achieved with a centralized "one-stop" service coordination agency (OECD Theme 3). If there is a strong labour-market board (Sweden, Germany) this agency can be lodged there, so maximum information about work can be readily tapped and a work orientation emphasized.

Thus, the OECD theme "Partial benefits may become an easy bridge into benefit dependence" (OECD themes, p. 5) is true only if you require nothing in rehabilitation, training/education, therapy, etc and only if you rely on cash support instead of wage subsidies as an alternative to partial disability. I would not "use the philosophy of unemployment programmes" (OECD, p. 3) as a model. With only a few exceptions, rich democracies are quite passive in these programmes, not active; they cannot successfully tie benefits to participation in active labour-market programmes because the latter are non-existent or poorly funded or poorly organized. The infrastructure for work-oriented programmes is missing.

3   "Unbundling" Disability Status and Benefits of Medication, Care, or Transportation

*   These reflections are based on Wilensky, H.L. (2002) *Rich Democracies: Political Economy, Public Policy, and Performance.* Berkeley: University of California Press.

"*Unbundling*" *disability status and benefits of medication, care, or transportation,* another good OECD idea (p. 1), depends on the avoidance of means-testing for both cash benefits and service delivery. Both cost containment and "individual participation packages" (fitting the highly diverse needs of various types and degrees of disability) are best accomplished by combining universal rights and light income tests, the simpler the better. The model might be another population that has proved popular – working parents. The leading nations in publicly subsidized child care generally provide child care services categorically as a social right with graded co-payments to constrain costs and make the spending politically acceptable. The principle might be applied to the disabled: Everyone in the category should be assured of a minimum income that increases with increments of impairment. If the total cash income of the household is quite high, an income test should be applied, as with the universal right of working parents to costly day care for their children. The income test, if any, should be applied to the household income of the disabled, not to all non-resident ascendant and descendant relatives. The package of services relevant to the condition of the recipient, however, should be separate from any income test and administered without an elaborate investigatory and surveillance apparatus. Periodic review should not degenerate into sustained harassment.

A word about the hazards of science-based decisions about who is disabled and how much. I see no solution to the notoriously slippery definitions of "disabled". The invalidity of clinical diagnoses is apparent everywhere – one reason the growth in these programmes seems unrelated to the incidence of real disabilities. I would not worry about this. What politicians and agency administrators need is a decision rule that sounds fair and equitable, is publically acceptable, and does not break the bank. Science-based clinical judgments can be little more than a partner in tactics for public acceptability.

4 Country Variations

Four countries illustrate these themes of active work orientation, balancing rights and obligations, the interdependence of social, economic, and labour-market policies, and "unbundling" – The Netherlands, Sweden, Germany, and the USA. For the cost-conscious, *The Netherlands* until the mid-1990s was the symbol of what not to do: the combination of wildly loose definitions of disability, indulgent administration, and an almost exclusive focus on passive cash benefits made it tops in total disability claims and spending, with the lowest average age of first-time claimants (42 years old), and the lowest labour-force participation rate of 55-64 year-old males. A high unemployment rate did not help. *Sweden* is the opposite extreme: Although it does not run up the total bill as much as the Netherlands, it is tops in interrelated work-oriented rehabilitation, ALMP, and family policies designed to facilitate work; the result is the highest rate of labour force participation for all adults – and three times the Dutch rate for age 60-64. All these policies indirectly help the disabled to contribute to the economy and polity while they achieve a more independent life. Among the direct measures promoting independence are a legal right to benefits, including counselling and training, support for individuals as well as parents with disabled children, escort services, housing with special service, support for minor handicaps, interpreter services for the deaf and blind, and more. When these services to promote autonomy were expanded in the mid-1990s, eligibility standards were tightened to contain costs. The *Germans* are in the middle: they combine the Swedish accent on rehabilitation for work with more cost control. However, offsetting their incentives for work and rehabilitation, they encourage early retirement by giving unemployed workers over 60 full disability. So their disability recipients per 1,000 60-64 year-olds in 1990 was almost twice the Swedish rate. The *USA*, for various structural reasons, keeps marginally productive workers, including the disabled, at low wages in a market-driven system. There is little connection between clinical disability evaluation and job-finding services (meagre effort at ALMP). Periodic and erratic efforts to crack down on rising costs bring loud protests, much judicial action (adversary legalism), and a rise in spending but little rehabilitation and job creation for the disabled.

A growing social problem that poses an issue for the disabled is the interaction of two long-term trends common to all rich democracies: an increase in healthy older populations and a steady decrease in age of exit from the labour force. At the root of the problem is management and union desire to ease out older workers. Managers prefer younger, cheaper men and women and middle-aged women and if the state can pick up the tab, they will help older workers into an early retirement; unions go along because they want to reduce unemployment and make way for younger members. In trying to contain exploding costs of pensions while they cope with an oversupply of healthy displaced older workers who prefer to work at least part-time, many governments have tried to devise flexible retirement systems. Surely it is good public policy to transform the healthy aged who want to work into taxpayers, part-time workers, and partial pensioners rather than pressuring them to retire fully. But it is extraordinarily difficult both technically and politically to craft social security systems that would reverse the long-term slide in the age of exit from work. One obstacle is the prevalence of disabilities of various kinds among the aged. The trick is to find the balance between reductions in benefits for very early retirement and generous partial pensions for continued part-time work for aged say 60-70 while avoiding pressure on the worn-out workers in the least attractive jobs to postpone retirement. As in the case of the partially-disabled, this necessitates adequate income and medical supports; or if rehabilitation is the focus, a reallocation of funds toward work-oriented rehabilitation and a tight connection to an active labour market policy. As countries moving toward flexible retirement – especially Finland and Sweden – discovered, pension reform, labour-market reform, and disability programme reform go hand-in-hand. Flexible retirement systems cannot be crafted without attention to disability pensions and job creation, as well as part-time pensions and a right to rehabilitation.

5   Lessons from These Observations

If we want to balance the generosity of benefits that make life better for the handicapped with the goal of cost containment, the middle way between Sweden and the United States, with a bias toward Sweden, makes sense. Avoid the United States' low, litigious, and erratic benefits and USA's and Britain's limited commitment to rehabilitation; adopt the Swedes' commitment to an active labour-market policy and a work-oriented range of services and incentives, but avoid what they have gradually abandoned – overgenerous sick pay; and, above all, avoid the Netherlands' penchant for disability design that has promoted permanent disability as an answer to unemployment and underemployment. Adopt German quotas with fines, but avoid their strong incentives for an early retirement. Adopt the Finn's flexible pension reform of 2003, an heroic effort toward consensus that combines reform of disability pensions, promotes work among all reasonably healthy older workers without punishing the less able young-old. Finally, retain the German, Swedish, and Finnish commitment to tripartite consultation and administration. When union, management, and public input is built into the system at every level, there is a greater chance of adequate representation of laymen's interests *vis-à-vis* agency or lawyers' interests or professionals' (doctors, social workers) interests – and substantive justice is a more likely outcome.

What Should and What Can Employers Do?

Key Issues

1. Often systems make it too easy for employers to use the disability benefit scheme as a workforce management tool. The result of this is a large number of older workers permanently leaving the labour market through such benefits.
2. Employers are usually not sufficiently involved in the (re)integration process of their own and other (potential) employees. In few countries are employers given any role in the process of vocational rehabilitation and training, and mandates to accommodate work or the workplace are also exceptional. Where they exist, they are rarely effectively enforced.
3. Obligations to pay sick leave or continue (full) wage payment during a certain period of sickness absence are more widespread, and are meant to encourage employers to invest in preventive measures.
4. Different employment promotion policy approaches have similar effects. Whether policy is rights-based (anti-discrimination legislation), obligations-based (employment quota) or incentives-based (voluntary action), it is predominantly current employees who receive protection, not those seeking work.
5. Regulations which oblige the employer to make an effort for disabled employees are difficult to enforce, despite sanctions. Most regulations contain wording that is open to interpretation, and it has to be deter-

mined from case to case what constitutes undue hardship on the employer or whether it is impossible to accommodate a person's disabling condition in the company. Fines are often so low that employers may find it easier to pay than make any effort.

OECD Policy Conclusions

- Existing employer-employee relationships should be utilised as much as possible, both through positive incentives and through mandated obligations. Involving the employers is crucial for the (re)integration of disabled persons.
- The effectiveness of any measure will depend on the willingness of employers to help disabled persons stay in or enter work, and on possibilities of circumventing legislation. Proper sanctions for employers not fulfilling their obligations and adequate instruments to implement these sanctions are important. It is the existence of these two elements which could guarantee that either anti-discrimination laws or mandatory employment quotas are effective in requiring employers to satisfy their responsibilities.
- To strike the balance between promotion of employment and imposing undue hardship on employers is a major policy challenge. Special attention needs to be given to the fact that retention measures can lead to discrimination of those disabled persons seeking work.
- Therefore, it is essential to recognise that employers need help to fulfil their obligations. Workplace and job adjustments generally require small financial investments. More crucial are technical assistance and guidance, assessment of the problem and development of an intervention strategy for the participation plan.
- Employers who make an effort to (re)employ disabled persons should not be penalised financially *vis-à-vis* employers who fail to make an effort.

292

Transforming Disability into Ability: What Can Employers Do?

Christoph M. Schmidt

The OECD Report and its Policy Conclusions

Much of the discussion in this conference *Transforming Disability into Ability* is about the dual objectives of disability policy, about (i) ways to prevent the exclusion of disabled citizens from economic and social life, particularly from the regular labour market, and (ii) measures to ensure that those who suffer from a disability have a secure income and do not fall into poverty. This discussion has already come a long way, since it is hardly disputable any longer that disability and, similarly, early retirement programmes – in their intention to provide income security – thwart workers' incentives to pursue integration, while offering employers an inexpensive tool for workforce management. Yet, the debate on what to do exactly is also far from resolved. What has become clear is that these two principal objectives – while important contradictory elements continue to present severe challenges for the design, implementation, and evaluation of disability policy – to a large extent go hand in hand.

Specifically, the new OECD report advocates very strongly that an approach emphasizing activation seems to be the best way to proceed, in an ideal form with measures which are individually tailored to the impediments faced by the disabled person and which are set into operation as close as possible to the commencement of the problem. Most importantly, the report amasses a range of arguments for the perspective that this approach should introduce and strengthen a culture of mutual obligation, generating the requirement to both offer incentives to disabled workers to supply their labour to the market, and to involve employers. The conference panel "What Can Employers Do?" addresses the obligations held and incentives faced by employers in this context.

Across the OECD a large variety of approaches pursues the involvement of employers, ranging from mandating employment quotas over anti-discrimination legislation to the provision of incentives. The principal route taken by different countries very much reflects their underlying attitude to societal issues. In societies favouring an approach based on civil rights – specifically, in the US, Australia and Canada – we tend to find chapters regarding disabled people which are included as integral parts of their anti-discrimination legislation. Typically, employers are obliged to accommodate disabled workers able to fulfill the job requirements at the workplace, unless they can prove that this would cause undue hardship. In practice, it is difficult for any refused job applicant to prove that discrimination was the cause of the rejection. To put it bluntly, employers are merely forced to refuse disabled workers with sufficient legal prudence, rather than provided with a genuine incentive to hire them.

294

Many other countries – Austria, France, Germany and Italy, to name a few prominent examples – rely on mandatory employment quotas, requesting employers to retain a certain proportion of disabled workers among their staff. While employers failing to comply with anti-discrimination legislation face litigation under the civil rights approach, under this obligations-based approach employers missing the specified employment quota will be fined. This makes, in addition to the courts, a regulatory authority necessary. Another element of red tape is introduced by the unavoidable fact that legislated quotas need to rely on the presentation of suitable documents by *registered* disabled people. Typically, the introduction of quotas seems to achieve that employed workers who become disabled are more likely to be retained in their job, but it also seems that it reduces the hiring rates of job seekers who are disabled or who are likely to become disabled in the foreseeable future.

Anti-discrimination legislation may contain special employment provisions, and such obligations may also be part of the mandate of employment quotas. Specifically, employers may be requested to adjust the workplace and the associated equipment to provide equal access to the workplace to disabled workers, and to adapt the work schedule. How binding these provisions are for employers naturally depends on their enforcement and on the financial consequence of any failure to comply with them.

More fundamentally, any set of rules and regulations can only be as effective as its enforcement procedures, and any intervention into the functioning of the market might entail positive as well as (unintended) negative consequences.

Medical and Vocational Rehabilitation

A key element of any promising perspective on disability policy is the recognition of the variegated nature of the problem. Specifically, disability is not at all a dichotomous characteristic in which one is fully disabled and therefore out of the workforce, or not disabled and thus perfectly integrated in the labour market. Rather, disability is a gradual and often temporary phenomenon. Moreover, whether a health impediment turns into a permanent disability very much depends on the way the problem is dealt with. Consequently, there is an important role for medical as well as vocational rehabilitation and all systematic efforts to foster re-integration into the workforce.

295

In fact, in advanced economies more than 10% of adult men report some sort of disability, with growing shares over time. These disabilities comprise (i) physical disabilities, most prominently back problems, missing limbs, and vision and hearing impairments, (ii) mental disabilities including substance abuse, and (iii) other disabilities, such as heart problems, asthma, and diabetes. Clearly, most of these conditions do not preclude at least a modest participation in the labour market or in societal activities. Many of them might only present a transitory obstacle to full participation. Other conditions might or might not become impediments to social inclusion, depending on the timing of any treatment or rehabilitation activity.

Standard statistical indicators do not present a completely satisfactory account of the issue. Clearly, there has been a long-term trend towards higher participation in disability insurance programmes, i.e. towards lower labour supply, and towards lower employment rates specifically among older men. In European countries the share of disabled people of working age is relatively high, with the Netherlands displaying particularly high figures. Yet, it is not clear to what extent this genuinely reflects the deterioration of health associated with modern work life and population aging, or the decline of gatekeepers' standards and, thus, disguised unemployment. While promising empirical research could exploit time series and cross-state variation in eligibility and denial rates to address these issues, this evidence is scarce.

What seems to emerge quite clearly, though, is that the success of measures pursuing medical and vocational rehabilitation critically depends on their timing. Experience with previous attempts indicates that the earlier in a phase of insufficient health any rehabilitation efforts commence, the more promising their assessment. What we do observe in the moment, though, is that disabled workers display low outflow rates from disability, i.e. permanency of the disability status for most individuals who are afflicted with a serious health impediment. A strategy for change necessarily needs to target this aspect. In turn, this makes the involvement of employers in the rehabilitation process another important element of disability policy.

Finally, whenever market outcomes lead to results which entail an undesirable distributional outcome for a particular group of society, there might be a case for direct government intervention. Disability, and specifically rehabilitation are a case in point, since – at least according to current experience – too often spells of poor health turn into permanent disability and, thus, exclusion from the workforce. Thus, it might be advisable to introduce targeted public-sector programmes for re-integration. Yet, the analogous case of active labour market policy to combat unemployment suggests some important lessons. Most importantly, interventions by the state tend to be far more promising, when they involve employers in their design and their implementation. Again, this makes the involvement of employers in the rehabilitation process another important element of disability policy.

Future Disability Policy

The major, and from my perspective very convincing, recommendation for future disability policy which is emerging from the OECD report is a request for a fundamental change in paradigm. Old-fashioned disability policy tended to equate disability and inability to participate in the labour market, and reduced the role of society to the provision of income support and, with lower emphasis, to the design of targeted re-integration programmes run by the public sector. This income support tended to be linked to the previous payment of contributions, in analogy to other insurance schemes.

The report advocates a change of attitude, leading to the active participation of all relevant groups of actors in the endeavor of re-integration. Specifically, in addition to a stronger role for informed disability gatekeepers and improved co-ordination of all relevant authorities, this approach asks for the co-operation of disabled individuals and employers alike. While the disabled individual remains eligible for income support, the principal aim should be re-integration into the labour market and self-sufficiency. Only to the extent that re-integration efforts do not succeed, should income support receive a higher emphasis. In the typical course of events authorities should provide a mix of (early) activation measures, cash transfers and re-integration services, while the disabled individual is actively working towards re-integration him-/herself.

Thereby, the provision of re-integration efforts and the obligation to strive for self-sufficiency should be closely tied together, for instance through a set of positive incentives and sanctions. This also implies that income-testing and the assessment of a disabled individual's capacity to work should be connected more closely than before. Moreover, since disability is recognized as a very heterogeneous condition, the ideal rehabilitation strategy should entail a package individually tailored to the disabled individual. In any case, since re-integration into the workforce is a target to be pursued adamantly, the implicit tax rate for taking up work which is embodied in the financial benefit scheme should be small. Otherwise individuals experience a penalty for taking up work and, consequently, a low rate of re-integration. This recommendation certainly holds also for in-kind benefits such as eligibility for free health care.

In this new approach, the clear emphasis on re-integration also requires employers to be actively involved. Yet, the challenge for economic policy is to devise promising ways to achieve this objective. Two principal routes could be taken to achieve a more serious involvement of employers. One could rely on more intense regulation, together with effective – and costly – enforcement activities and serious financial sanctions. This policy could easily backfire, though, as it might make job creation and the hiring of disabled workers – or those likely to become disabled – less attractive. Alternatively, in my opinion clearly the preferable route, one could rely on the provision of better incentives for employer participation.

A range of suggestions exists that fills these principal guidelines for future disability policy with life. For instance, a clear suggestion emerging from the report is that generally small-scale targeted programmes with a close link to employers are to be preferred to large-scale, more diffuse alternatives. Furthermore, employers retaining or hiring disabled workers frequently need support in their integration efforts, perhaps even permanently. Similarly, employers actively involved in early interventions aiming at re-integration often need guidance and technical assistance. Moreover, employers' involvement can take other routes that retaining disabled staff and working at their re-integration. An important avenue for their contribution lies in the promotion of preventive measures and injury prevention programmes. An instrument that is already in use for providing incentives in this direction is the obligation to employers in many countries to pay the medical cost of their workers through an initial phase of sickness and disability.

Clearly, any successful set of measures aiming at the improved re-integration of disabled workers would have to rely on an overall economic climate favouring initiative and entrepreneurship. Re-integration of disabled workers will be more difficult in times of high unemployment, and in labour markets plagued by rigidities. Yet, contrary to common practice, it is not at all advisable to compromise the re-integrative approach by shifting part of the burden arising from an unfavourable macro-economic situation to disability policy. On the surface, counting unemployed workers as disabled seems to relieve the labour market, but by doing so not a single worker treated in this fashion does become re-employed. Rather, the status of being out-of-the-workforce is cemented for these workers. Thus, frequent practice of regarding workers beyond, say, 45 or 50 as difficult to re-integrate, and denying them any effort at re-habilitation and re-integration, is very unfortunate. This conclusion holds even more strongly in the future, as all major economies are aging rapidly.

Yet, this discussion touches upon a broader, less well researched issue: What approaches to re-integration do work and which do not? Only if we were to assess quite accurately, in terms of direct and indirect costs and re-integration success, what alternative ways to allocate the budget can achieve, could we satisfactorily solve the intricate problem of finding an optimal budget allocation. In that case, one might for instance opt for a concentrated effort on those disabled workers with the highest chances of re-integration, or for the targeting of those individuals which are hit hardest by disability. One could easily imagine that considerable activity would be allocated to older workers, quite in contrast to current practice. Unfortunately, we do know very little about this issue, due to insufficient evaluation efforts.

The report argues correctly that in addressing this issue, a very fruitful area to look for precedence is the evaluation of active labour market policies. During the last couple of years, a large body of literature has documented the intricate nature of the evaluation of policy interventions. We do know today that the success of policy instruments depends on a variety of aspects, among them the characteristics of the target group, the way the instruments are implemented, and the economic and social environment. In any case, one should not confuse take-up rates or funds disbursed with the success of any measure, but rather try to identify the genuine, incremental effect of the intervention over and above what targeted individuals would have experienced without them. In general, this literature suggests to generally be skeptical regarding the potential of government interventions into the labour market.

Although this literature has also devised powerful ways to deal with the inherently non-experimental nature of many studies, important uncertainties remain. Similarly, the assessment of health status is plagued with measurement problems. Not unlike statistical estimation procedures these efforts are prone to type I and type II error, i.e. disabled workers might not be recognized as such and other workers who are not genuinely disabled are classified as disabled workers. Therefore, it is important that regular, and not too infrequent reviews of the medical condition of individuals with health impediments might be leading to a revised assessment of disability status. Yet, the problem most seriously generating uncertainty as to the best strategy is the obvious trade off between offering benefits and opportunities to employed workers becoming disabled, and to potential workers currently not employed, yet likely to experience the onset of a disability spell during the short- to medium-term future.

The Structure of the Session

The current experience suggests that both principal approaches to request employers to fulfill their obligations – regulation and incentives – may have unintended consequences. Disabled citizens' welfare may be lower rather than being enhanced by these disability policies. Given that both strategies generate considerable costs, it is therefore indispensable to learn more about which approaches do work – to weed out the unsatisfactory strategies and instruments, and to identify those which should be pursued more intensively. To this end, this session of the conference has drawn together experts on the nexus of disability policy and workplace organization.

The first individual contribution has been by Professor *Richard V. Burkhauser* (Cornell University), one of the most prominent and productive contributors to the economic literature on disability policy. His presentation addressed more detailed aspects of the problem. Professor *Philippe Askenazy* (CNRS and CEPREMAP, Paris), a renowned French expert on modern work life, discussed how innovative workplace organization might decrease as well as increase the quality of work, with a specific eye on the stress-increasing aspects of modern workplace organization. Professor *Carlo Castellano* (BIAC, Italy), an experienced entrepreneur, provided an example for promising initiatives set into operation by employers, a project attempting to exploit the strategic opportunity offered by recruiting qualified ICT personnel.

The two subsequent contributions outlined the legislative and regulatory experiences of selected European countries. *Dr. Hartmut Haines* (German Ministry of Health and Social Security), a senior ministerial expert in the fields of rehabilitation, integration, and participation of disabled individuals, described the German system of obligations and incentives for employers towards disabled employees. Professor *Bjorn Hvinden* (Norwegian University of Science and Technology, Oslo), a professor of sociology, discussed the Norwegian perspective.

Finally, Professor *Rick van der Ploeg* (European University Institute, Florence) described the problems arising from an ill-designed disability policy, using the case of the Netherlands as his example. In his contribution, Professor van der Ploeg could draw from an extensive experience both as a high-level active policy-maker and as a renowned scientist. On the basis of historical experience he addressed crucial design issues for improving upon current policy, in particular regarding ways to involve employers in the process of rehabilitation and re-integration.

A Summary of the Plenary Discussion

The plenary discussion evolved around three intimately related major themes, (i) the lessons to be drawn from existing disability policies, (ii) the involvement of employers, and (iii) the trade-off between job retention and new hires.

Existing Policies to Remove Barriers to Employment

The Americans with Disabilities Act of 1990 (ADA) is a prototype for employment mandates aiming at the elimination of the employment barriers faced by people with disabilities. In its design it follows two objectives. One objective is to ensure that disabled workers have access to all areas of employment, mandating that equally qualified individuals with a disability are not discriminated against in wages and employment. The second objective is to increase the labour market opportunities for disabled workers by the requirement that employers provide "reasonable accommodation" to their disabled workers. While in many cases the cost of this requirement is low, its financial consequences to the employer can become substantial in individual instances.

Taking the key objective of integration into the workforce as the starting point of his assessment, Professor Burkhauser contrasted the recent experience of disabled workers, i.e. the decade after the passing of the ADA, with the apparent success of policies intended to integrate lone mothers into the American workforce during the same period. Against this benchmark, US disability policy does not seem to have operated successfully at all, despite the strong and protracted economic growth of the US economy. In fact, for much of the last decade the employment rates of working age men and women with disabilities have declined absolutely and relatively to comparable workers without a disability. Professor Burkhauser concluded on the basis of a wide range of thorough empirical analyses that these patterns were predominantly caused by changes in the social environment – specifically by the increased generosity and ease of entry onto social assistance programmes –, not by deteriorating health.

It has to be emphasized that there are contrasting approaches in other countries, also leading to somewhat disappointing results. Clearly outspoken in his conclusions on how disability should not be set up, Professor van der Ploeg discussed the relatively high share of registered disabled in the Netherlands, corresponding to high spending on disability benefits. Since it is quite unlikely that the Dutch population suffers more severely from health impediments than that of other European countries, entering a phase of disability benefits seems to be a permanent exit route from the labour market for reasons other than health, i.e. disguised unemployment. Corroborative evidence stems from the observation that many of the registered disabled enter disability for the reason of psychiatric and back problems, both relatively subjective impairments.

This situation arises, since taking this route has been made attractive to both workers and their employers. Workers prefer a permanent exit from the labour market on relatively generous terms. Employers, on the other hand, cherish the opportunity to eliminate less productive, typically older workers, from their payroll. Yet, the bill is ultimately paid by the workers who do not get a real chance to re-integrate themselves into the workforce, and by the taxpayers at large. Professor van der Ploeg argued that attempts at the alleviation of this problem should concentrate on the process of establishing eligibility and on increasing efforts at providing opportunities for rehabilitation and re-integration. He viewed reductions in the generosity of disability benefits, once disability has become established thoroughly for the individual, with considerably more skepticism.

Involving Employers

Also, in his argument for involving employers more intensely, Professor van der Ploeg was clear that all these efforts should keep possible hardship arising for employers seriously. One aspect could be collective bargaining agreement entailing lower wages for disabled workers. Another fruitful avenue, in his view, is the improved prevention of the transition from sickness into disability. This could be supported by incentives, such as experience rating of disability insurance premia and the requirement to pay the wages of sick workers for an initial period of their sickness spell – but one should also beware of adverse effects on hiring. Most difficult, yet crucial is the enforcement of any obligation, once established, to avoid free riding.

Addressing what he characterizes as the basic conflict between individual firms' profit maximization objective and a society's rational desire to integrate disabled citizens, Professor Hvinden clearly advocated a strengthening of the obligation approach. In his view, discrimination should be prevented by obliging employers to avoid it – this could only be implemented by political leaders willing to enforce measures. As a complementary activity, the state could offer cost-sharing schemes for employers accommodating disabled workers, perhaps even accepting that some employers receive funds who would have provided accommodation anyway. His emphasis was clearly on the enforcement of obligations.

Similarly, Dr. Haines outlines the comprehensive set of obligations for German employers, set in operation with the aim of a step-by-step re-integration of workers with health impediments into the labour market. Among these are a special protection of disabled workers against dismissal, an employment quota of 5%, and anti-discrimination and workplace accommodation requirements. Moreover, he saw an important role played by worker representatives who must be involved in questions of hiring, dismissal and re-integration.

Quite a different route was suggested by Professor Castellano who documented the positive impetus stemming from direct employer initiative. Similar to Professor Askenazy he emphasized that employers who do feel that an involvement into rehabilitation and re-integration is to their economic advantage can be incorporated into the process most fruitfully. Along the same lines, Professor Burkhauser advocated that one should use government funds to support those employers financially who co-operate in rehabilitation, as a better route to achieve this co-operation than imposing the co-operation costs onto them via regulation.

The Trade-off Between Job Retention and New Hirings

Employment provisions intend to increase the relative demand for protected workers artificially. Yet, they also impose costs on firms which may decrease the genuine relative demand for all workers who are disabled or who are likely to fall into a spell of protracted health problems. Specifically, firms and workers cannot share the expenses associated with the specific investments into the human capital of disabled workers because of equal-pay provisions. Thus, the ultimate effect of the provisions are an empirical question. This issue was ultimately the most hotly-debated topic in the session, yet left also the largest room for further research.

Regarding the effects of the ADA on employment retention and new hires, Professor Burkhauser argued that the current evidence is mixed. On balance, the ADA seems to have exerted negative employment effects on disabled workers, while at the same time the ease of entry onto the disability roles has increased. As an alternative to obligations, advocated for instance by Professor Burkhauser, expanding the Earned Income Tax Credit (EITC) for disabled workers into a Disabled Worker Tax Credit (DWTC) would provide a wage subsidy encouraging disabled workers to remain or enter the labour market after becoming disabled. Employers' costs of hiring workers would effectively be diminished, since they could reflect productivities directly, by contrast to, say, the alternative of a mandated minimum wage. This would make workers more competitive in the labour market, fostering their re-integration.

The Agenda for Further Research and Discussion

Since – in addition to the general limitations arising for such an approach – the experience with the United States' ADA documents the importance of the social environment for the effectiveness of a disability policy relying on obligations, and since the current European experience demonstrates how unfortunately designed disability policy can contribute to transforming impaired health into permanent disability, we are far from possessing an ideal set of instruments for an integrative disability policy. One of the key issues for further research has been identified in this session of the conference. This question is how to ensure an increased contribution by employers to the processes of rehabilitation and re-integration.

It has become more than clear that in attempts at answering this question one should consider strengthening incentives as an important alternative to obligations. Further research has to clarify whether the provision of incentives is indeed easier to administer and offers better cost-benefit ratios, as much of the discussion in the session suggests. We also do not know too well which are the best ways to provide such incentives. One interesting approach at making work more attractive to workers on partial benefits is introducing a variant of the EITC. Employers should also receive incentives to participate in rehabilitation measures and engage in an improved workplace organization generally. The key issue is here, whether it is possible to provide a package of policy elements to employers such that rehabilitation and organizational changes fostering the quality of work are in employers' interest. Finally, it would be preferable to think of policy packages that take business cycle fluctuations into account.

For the design of better policy, we would also have to receive more informed evidence, preferably from a life-cycle perspective. At the heart of a better grasp of the stylized facts would be an improved understanding of the processes ultimately leading to disability. Do workers typically become disabled on or off the job? What are the employment consequences of entry into a major health impediment for workers vs. non-workers? These are genuinely longitudinal or life cycle-related questions that cannot be addressed satisfactorily by snapshot analyses of cross-sectional data. We seem to understand that it is relatively easy to protect workers in existing jobs, but perhaps at the expense of disabled workers seeking jobs. How could this trade-off be avoided or at least be solved more satisfactorily? Again, the provision of appropriate incentives might be the key.

The disabled are clearly disadvantaged economically, with an average real annual income of disabled men comprising less than of non-disabled men. Specifically, men with disabilities are less likely to work than non-disabled men, and when they do work, disabled men earn lower wages than men without disabilities. Moreover, disabled men are more likely to be on social assistance than men without disabilities. These patterns might reflect labour market barriers as well as reduced productivity, since disabled men are generally less educated, older, and working in blue-collar occupations. We should learn more about the interaction between disability and economic circumstances, though. This will require detailed multivariate analyses, preferably even from a cross-country comparative perspective.

Finally, there is a clear need for scientific evaluation of policy interventions. We do understand that gross job creation is not the causal effect of the programme. But how do we convince policy-makers that it is instructive but insufficient to look at the growing literature on active labour market policy? And what would be the convincing study design for the evaluation of interventions in the area of disability policy? A good example for the unfortunate misunderstanding that correlation indicates causality is the account of the experiences with the reformed German regulations presented by one of the panelists.

Clearly, to assess the causal effects of any reform, one must answer the question "what would have happened to the relevant outcome variables in the hypothetical case in which the reform would not have been enacted?" Only if the answer were that the development would have been quite different, could we attribute the difference to the reform. The mere statement that *after* the reform unemployment of severely disabled individuals fell considerably, is quite useless. There is still a lot of work to be done until policy-makers and administrators will understand that both asking the right question is necessary and that its answer requires the construction of counterfactual situations by competent researchers. Only on this basis will it be possible to advance our understanding of these issues, since progress requires the intimate co-operation of policy-makers, administrators, and researchers.

Employers and Disability: Adapting Modern Work Organizations

Philippe Askenazy

A. Trends in Disability and Working Conditions

Because the outflow from disability benefit remains extremely low, the debate on the actions of employers mainly focuses on their role for improving the accessibility to jobs for disabled people.

But at the other extremity of the stock of recipients of disability benefits, despite the reforms affecting benefit access, the inflow rate was stable in the last decade. In addition, the composition of this inflow has been distorted: the proportions of youths, of persons with a mental disability and of ex-working recipients, as well as the number of early retirements have increased (see the OECD report for detailed statistics).

These evolutions are consistent with trends shown by the working conditions surveys undertaken in Europe by national statistical institutes or by the European Foundation for the Improvement of Living and Working Conditions at Dublin (Landsbergis et al., 1999). While the manufacturing sector continuously declines, physical constraints at work are still significant and even increasing. The share of European workers who report working at very high speed (respectively to have to meet tight deadlines) reached 56% in 2000 (resp. 60%) as compared to 48% in 1990 (resp. 50%). At the same time, an increasing proportion of workers reports work-related health problems; between 1995 and 2000, fatigue as well as the proportion of backache (from 30% to 33%) have increased. as have musculoskeletal disorders (e.g. MSDs). Concurrently, new constraints associated to mental stress such as clients' pressure seem to extend and thus to increase mental strain, especially among young workers. Finally, in several countries, some occupational illnesses including cumulative trauma disorders (CTDs) and musculoskeletal disorders (MSDs) exponentially spread. For instance, the number of CTD or MSD has increased tenfold in the U.S. between 1984 and 1994 and in France between 1991 and 2001. This phenomenon particularly hurts women and occupations such as supermarket cashiers. Globally, we would thus observe an intensification of work (Green/McIntosh, 2001) that has been confirmed by numerous researchers from various disciplines during an international conference in Paris.[1]

If working becomes more and more hard and intense, this should not only strengthen the obstacles for disabled people but also keep up the flow from work to disability. In face of global firm reorganizations, the workers, disabled or non-disabled, should be concerned.

B. Modern Work Organization and Working Conditions

However, this idea of damaged working conditions can seem puzzling because jobs are more and more concentrated in tertiary activities and because firms have developed modern workplace practices – multitask jobs, job rotation, quality management ... – that are generally known to virtually improve quality of work and to offer more interesting jobs.

"Taylorist" organizations were based on hierarchical communication and required specialised skills from their employees consistent with the standardization of the production process. "Modern" firms have more horizontal communication channels and favour multiskilling as opposed to specialization. Modern work practices mainly respond to globalization and changes in the technological environment which make information processing, adaptability and product quality key for firms' competitiveness. Basically, modern work practices encompass complementary types of changes:

- The modern management model is often associated with making production processes "lean" and more responsive to market changes. Total Quality Management (TQM) emphasises continuous quality improvement and cost reduction.
- Just-in-time (JIT) systems are also part of the new lean production model. JIT is used not only to improve clients' satisfaction by shortening delivery time and by quickly responding to changes in tastes, but also to cut production costs by reducing stocks. JIT production can be achieved through functional flexibility; in continental Europe it also relies on the development of working time flexibility.

- Decentralization of decision-making aiming at improving the information flow between management and workers. Self-directed work teams and a flattened hierarchy induce some delegation of responsibility to groups of workers. Both decentralization of decision-making and lean production imply that workers are involved in job rotation.

This modern work organization has spread extensively among manufacturing and services in numerous OECD countries, especially across U.S. businesses since the early 1990s; most occupations are affected, from clerks to managers (see Amal/Torres 2001, OECD 1999 and Ostermann 2000 for evidence). In France that is representative of the OECD average, the share of private establishments using multi-task training went up from 12 to 34% between 1992 and 1998 while that of establishments not providing it dropped from 44% to 26%. Similar extensions hold in other countries like Germany, Italy, or the UK.

An important literature in ergonomics, psychology, occupational medicine or sociology has been devoted to the consequences of changing workplace organization for the well-being of workers. Most works take the form of theoretical analysis or cases. They underline the extreme heterogeneity of the impact of new forms of workplace organization across industries, firms and occupations and that these workplace changes are not necessary virtuous (e.g. Wayne/Robertson 1996 and Hägg 2003). For the sake of simplicity, they can be divided into two groups defending differing, although not necessarily exclusive, views:

a) In the modern production model, there is synergy between performance of firms and workers' health and safety.
    - Optimizing the production process requires to reduce one of the main sources of waste, i.e. absenteeism due to occupational hazards, workers' stress and the costs of related incidents
    - Quality management and norms help reduce failures in the production process that induce risks of injury in the workplace and factors of mental strain.
    - Job rotation and delegation of authority make work more diversified and therefore potentially more interesting. It should also help reduce work injuries and stress given that repetition and boredom are important factors of risk.
b) An opposite line of results stresses that modern practices increase the pressure exerted on workers for performance.
    - Quality control is an additional source of mental strain.

      – Job rotation and management reduce slack time, thus raising the pace of work.
      – Workers used to build up personal routines which improved their safety and reduced their efforts through a learning-by-doing process. Job rotation, continuous process improvement and changes in the production process are frequent product changes and consequently detrimental to the building-up of such safety mechanisms.

Working time flexibility is likely to disturb the planning of people's life. Moreover, it implies that short working days may be followed by very long ones while it is well-known that mental strain and environmental tensions increase more than proportionally with the number of hours worked per day.

    As shown by this discussion, the impact of modern work organization on working conditions, health and safety is a priori complex and ambiguous. Some statistical or econometric studies have tried to evaluate the net impact of these practices on working conditions and occupational health and safety. Despite large methodological difference, they find convergent results (see Askenazy/Caroli 2002 for a review). For instance, on the U.S., Brenner et al. (2001) match the representative establishment survey SEPT (survey of employers providing training) and the establishment logs of the OSHA (Office of Safety and Health Administration); they find that Just-In-Time and quality circle induce an increase by 20 to 65% in the frequency of Cumulative Trauma Disorders. In that line of research, the French working conditions survey 1998 is an unique tool for exploring this issue (see Askenazy/Caroli 2002 and Askenazy et al. 2002). It is a complementary survey of the French labour force survey. It provides detailed information for a large (20,000) and representative sample of the French labour force: workplace practices, working conditions, mental strain (receiving contradictory orders, isolation, tensions with colleagues, hierarchy or customers, time pressure...), occupational injuries, plus age, gender, nationality, education, seniority, family status and composition etc. It enables us to perform robust statistical treatment, especially to partly correct for selection biases that are substantial when one studies the determinants of health and safety. Table 1 reports some main results.

    Even after corrections, in France, at the end of the 1990s, modern work practices such as job rotation, quality norms, and working time flexibility are each associated with, not only, additional mental strain or factors of stress, but also, a 20% surplus of occupational injuries (especially benign ones).

These results are consistent with the view that the intensification of work is not only a statistical artefact due to higher social standards but the outcome of the changing workplace environment. This can explain the growing share of mental disabilities among individuals that have previously worked.

Contrary to the common belief that "transforming disability into ability" is slowed by generous benefits for disabled peoples, this piece of literature also suggests that "involuntary" disability can be massive; strain at work (stress, tension between workers, hierarchy...) in firms is a barrier to return to work.

Table 1: Connections between Workplace Practices, Mental Strain and Occupational Injuries In France in 1998 (propensy score methods)

%	Quality norms	Job rotation	Flexible working time	Net technology
Dependant variables				
Tensions				
(colleagues, ...)	+10 to +20	+10 to +20	+10 to +15	n.s.
Uncertainty (contra-				
dictory orders ...)	+10 to +20	+10 to +20	n.s.	0 to +20
Isolation	+10	+10	n.s.	-10 to -20
Temporal pressure	n.s.	n.s.	+10 to +20	0 to +20
Occupational risks	+20	+20	+10 to +20	-15 to -25
Occupational Injuries	+25	+20	n.s.	-15

Source: Conditions de travail 1998. Workers with tenure above one year.

C. Improving Work Organization

What can employers do? Actually, connections between organization and damages in safety or health are not a fatality; they result from the non-integration of the working conditions problem during the implementation of a new organization. Modern work practices are not necessarily "pathogen". Employers can invest in order to improve the overall quality of life at work:

- First, case-studies suggest that if modern practices induce real autonomy, quality of life at work recovers.
- Second, employers can use the services of professionals, such as occupational physicians, human factor consultants and ergonomists; they can help to dramatically improve workplace organization for both disabled and non-disabled. Some firms have developed "good prac-

tices". For example, a rational use of job rotation can both increase productivity and reduce work strain; this practice is successfully[2] used to ensure a progressive return to work of injured workers. More generally, corporate ergonomics programmes, including training and overall analysis of the workplace environment, are usually efficient (see Hägg 2003 for a review).

- Third, case-studies also prove that new information and communication technology, especially "net" or web technology, can lower mental strain and physical risks at work. Indeed, they facilitate communication and reduce isolation of workers. This observation is partially confirmed by the data from the French working conditions survey (see the last column of Table 1). This technology can also simplify the integration of disable people in the labour force.

Recent American experience illustrates that employers can effectively improve the workplace environment. Firms have been aware of the issue of working conditions, mainly because of costs of workplace hazards and the pressure of insurance companies and unions. They have thus conducted ergonomic programmes, invested in training, massively introduced net technologies etc. At a macro level, the output is extremely positive. According to the BLS data, the frequency of occupational injuries and CTDs in the US since 1994 has dropped by 30 to 40%; this decline is exceptional because the high economic growth during the "new economy" decade should have theoretically induced an opposite trend. The return-to-work has been improved: among lost workday hazards, the proportion of cases with a simple restriction of work (not inducing days away from work) is now 40% compared to 20% ten years ago. Using ergonomic prevention, industries seem to achieve both safer workplace conditions and productivity recovery (Conway/ Svenson, 2001).

Conclusion

These analyses suggest that it would be worthwhile for employers, in association with workers or their representatives, to focus more on and to efficiently invest in health, safety and ergonomics of their workplace, especially when implementing innovative organization. Such prevention can reduce the "work pressure" in firms. This in turn should help to not discourage some disability benefit recipients to work, to improve their integration or return to work in the firm, and finally to reduce the flow from ability to disability.

Notes

1   See http://www.cee-recherche.fr/fr/colloque_intensification/intensification.htm for
      the proceedings.
2   For instance, in Quebec (Canada), this practice is an important tool used by firms that
      since the 1985 law on occupational injuries and illnesses, have to guarantee the return to
      work for their workers.

References

Arnal, E./Ok, W./Torres, R. (2001) "Knowledge, Work Organisation and Economic Growth",
      http://www.olis.oecd.org/OLIS/2001DOC.NSF, Labour Market and Social Policy Pa-
      per N°50, DEELSA-OECD.

Askenazy, P./Caroli, E. (2002) "Innovative Practices, Technology and Well-Being at Work:
      Additional Evidence for France in 1998", http://www.cepremap.ens.fr/~askenazy/
      eale3b.pdf mimeo Cepremap.

Askenazy, P./Caroli, E./Marcus, V. (2002) 'New Organizational Practices and Working Condi-
      tions: Evidence from France in the 1990's', *Louvain Economic Review*, 68 (1-2).

Brenner, M./Fairris, D./Ruser, J. (2001) 'Flexible Work Practices and Occupational Safety and
      Health', forthcoming in *Industrial Relations*.

Conway, H./Svenson, J. (2001) 'Musculoskeletal Disorders and Productivity', *Journal of Labor
      Research*, 22 (1): 29-54.

Green, F./McIntosh, S. (2001) 'The Intensification of Work in Europe', *Labour Economics*, 8: 291-
      308.

Hägg, Güran (2003) 'Corporate Initiatives in Ergonomics – An Introduction', *Applied Ergonom-
      ics*, 34: 3-15.

Landsbergis, P.A./Cahill, J./Schnall, P. (1999) 'The Impact of Lean Production and Related New
      Systems of Work Organization on Worker Health', *Journal of Occupational Health Psychol-
      ogy*, 4 (2): 108-130.

Lewchuk, Wayne/Robertson, David (1996) 'Working Conditions Under Lean Production: A
      Worker-based Benchmark Study', *Asia Pacific Business Review*, Summer: 60-81.

Merlié, D./Paoli, P. (2001) *Third European Survey on Working Conditions 2000.* Luxembourg: Of-
      fice for Official Publications of the European Communities.

OECD (1999) 'New Enterprise Work Practices and their Labour Market Implications', *OCDE
      Employment Outlook*, Chapter. 4, pp. 195-241.

Osterman, P. (2000) 'Work Reorganization in an Era of Restructuring: Trends in Diffusion and
      Effects on Employee Welfare', *Industrial and Labor Relations Review*, 53 (2): 179-196.

313

What Should and What Can Employers Do?
A German Government Perspective

Hartmut Haines

What should and what can employers do? My contribution reflects the government's perspective on this issue. And this perspective, at least concerning Germany, cannot be understood without a short overview of our rehabilitation and workforce participation framework.

In Germany, the title of this conference *Transforming Disability into Ability* has been a major political and legal goal for decades. During the last parliamentary period, contingent legislation has sharpened and strengthened the instruments to reach this objective.

The guiding principles of rehabilitation and participation policy in Germany are (see also Figure 1):

- participation of disabled persons in society,
- intervention at the earliest possible stage of disability, and
- provision of individual assistance, tailored to the actual needs, irrespective of the cause of the disability.

The following factors are considered important for the participation of disabled persons:

- information of all persons involved,
- tailoring the living conditions of disabled persons,
- "necessary help" in the form of (public) benefits,
- personal commitment/motivation of those concerned, and
- participation management where necessary.

In an open labour market, the central responsibility for getting and keeping disabled and non-disabled workers in employment rests with the employers. Regarding labour force participation of persons with disabilities, Germany applies a concept of shared responsibility. The responsibility of em-

Figure 1:   Disability and Intervention

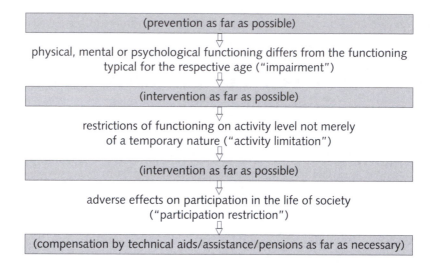

ployers is to provide equal opportunities for persons with and without disabilities and not to discriminate against persons with disabilities. The responsibility of government in this area is to lend "moral" support to employers to help them fulfil their role and provide a collectively financed public benefit for the financing of extraordinary burdens arising out of the employment of persons with disabilities.

This concept of shared responsibility is the basis for the regulations in the German Social Code Book #9 which has been in force since July 2001:

• Part 1 of Book #9 comprises common regulations on participation-oriented benefits (applicable uniformly to funds concerned),

• Part 2 of Book #9 includes special regulations to promote participation of severely disabled persons in working life.

The general objective of the participation-oriented benefit is to promote self-determination and equal opportunity for participation in society, and to avoid and remove disadvantages of persons with disabilities. This policy is applied with strong involvement of the disabled persons and of persons who are threatened by a disability, on an individual level as well as via their organisations.

The specific aims of participation-oriented benefits are: (i) to avert, eliminate, alleviate the disability or to prevent its aggravation and reduce its effect, (ii) to avoid restrictions in the earnings capacity and need of care of a person with disabilities, (iii) to secure participation in working life in accordance with personal preferences and abilities, and (iv) to promote the personal development of the beneficiary and facilitate full participation in society by leading a life as independent and self-determined as possible.

The benefits necessary to meet these objectives are not written down in a detailed list. In order to facilitate participation in working life, health-related benefits as well as work-related benefits are available, including wage subsidies and personal assistance, according to individual needs. The decision which benefits are "necessary" needs to be taken by considering the following dimensions: the usefulness of the benefit to meet the above-mentioned goals, the determination of a particular benefit as the best way to meet these goals and the importance of acting in the shortest possible time.

Figure 2:   Participation-oriented Benefits by (Groups of) Funds

Benefits aimed at	Industrial accident insurance	Social compensation e.g. for war victims	Health insurance	Pension insurance	Federal Employment Service	Social assistance	Youth assistance
medical rehabilitation	■	■	■			■	■
participation in working life	■	■		■	■	■	■
participation in social life	■	■				■	■

Germany accords an absolute priority to prevention, in particular before granting pensions and long-term care benefits, but also with respect to other passive social benefits. Before a cash benefit is awarded all other possibilities to avoid and overcome disabilities must have been exhausted. The responsible fund has to check whether participation measures could successfully be applied before making any decision to pay a benefit. It is the responsibility of the respective fund to tailor a package out of the range of available participation measures and coordinate these benefits for each individual case.

A series of special provisions exists for severely disabled persons. They are specially protected against unlawful dismissal, and elected representa-

tives protect the interests of all severely disabled persons at work. Employers are obliged to fill 5% of the positions in their company with severely
disabled persons; if they fail to do so they must pay a compensatory levy.
Further, supplementary benefits are paid for participation in working life.

The employers' duties with respect to severely disabled persons are:
not to disadvantage (discriminate) persons with disabilities, to provide
workplace accommodation, to enable severely disabled persons to fully develop and use their knowledge and skills, and to enable participation in
vocational training.

The shop-floor representatives of severely disabled persons must be
fully informed and heard before any measures are taken at the enterprise
level. Measures taken without their involvement must be suspended. They
must also be included in monthly discussions between employer and representatives of employee interests, and consulted as to whether vacancies
are suitable for severely disabled persons. Finally, the representatives are
required to cooperate and liaise closely with the Federal Employment Service and the Regional Integration Service.

Integration and advancement of persons with severe disabilities in the
work sphere is also promoted through agreements between employers and
representatives of severely disabled persons. These agreements cover areas
such as personnel planning, work(place) organisation, and gender
mainstreaming.

If problems or difficulties in the employment of a person with disabilities arise, the employer discusses possible solutions for a continuation of
employment with representatives of both the severely disabled persons and
of all employees. If a (severely) disabled person is sick, i.e. out of work, for
three months or if employment is at risk for medical reasons, the employer
will discuss possible solutions with these representatives, with the consent
of the disabled person. Summing up, one can say that in Germany management of disability at the workplace is possible. The tools exist; and the tools
are waiting for users.

Recently, some new or strengthened obligations and incentives for
employers were introduced in Germany regarding the situation of disabled
employees. Every district now offers integration services in order to assist
employers and employment services in particularly difficult cases where
advice may be needed. There are also new benefits for workplace assistance
and there is the right to part-time work for those who need it because of

their disability. Administration of integration benefits has been made easier and influence of shop-floor representatives of severely disabled persons has been increased.

It was decided to reduce the quota for the employment of severely disabled persons from 6% to 5% provided that the overall number of unemployed severely disabled persons is reduced by 25%. A schedule of different compensatory levy rates according to quota fulfilment was introduced and a wide public campaign under the banner "50,000 jobs for severely disabled persons" was launched.

The first experiences with those new regulations have been encouraging. 150,000 new jobs for severely disabled persons were offered within three years time, of which 55,000 received financial support. The number of unemployed persons with severe disabilities was cut by 45,305, from 189,766 in October 1999 to 144,461 in October 2002. Overall, the evolution of the employment situation has been more favourable for severely disabled persons than for other groups.

In my view, these effects are surely influenced by the new legal instruments, but they are, to a great degree, the results of "law enforcement", including the campaign.

Employing Those Not Expected to Work: The Stunning Changes in the Employment of Single Mothers and People with Disabilities in the United States in the 1990s*

Richard V. Burkhauser and David C. Stapleton

Over the last two decades of the 20th century, but especially in the 1990s, United States social welfare rhetoric dramatically shifted with respect to two poor working-age populations that had traditionally been eligible for categorical cash benefits and who were "not expected to seek work" to receive them – single women with children and people with disabilities. In the case of mothers, these "deserving poor" were not expected to seek work because their socially expected role was to spend time at home raising their children. Those with disabilities were not expected to work because their health-based impairments presumably prevented them from performing any substantial gainful activity.

The levels of their government benefits (primarily Aid to Families with Dependent Children [AFDC] for single mothers and Supplemental Security Income [SSI] and Social Security Disability Insurance [DI] benefits for those with disabilities) were not high by Western European standards. But these benefits were significantly higher and longer term than the benefits available to those who were poor but "expected to seek work" – non-disabled working-age men and non-disabled working-age women without children – because the United States has no universal minimum social safety net for those below age 65.

* Partial funding for the work reported in this paper came from the United States Department of Education, National Institute of Disability and Rehabilitation Research, cooperative agreement No. 13313980038. We thank Rachael Dunifon and Mary Daly for their comments on this paper.

During the 1990s, both groups experienced very large changes in employment and dependence on programme benefits; indeed, they were "stunning". Even more stunning, changes for the two groups were in opposite directions. This remarkable development can be largely attributed to policy developments, and much can be learned from comparing them by those considering a change in the "mutual obligations" of persons with and without disabilities, as discussed in *Transforming Disability into Ability: Policies to Promote Work and Income Security for Disabled People*.

The Integration of Single Women with Children into the Labour Force

The dramatic increase in the employment of women in general and married women with children in particular over the past 40 years is evidence of the changing social expectations of women with respect to labour force participation in the United States. Hence, it was not surprising that social expectations with respect to single mothers on welfare would also change. But the results of that change as expressed in the Personal Responsibility and Work Opportunity Reconciliation Act (PRWORA) of 1996 were surprising. This Act, together with other changes in welfare policy in the 1990s, especially the dramatic increases in the generosity of the Earned Income Tax Credit (EITC) for low-income working families with children in 1993, fundamentally altered the structure of United States welfare payments to low-income men and, especially, women with children. Those who study this period all agree that the welfare reforms, the EITC expansion, and seven years of strong economic growth between 1993 and 2000 each contributed substantially to stunning increases in employment for single women with children and stunning declines in welfare programme participation, although there is disagreement about the relative importance of these three factors (Blank, 2002; Moffitt, 2002; Besharov, 2003; and Hotz/Scholz, forthcoming).

As discussed in Blank (2002: 1115): "At the same time as major changes in programme structure occurred during the 1990s, there were also stunning changes in behavior. Strong adjectives are appropriate to describe these behavior changes. Nobody – of any political persuasion – predicted or would have believed possible the magnitude of change that occurred in the behavior of low-income single-parent families over this decade."

Figure 1 from Blank (2002) shows the stunning decline in households receiving AFDC prior to 1996 and its replacement, Temporary Assistance for
Needy Families (TANF), after 1996. Between 1994 and 2000, the caseload
declined by 56.5%. Figure 2 shows the dramatic change in the labour force
participation rate of single women with children under the age of 18 before
and after 1994 compared to other women. While the labour force participation rate of single women without children is uniformly high over the period and the labour force participation rate of married women with and
without children rises over the entire period, the labour force participation
of single women with children shows little change prior to 1994 but soars
thereafter. Blank (2002) further documents that the poverty rates of single
female householders after rising over the 1980s business cycle from 30.4%
in the business cycle peak year of 1979 to 32.2% in the business cycle peak
year of 1989, fell to 24.7% by the business cycle peak year of 2000, with all of
the decrease occurring after 1992.

These are changes in real outcomes – programme participation, labour
force participation rates, and economic well-being – that match political
rhetoric. President Clinton promised that he would "change welfare as we
knew it" and he, with bi-partisan help from a Republican-controlled Con-

Figure 1:   Total AFDC/TANF Caseloads in 1970-2000

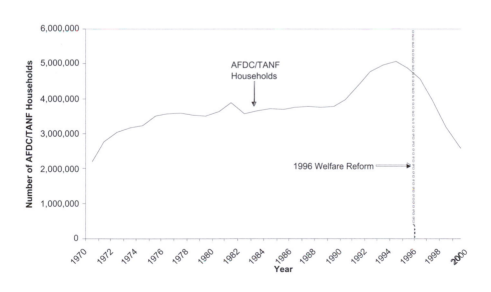

Source: Blank, 2002.

gress, delivered on that promise. Although the relative importance of the improved economy versus changes in public policy remains uncertain, the combination of programmes aimed at increasing labour force participation of single mothers via carrots (a more generous EITC, increases in subsidised child care, better access to subsidised medical insurance, employment services, etc.) and as sticks (a five-year maximum life time limit on TANF benefits, restrictions on other funded transfers, etc.) had an important impact on these outcomes. Another aspect of the welfare reforms that likely contributed to these changes is that they gave States both greater freedom in how they designed their programmes and greater incentives to increase employment of adult recipients and reduce welfare caseloads. One of the important consequences of these procedural changes is that most states are engaged in substantial, and reportedly successful, efforts to help needy families before the families must resort to welfare. These "diversion" efforts often provide assistance that a parent might need to retain an existing job or return to work quickly following the loss of a job.

324

United States policy-makers were successful in increasing the willingness of single mothers with children to seek employment by consistently shifting programme incentives to favour earnings from work over welfare

Figure 2:   Labour Force Participation Rates for Women by Marital Status and Children (Ages 20-65)

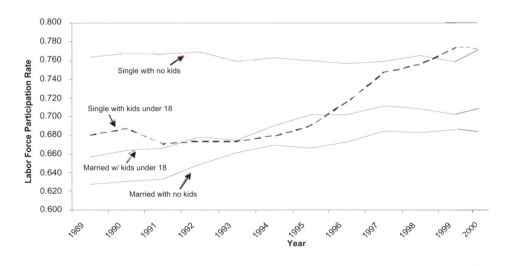

Source: Blank, 2002.

benefits from not working. The sum of these marginal programme changes was a major change in single mother's expectations with respect to work that more closely matched the changing expectations of American society with respect to the role of women. But equally importantly, policy-makers changed the expectations of gatekeepers who administered these programmes with respect to how success was measured. Single women with children are now expected to work. While they continue to be eligible for temporary benefits, programme success is now defined as their integration into the labour force.

But even this was not enough to assure that these expectations would be met. Single mothers' changing expectations about seeking work had to be met with effective private sector demand for that work. Importantly, the EITC, one of the major pro-work mechanisms used to encourage work, did so via a tax transfer. Hence, unlike an increase in the minimum wage, it did not undercut employer demand for single mothers with low work skills by artificially increasing the wages private sector firms had to pay for their services. That shift in policy plus the strong economy between 1993 and 2000, assured that private sector jobs were available for these new workers.

Despite the welfare caseload decline, total government spending on low-income families, which also includes spending for the EITC, health care, child care, and many other supports, has continued to grow, as has the number of families receiving some benefits (Besharov, 2003: 17-19). An important lesson of the reforms is that spending to support low-income families receives much stronger political support when it is tied to work than when it is not.

One final, important, observation is that, although there were demonstrable improvements in economic well-being for most single mothers and their children, there remains much concern about the status of those mothers who are least capable of entering, and staying attached to, the labour force.

The Integration of People with Disabilities into the Work Force

The passage of the Americans with Disabilities Act (ADA) of 1990 was a major political victory for those who believe that working-age people with disabilities should be fully integrated into society, in general, and into the workforce, in particular. The intellectual underpinnings of this belief are first, that the most promising path to economic independence is through market work, and second that the social environment is a more powerful factor in determining employment outcomes than is an individual's impairment. The ADA aims to change the workplace environment and, hence, to increase the employment of people with disabilities by a) mandating that their employers provide them with reasonable accommodations, and b) protecting them from employment discrimination.[1] The rhetoric across the federal government now embraces the notion that environment rather than impairment is critical to employment outcomes for the majority of people with disabilities. Yet the implication of this insight with respect to the incentives that government programmes play on these outcomes has not been broadly accepted, let alone acted upon.

The consequences of the mixed signals of current social policy are evident in the programme participation and employment rates of working-age people with disabilities over the 1990s. Figure 3 taken from Burkhauser and Daly (2002) shows that, in sharp contrast to the stunning decline in AFDC/TANF rolls in the 1990s, the SSDI and SSI-disability rolls experiences stunning increases. Also in sharp contrast to single women with children, the

Figure 3: **Disability Benefit Roll and Employment Rate Among Working-Age Men and Women with Disabilities**

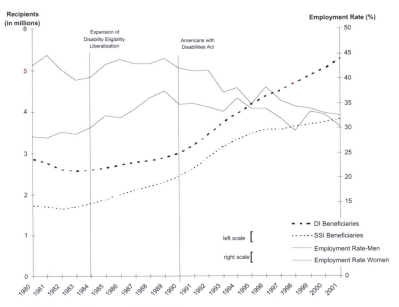

Source: Updated from Burkhauser and Daly, 2002.

employment rates of men and women stunningly declined over the 1990s business cycle after rising over the 1980s business cycle. Most discouraging of all, during the great economic expansion after 1992, the employment rates of both men and women with work limitations continued to fall so that they were actually lower in 2000 than they were in 1992, the trough year of the 1990s business cycle.

We have just completed editing a book that focuses on this period and disentangling the various factors that caused the stunning change in programme participation and employment of people with disabilities (Stapleton/Burkhauser, 2003). Some of the findings reported in the book establish that the data used to measure employment in this population is valid. While the definition used by Blank and others to document the employment and economic well-being of single women with children is not controversial, the use of these same Current Population Survey (CPS) data to capture the population with disabilities is. For instance, with reference to studies using the CPS, the National Council on Disability, in their report of July 26, 2002, recommended that "the Federal Government should not encourage or support the dissemination of employment data until a methodology for assessing employment rates among people with disabilities that is acceptable to leading researchers and demographers in the field and credible to persons with disabilities can be developed." (National Council on Disability, 2002: 20)

Burkhauser, Houtenville, and Wittenburg (2003) demonstrate that, although the use of a work limitation-based question such as the one used in the CPS to capture the population with disabilities is not a perfect measure, the employment trends in this CPS population are not significantly different from employment trends using other measures (severe impairment, housework limitations, etc.) and other data sets (National Health Interview Survey, Survey of Income and Program Participation) to capture employment rates in a consistently defined population over time. Houtenville and Daly (2003) demonstrate that employment rate declines in the CPS working-age population with disabilities in the 1990s are not caused by compositional changes in that population. Rather, they are found in all education, race, gender and age sub-categories of that population.

Having established that the trends in the 1990s are both real and stunningly different from those in the 1980s, the rest of the chapters in the book focus on the causes for this change. Burkhauser and Stapleton (2003) conclude that changes in social policies rather than in the severity of the underlying impairments in this population are responsible for the decade-long decline in the employment of working-age people with disabilities.

The primary social policy change we focus on is the substantial increase in the ease of access to and benefits from SSDI and SSI relative to work. We are especially convinced by evidence reviewed in Goodman and Waidmann (2003) that: 1) increases in the SSDI rolls closely track the employment of those who say they cannot work because of an impairment or health condition (Bound/Waidmann, 2002); 2) eligibility primarily expanded via a lowering of the eligibility criteria for the two impairment groups (musculoskeletal and psychiatric) that also account for a very large share of growth in those who reported an inability to work at all; 3) growth in low-wage workers on the SSDI rolls was much greater than for others, reflecting unintended increases in their replacement rate (Autor/Duggan, 2003).

The second policy change we focus on is the ADA. Burkhauser, Butler, and Weathers (2002) have shown that employers' accommodation of workers with disabilities significantly extends their time in the labour force and postpones their movement onto the disability rolls. But DeLeire (2003), in his review of the evidence developed primarily by himself and Acemoglu and Angrist (2001), argues that, although the ADA is likely to have increased job duration of those with disabilities who are already working, a lack of enforcement with respect to new hires, coupled with the cost of accommodations, could actually have the "unintended consequence" of reducing the overall employment of people with disabilities. He believes that this is the cause of the decline of people with disabilities since 1992. He reports that: 1) employment declines for workers with disabilities in medium-sized firms were greater than in smaller firms that were exempt from the ADA and in large firms where the costs of compliance are smaller; 2) relatively high employment declines in states where ADA enforcement actions are relatively high; and 3) declines in employment even after excluding SSDI beneficiaries from the sample.

There is still room for debate as to which of these explanations lay behind the decline in the employment rates of working-age people with disabilities. But the stark contrast between the stunning increases in the employment rates of single mothers with children over the growth years of the 1990s and the equally stunning decreases in employment rates of working-age people with disabilities over those same growth years demonstrates that the rhetoric related to policy changes aimed at integrating people with disabilities has not matched reality. The passage of the ADA did not achieve this goal and in contrast to the welfare reforms of 1996 with respect to single mothers, the changes in SSDI and SSI policies over the 1990s reduced the incentives of those with disabilities to work.

Pro-Work Policies for People with Disabilities

Historically, the federal government's approach to providing economic security for people with disabilities has been dominated by a caretaker approach, reflecting the outdated view that disability is solely a medical issue. At the insistence of advocates and others, the government has launched a multi-faceted effort to change that, epitomised by the passage of the ADA, but also reflected in other legislation, such as the 1998 Individuals with Disabilities Education Act, the 1998 Workforce Investment Act, the 1999 Ticket to Work and Work Incentive Improvement Act (TWWIIA) and in various presidential initiatives. These new pro-work policy initiatives focus on increasing investment in "human capital" of people with disabilities (i.e. the market skills they have), or in breaking down institutional and physical barriers to the use of their existing human capital.

329

But a glance at the budget numbers shows that cash transfers and medical care (SSDI, SSI, Medicare, and Medicaid) expenditures dwarf expenditures for efforts to integrate those with disabilities into the labour force. And the eligibility rules for these programmes discourage work. These programmes continue to have the following dominate feature: they are strongly conditional on earnings – the more you earn, the less likely you are to be eligible for benefits, or the lower are your benefit payments. The message they send to people with disabilities who can work is that "we will help you as long you don't help yourself." That message needs to be changed to one of "we will help you, but we expect you to help yourself, and we will reward you for doing so." If we are serious about changing the approach to economic security for people with disabilities to one that emphasises taking advantage of their abilities, through employment, we need a coordinated set of marginal changes in support programmes that will both fundamentally change the expectations of those with disabilities and the gatekeepers of these programmes to view work as the primary measure of policy success.

The main lesson from welfare reform is that a three-pronged change is needed for people with disabilities if we are ever to achieve comparable success:

1. More assistance to help them stay in their current jobs, or to find a new job when they lose it.

2. An expanded EITC for those who work but have very low earnings.[2] (See Burkhauser/Wittenburg, 1996 for a detailed discussion of the implicit taxes that disability recipients face on their earnings, and how an EITC could offset those taxes.)

3. For at least a substantial share, an expectation that they will work and that government's role is to help them support themselves through work – an expectation that seems in line with the intent of the ADA.

Such policy changes would complement efforts to increase the human capital of people with disabilities and break down barriers to its use. It would not only help to ensure that increased human capital and reductions in barriers to its use would actually increase employment and reduce economic dependence, but would also create incentives for people with disabilities to invest more in themselves. The dramatic differences in the work outcomes of single mothers with children and working-age people with disabilities shows that even during a sustained period of economic growth rhetoric alone is not sufficient to integrate populations "not expected to work" into the labour market. To successfully integrate people with disabilities into the workforce, policy-makers must make marginal changes in policies and programmes that are consistent with providing support for work, making work pay, and expecting people with disabilities to do what they reasonably can to support themselves. The recent experience of single mothers in the United States suggests that reforms with these three features, appropriately balanced, can both improve the lives of many people with disabilities and achieve broad-based political support.

Notes

1   See Krieger, 2000 for a discussion of the ADA, its legislative history, and its treatment by the courts.

2   Workers with disabilities in the United States already qualify for an EITC if their incomes are sufficiently low, but the size of the credit is very small unless they also have dependent children.

References

Acemoglu, Daron/Angrist, Joshua (2001) 'Consequences of Employment Protection? The Case of the Americans with Disabilities Act', *Journal of Political Economy,* 109 (5): 915-957.

Autor, David/Duggan, Mark (2003) 'The Rise in Disability Recipiency and the Decline in Unemployment', *Quarterly Journal of Economics.*

Besharov, Douglas J. (2003) 'The Past and Future of Welfare Reform', *The Public Interest,* Winter, 4-21.

Blank, Rebecca M. (2002) 'Evaluating Welfare Reform in the United States', *Journal of Economic Literature,* 40 (4): 1105-1166.

Bound, John/Waidmann, Timothy (2002) 'Accounting for Recent Declines in Employment Rates Among the Working-Aged Disabled', *Journal of Human Resources,* 37 (2): 231-250.

Burkhauser, Richard V./Butler, J.S./Weathers II, Robert R. (2002) 'How Policy Variables Influence the Timing of Social Security Disability Insurance Applications', *Social Security Bulletin,* 64 (1): 52-83.

Burkhauser, Richard V./Daly, Mary C. (2002) 'U.S. Disability Policy in a Changing Environment', *Journal of Economic Perspectives,* 16 (1): 213-224.

Burkhauser, Richard V./Houtenville, Andrew J./Wittenburg, David C. (2003) 'A User's Guide to Current Statistics on the Employment of People with Disabilities', in: Stapleton, David/ Burkhauser, Richard V. (eds.), *The Decline in Employment of People with Disabilities: A Policy Puzzle.* Kalamazoo, MI: W.E. UpJohn Institute for Employment Research.

Burkhauser, Richard V./Stapleton, David (2003) 'Conclusion', in: Stapleton, David/Burkhauser, Richard V. (eds.), *The Decline in Employment of People with Disabilities: A Policy Puzzle.* Kalamazoo, MI: W.E. UpJohn Institute for Employment Research.

Burkhauser, Richard V./Wittenburg, David C. (1996) 'How Current Disability Transfer Policies Discourage Work: Analysis from the 1990 SIPP', *Journal of Vocational Rehabilitation,* 7 (August): 9-27.

DeLeire, Thomas (2003) 'The Americans with Disabilities Act and the Employment of People with Disabilities', in: Stapleton, David/Burkhauser, Richard V. (eds.), *The Decline in Employment of People with Disabilities: A Policy Puzzle.* Kalamazoo, MI: W.E. UpJohn Institute for Employment Research.

Goodman, Nanette/Waidman, Timothy (2003) 'The Role of Disability Insurance in Explaining the Recent Decline in the Employment Rate of People with Disabilities', in: Stapleton, David/Burkhauser, Richard V. (eds.), *The Decline in Employment of People with Disabilities: A Policy Puzzle.* Kalamazoo, MI: W.E. UpJohn Institute for Employment Research.

Hotz, V. Joseph/Scholz, J. Karl (Forthcoming) 'The Earned Income Tax Credit', in: Moffitt, Robert (ed.), *Mean-Tested Transfer Programs in the U.S.* The University of Chicago Press and NBER.

Houtenville, Andrew/Daly, Mary C. (2003) 'Employment Declines Among People with Disabilities: Population Movements. Isolated Experience, or Broad Policy Concern?', in: Stapleton, David/Burkhauser, Richard V. (eds.), *The Decline in Employment of People with Disabilities: A Policy Puzzle.* Kalamazoo, MI: W.E. UpJohn Institute for Employment Research.

Krieger, Linda H. (2000) 'Forward-Backlash Against the ADA: Interdisciplinary Perspectives and Implications for Social Justice Strategies', *Berkeley Journal of Employment and Labour Law,* 21 (1): 1-8.

Moffitt, Robert A. (2002) 'From Welfare to Work, What the Evidence Shows', Policy Brief No. 13, *Welfare Reforms and Beyond,* the Brookings Institute.

National Council on Disability (2002) 'A Carefully Constructed Law', The Americans with disabilities Act Policy Brief Series: Righting the ADA. October 30. NCD. http://www.ncd.gov/newsroom/publications/carefullyconstructedlaw.html.

Stapleton, David/Burkhauser, Richard V. (eds.) (2003) *The Decline in Employment of People with Disabilities: A Policy Puzzle*. Kalamazoo, MI: W.E. UpJohn Institute for Employment Research.

How to Get Employers to Take on Greater Responsibility for the Inclusion of Disabled People in Working Life?

Bjørn Hvinden

What Are the Key Issues?

The organisers of the Vienna conference ask "What should and what can employers do?" The simple answer is that employers should and can to a greater extent

- hire job applicants with impairments,
- provide good and safe working conditions to all their employees,
- adopt the principles of universal design in the construction of work premises,
- and if required, make the appropriate particular adjustments in job arrangements to enable an individual to take up or continue in work.

In other words, employers should not discriminate people on the grounds of disability. Accessibility and suitability should primarily be achieved through universal design. In those cases where this is not sufficient employers should accommodate the work situation to the requirements of the person in question. They may achieve this by installing specially-adjusted technical equipment or adopting particular working time arrangements. Moreover, employers should apply general principles of good human resource management, upgrade employees' competence and skills, facilitate their internal advancement and so on, also in relation to employees with impairments. Employers should provide these employees with the same degree of job security and protection against unfair dismissal that other employees enjoy. There is an extensive literature and an established expertise on how to find practical solutions to these tasks. Admittedly, there are some issues around the sharing of the costs of workplace accommodation or compensating for the diminished productivity of some employees that one needs to address. Yet, the key question is not really what employers *can* do; it is quite clear and well-known what employers can do in organisational and practical terms. And it should be added, so are also a fair number of employers doing already.

Rather the key question is *why* employers are not to a greater extent doing what may be legitimately expected from them in this area: Why are employers not recruiting *more* people with impairments? Why do they not *more often* make workplaces accessible for all and adjust work conditions when that is required? Why is this not seen as an important part of the social responsibility of the enterprise? Although the OECD report *Transforming Disability into Ability* makes a number of important points about what should be responsibilities and obligations of employers, it does not really help us to understand why so many employers fail to do what could have been their contribution to securing people with impairments equal opportunities in employment.

How to Meet the Social Implications of Market Competition?

Arguably, the underlying issue is *the social consequences of market competition*. This competition leads to the kind of individual actor adjustments that have been stylised in Game Theory. When a large number of firms are competing with each other, they struggle to achieve a maximally productive, flexible and qualified workforce, and minimise what they perceive as production costs and associated risks. Consequently, each employer is stimulated to make adjustments and choices that are rational and sensible on the individual or micro level but deeply irrational and counterproductive on societal or macro level. The individual firm will for instance be reluctant to choose disabled job applicants or to incur the costs of making workplaces accessible and accommodating for people with impairments because this is perceived to put the firm in *a competitive disadvantage*. The management of each firm will fear that its competitors will have a more efficient and flexible workforce because they do not recruit people with impairments, and that they will avoid the commitment of resources, outlays and attention associated with making the workplace accessible and accommodating. (This also means that the underlying assumptions about employees with impairments as potential liabilities rather than resources for the firm remain untested empirically.) The OECD hints to these consequences of market competition when it states: "Employers who make an effort to (re) employ disabled persons should not be penalised financially *vis-à-vis* employers who fail to make an effort" (p. 164).

We are living in a world where the forces of market competition are becoming stronger and more wide-ranging. Let me here only refer to the evolving single market in Europe, the ongoing liberalisation of world trade for commodities, financial and other services, and other aspects of economic internationalisation and globalisation. In my view stronger market competition makes it necessary to introduce new and stricter social regulation policies. This is less of a paradox than it appears. To be more specific, there is a need for national and transnational legal regulations to protect people with impairments against discrimination and promote equal opportunities in employment and occupation. The rationale is that if all relevant players in a competitive market have the same legal obligation not to discriminate disabled people and the same duty to make workplaces accessible and accommodating, each individual player will have less reason to fear that he/she will be put at a competitive disadvantage when they comply with these obligations. In other words, there should be less risk involved for each player if he/she acts in a non-discriminating, including and accommodating way *vis-à-vis* job applicants with impairments or employees who become disabled. As part of this kind of social regulation policy one must also have in place appropriate institutions for supervising and monitoring employers' compliance with their legal obligations, and accessible procedures for filing complaints, eventually through the court system, for the individuals who see themselves discriminated against. The costs associated with litigation in this area should to a substantial extent be recoverable for the disabled person, either through schemes for legal support or financial aid channelled through the organisations of disabled people.

The need to complement enlarged and strengthened market competition with new forms of social regulation measures is what gives the current European Union disability strategy a particular significance. This strategy emphasises the principles of non-discrimination and universal design, as for instance followed up in a Framework Directive (2000/78/EC), a Community Action Programme, and the incorporation of considerations for the

335

needs of disabled people in the promotion and regulation of the single market. Of great importance are also the efforts currently made within the United Nations to develop a proposal for a legally-binding instrument on the rights and dignity of persons with disabilities. Especially as market competition is extended to an increasing part of the world through the forces of economic globalisation there is also a growing need for enforceable legal protection against discrimination and neglect of fundamental rights on an international level, and not just on a national or regional level. These ambitions may seem utopian today but the experiences with existing international and transnational conventions, for instance on the rights of women, children and ethnic minorities suggest that it would be rash and too hasty to dismiss them.

Some Cautions and Unsolved Issues

336   Even if there was general agreement on the need to give employers a stronger involvement in efforts to ensure that disabled people enjoy the same possibilities as other people to have a fulfilling work career this does not guarantee that this would be the outcome. There must be an appropriate *combination* of sticks and carrots; that is, a mix of legal obligations, financial incentives and communicative means promoting the awareness, knowledge and practical skills needed to make this involvement a reality. I would argue that each of these policy instruments will prove insufficient if not used together with the other two. Moreover, there must be a political will to use all three forms of instruments.

I will illustrate these general points with some examples from Norway. So far there has not been a general provision against discrimination of people with impairments in employment and occupation in Norwegian law. However, discrimination on the grounds of disability in recruitment (hiring) was made illegal in 2001. The government is currently drafting a bill to transpose the EU Frame Directive (2000/78/EC) into Norwegian law. Moreover, the experiences with two long-existing provisions within the National Insurance Scheme and the Work Environment Act are highly relevant, albeit not entirely encouraging, in this context. Here it may be worth mentioning that the situation of disabled people in Norway is paradoxical and ambiguous. On the one hand, available evidence (cf. Chart 5.4 in the OECD report on the employment rates of disabled persons and other OECD statistics on the labour market participation of people aged 55+) suggests that a comparatively high percentage of people with disabilities in Norway are in employment. This situation is unlikely to be the achievement of specific active integration efforts but probably to a great extent the outcome of a reasonably high quality of working conditions in Norway generally, promoted by a climate of cooperation between management and trade unions, and institutionalised and well-functioning systems of health and safety in most enterprises. On the other hand, the rate of people of working age receiving a disability pension is also higher in Norway than in most other countries (e.g. Chart 3.13 in the OECD report). There is clearly a strong expectation from the current political authorities in Norway that it is possible to reduce this rate *and* increase the number of people with impairments in employment. To the extent that it is realistic to achieve the latter objective, at least two important preconditions must be fulfilled:

First, there must be a political will to challenge what has conventionally been understood as "employers' prerogatives" and to acknowledge potential conflicts of interests: Since 1978 the Work Environment Act has contained legal provisions that appear to give the employer quite strong obligations for the practical adjustment or accommodation of working conditions for employees that become disabled while working for this employer. On closer examination the obligations turn out to be less clear and straightforward, as the Act contains formulations giving wide scope for discretionary judgments. More significantly, successive governments of different political colours have been hesitant or reluctant to provide binding regulations that could stipulate more specifically under what circumstances (e.g. in terms of the financial costs involved) employers are required to take particular measures. Given this, it is not too surprising that the body responsible for supervising the practical follow-up of the legal provision, the Directorate of Labour Inspection, has not made very strong or consistent attempts to enforce the employer's obligations in practice.

Thus it is tempting to ask whether this part of the Work Environment Act was really ever implemented or enforced. Relatively few cases have been taken to court, litigants have rarely been successful, and the organizations of disabled people have generally advised members not to file complaints because of the risks of losing their case. It is possible to draw various lessons from this situation. One is that Norwegian political authorities have not really wished to challenge the steering prerogatives of employers regarding internal firm issues, as these prerogatives have become understood within the Norwegian system of corporatist industrial relations and collective agreements between employers and trade unions. Arguably, one is not likely to make progress unless one acknowledges that there may be conflicts of interests in this area, not only between potential or actual employers and the individual with impairments, but also between the latter and the majority of employees without impairments. If there is no will to acknowledge this conflict and adopt the appropriate legal instruments to handle it, the two remaining types of policy instruments, financial incentives like wage subsidies and communicative means such as guidance, information and persuasion, will only be partially successful.

Second, one must find ways of sharing the costs related to accommodation between employer and government ("society"): Under the main social security scheme in Norway, the National Insurance Scheme, dating back to 1966, there have been legal provisions to provide financial support to finance or reimburse a part of the costs involved in on-the-job accommodation for workers with impairments. The rules have been designed to complement the legal provisions under the Work Environment Act just referred to. Thus, the National Insurance Act provisions are based on the premise that the employer has an obligation to accommodate the workplace to the requirements of an employee with an impairment, while acknowledging that the costs of making such adjustments may involve an unreasonable financial burden for the enterprise. This means that the National Insurance Scheme can under certain conditions cover expenses exceeding about NOK 27,000 (about 3,500 €). However, the full costs can be reimbursed if (a) the technical adaptation is necessary for enabling the person to take up paid work, (b) a completely new workplace has to be established to provide work for the person in question, or (c) the person has an impairment of a nature or degree that makes it possible for the employer to dismiss the person under the rules of the Work Environment Act. Moreover, the full costs may be reimbursed if the enterprise in question has signed a contract with the National Insurance Administration about joint efforts to promote a more inclusive working life, under the tripartite five-years agreement with the main partners in the labour market about such efforts.

However, on closer examination it turns out that there has been a striking underuse of the financial support available under the National Insurance Scheme. This seems partly to have been caused by an overzealous effort within local offices of the National Insurance Administration to prevent abuse of public funds. Partly this appears to be the result of a lack of coordination between the Directorate of Labour Inspection and the National Insurance Administration on how to promote an appropriate use of available resources, that is, facilitate on-the-job accommodation in circumstances where the full costs involved would represent an unreasonable burden for the employer. As a result, local level staff within the Labour Inspectorate appeared to lack basic knowledge about this possibility. Finally, there are reasons to assume that the lack of active and systematic enforcement of the obligations of employers has weakened their perceived need to involve themselves in accommodation efforts, including their incentives to explore possibilities for obtaining public support for the costs involved in such efforts. One implication of the underuse of provisions for supporting on-the-job accommodation is an imbalance in the overall use of public resources in this area. A disproportionate large part of these resources are used for replacing labour market income and for modifying the level and type of vocational qualifications of people with impairments. Both these objectives are important in themselves but the full potential of the spending of these resources is unlikely to be realised when one does not achieve more substantial changes *within* the working life where disabled people are supposed to find employment.

The Norwegian experiences outlined here have significant implications for the ongoing transposition and implementation of the EU Frame Directive (2000/78/EC). Under Article 5 of the Directive the employer is required to provide reasonable accommodation in order to comply with the principle of equal treatment in relation to persons with disabilities. "Reasonable" means that the costs of accommodation should not impose a disproportionate burden on the employer. However, Article 5 also says that "This burden shall not be disproportionate when it is sufficiently remedied by measures existing within the framework of the disability policy of the Member State concerned". This must imply that one shall take into account what possibilities there are for sharing the costs related to accommodation between the employer and the public purse. In other words, one will expect more from an employer in terms of taking measures to ensure equal treatment in a country like Norway where a part of the costs may be reimbursed by public schemes, than from an employer in countries where such schemes are non-existent. In order for provisions like under the National Insurance Scheme in Norway to have a positive effect, certain conditions must be fulfilled:

- All the relevant parties must be aware and knowledgeable about both sets of legal provisions (relating to the obligations of the employer *and* to the possibilities for having costs of accommodation reimbursed). These parties include the employer, the individual employee with an impairment, his/her trade union representative, and the front-line staff in the bodies responsible for implementation, supervision and enforcement of the legislation in question.

- There must be a firm commitment from the relevant public authorities and agencies to use the scope for action that legislation gives them.
- The organisations of disabled people, trade unions and other non-governmental actors must put pressure on the public authorities to ensure active use of this scope.
- Individuals who see themselves discriminated against must be given encouragement and support to filing complaints, and if necessary, take their case to court. Public funds must be available to cover the expenses related to litigation in test cases.
- There should be a systematic monitoring, assessment and public reporting of the implementation of these provisions. One of the important issues here is whether existing support schemes are geared towards the kind of accommodation that is required in a changing working life where an increasing number of people are employed in services occupations, in highly-qualified, information- and communication-intensive, high-performance jobs and "greedy organisations".

Finally, it is essential that public schemes for reimbursing the costs of on-the-job accommodation are designed in a way that is not seen to distort competition in the market, and thus comply with the rules on competition as laid down in the Treaty of the European Community. Thus it may be necessary to make it clear that such schemes provide a social right to the person with an impairment, and that they are not a hidden state aid or subsidy that would favour particular enterprises to the disadvantage of others (cf. Article 87 in the Treaty).

Role of Employers in Transforming Disability into Ability: Learning from Dutch Mistakes

Rick van der Ploeg[1]

The Netherlands until recently had a unique and, some would say, disastrous policy on disability benefits compared with most of the other European Union member states:

- general afflictions such as work stress or lower back problems are a ground for disability benefit, while Sweden, say, only acknowledges psychiatric problems if they are caused by traumatic events;
- the decision to grant a disability benefit is based on administrative considerations rather than on a health forecast and the ability to return to (part-time or adjusted) work;
- no lists of maximum duration of benefits for the various disabilities are used;
- the Netherlands have the lowest threshold (only 15% disabled) before one qualifies for a disability benefit (e.g. in Ireland and the UK it is 100%);
- the Netherlands is the only country which does not distinguish between "risque professionnel" and "risque sociale", but this may not much longer be allowed due to international agreements (see Article 121 of ILO);
- the level of the disability benefit is earnings-related (70%, used to be 80%), not a flat sum as in the UK, Ireland and Denmark or contributions-related as, say, in Germany;
- collective bargaining and extending the coverage of collective agreements by the Ministry of Social Affairs raises the level of the disability benefit for most to 100%;

- there is no period one needs to have worked before one qualifies for sickness benefit or (unique in Europe) disability benefit;
- in contrast to France, Germany, Austria, Italy and Spain, the Netherlands have no quota for the percentage of disabled employees to be employed in each firm (however, it is not clear that sanctions are enforced and fines are usually low).

Most of these features of Dutch disability policy provided no incentives whatsoever to get people back to work, rather the contrary. No wonder that Harold Wilensky (Berkeley) argues that the Netherlands was until the mid-1990s the symbol of what *not* to do: "the combination of wildly loose definitions of disability, indulgent administration, and an almost exclusive focus on passive cash benefits made it tops in total disability claims and spending, with the lowest average age of first-time claimants (42 years old), and the lowest labour-force participation rate of 55-64 year old males".

Do the Netherlands really have many more disabled people than other countries? Indeed, the Netherlands have a relatively large number of people on disability benefits ("wao"). In 1999 13% of the labour force had a disability pension. Excluding the self-employed and the chronically handicapped who never worked, in 1999 10.4% of the labour force was on disability benefits, compared with 11.3% in Sweden, 10.2% in France, 7.5% in Germany and 6.8% in Belgium.[2] The Netherlands have a total of slightly over 20% of the labour force on disability, unemployment and welfare benefits, a bit more than Sweden but much less than the UK, France, Denmark, Germany and especially Belgium (varying from 24 to 30%). Only Denmark has a greater proportion of people in work. In 1999 the inactivity ratio for the 15-64 age groups was 31% compared with 55% for Belgium, 48% for France and 40% for Germany. The Dutch problem is thus not unemployment or welfare, but the large number of people dependent on disability benefits.

In the 1980s there were 16.6 per 1,000 insured entering the ranks of the disabled (only 8.8 in Belgium and 9.5 in Germany) and in the early 1990s 5% of GDP was spent on disability benefits (2.2% of GDP average for the EU). The inactivity ratio for the population under 65 (persons on various kinds of benefit and without work divided by employment) is 0.8; which is average in Europe due to the relatively low unemployment rates. However, the share of sick and disabled people in total benefit years is with 61% extremely high (16% for Belgium, 30% for Germany, 26% for Great Britain, 27% for France).[3] The Netherlands have an excellent health system, so it seems unlikely that it is much more sick and disabled than the rest of Europe. The same comment applies to Norway, Sweden and to a lesser extent Denmark.

Many have argued that disability in the Netherlands is often disguised unemployment since a large proportion leaves the labour market permanently through such benefits. Workers prefer the higher and longer-lasting disability benefit to the unemployment benefit and firms find it an easy and cheap workforce management tool to get rid of less productive and older workers. However, after the large-scale dumping of employees in disability during the 1970s and 1980s, it turned out that disabled people are much less healthy than unemployed people. Still, the two most prevalent causes of disability are psychiatric and back problems, which are more difficult to diagnose and thus more open to manipulation. It is also odd that in recent years the proportion of disabled women between 20 and 35 has become three times the figure for their male counterparts.

Many argue that ill people are destined for disability pension. However, 65% is back to work within a week, 80% after two weeks, 90% after six weeks, and 95% after 13 weeks. Half of the remainder ends up in disability, so attention should be focused on people who are sick for more than, say, three months. It is also argued that disability is a dead end. A quarter is indeed 15 years or longer disabled, but of those who entered disability in 1998 40% started work within 2.5 years. Hence, some do manage to return.

Rather than slashing the duration and level of disability benefits (70% of wage but often raised to 100% through collective bargaining) attention should be focused on having a tough but just system with strict eligibility requirements ("high benefits only for those who really need it"). The objective should be to encourage investment in (re)integration of persons with a work handicap without imposing undue hardship on employers.

Since high incidence of longer-term sickness eventually implies a high incidence of disability, policy to transform disability into ability must focus on preventing and reducing sickness as well. In addition, it is important to stress mutual obligations in policy design and also to develop policies for empowering the disabled. Philip de Jong sets out the premises, principles and mutual obligations between the state and the disabled, on the one hand, and between employers and employees, on the other hand, that a more efficient system of disability should satisfy. The following policies have recently been designed to stimulate employers to take their responsibility in transforming disability into ability in the Netherlands:

A. Avoiding Free Riders

One could argue that much of the blame for the large rise in the number of disabled in the Netherlands must go the social partners, viz. the employers' organisations and trade unions. They often found it useful to take a free ride on the collective socially security system for the disabled by offloading their older, less productive workers without having to go through the bother and cost of firing. Topping up disability benefits through collective bargaining to 100% of last earnings has not improved incentives either. Nevertheless, bargaining at the central level between employers, employees and government may play a crucial role both in preventing disability and in reintegration of disabled workers. Agreements to avoid sickness among employees and to get sick employees back to work again ("arbo-convenanten") may help to prevent sick people sliding into disability. Also, agreements to not under all circumstances pay sick employees the full 100% of the wage they last earned seem to help. Extending coverage of collective bargaining outcomes between employers' federations and trade unions have, however, so far only played a marginal role in getting people on disability benefits back to work, since there have been few collective agreements about reserving jobs for disabled persons, stimulating reintegration, etc. Another problem has been that there was no explicit measure to see whether targets had been reached.

From 2003 onwards employers are responsible for reintegration, including vocational rehabilitation and training, not only within their own company, but also with other employers. This should be really effective in avoiding free-riding behaviour. Extending coverage can apply to the duration of the reintegration track with other employers and contents of contracts with reintegration companies, albeit that an employer must always have a choice of the reintegration company.

B. Sticks

Differentiation of disability insurance premiums ("pemba") punishes employers who have a lot of employees becoming disabled. Firms have to pay a substantial part of the costs of the disability arising in their firm for a period of 5 years, so firms have a strong financial incentive to prevent disability and to re-employ disabled workers. Of course, there is an offsetting effect as firms may be more hesitant to hire job applicants who are more likely to become disabled. This policy is the Dutch alternative to quota and is only in full operation from 2003 onwards. Signals so far suggest that this policy encourages firms to transform disability into ability.

Employers normally have an incentive to invest in measures preventing sickness, because they have to pay sick workers their full pay for a maximum of a year compared with 28 weeks in the UK, 12 weeks in Italy, 6 weeks in Germany, 12 weeks in France and 4 weeks in Belgium. If employers do too little to reduce sickness among their employees, according to the "Improvement of the Gatekeeper" bill (the "Wet verbetering poortwachter") from 1 April 2002, they can get sanctioned by having to pay the wage of sick employees for longer than a year with a maximum of two years. There are stiff fines, but it is too early to tell whether this policy will be properly enforced. Nevertheless, it provides strong financial incentives for employers to get sick employees back to work because they have to foot the bill.

Sick employees who try to get reintegrated cannot be fired for two years. If they become fully disabled after a year, they get a disability benefit and leave the firm. Making it more difficult to fire partially disabled people encourages employers to find suitable work for them, but also makes them more hesitant in hiring new employees with a higher chance of becoming sick and disabled. To avoid this type of adverse selection, employers do not incur any financial risk if they hire registered people who are handicapped for work (registered disabled and others that are designated as such).

C.   Carrots

Employers who keep employees (or hire applicants) with a work handicap in service can receive a one-off reduction of 2,042 euro (or at most three yearly reductions of 2,042 euro) on their sickness and disability insurance premiums, which is like the Return to Work Credit of 40 pounds a week for a maximum of 52 weeks the UK is introducing. If the adjustment costs for such employees (schooling, training, coaching, help of such employees, making the workplace suitable, etc.) are higher, they are eligible for an extra subsidy. Employers also receive half of the costs of a reintegration trajectory to another employer and the other half when the employee with a work handicap gets a job of at least half a year. Employers who take on a person with a work handicap receive a no-risk insurance contract, i.e. if such a person becomes sick or disabled during the first five years, the employers do not have to continue paying their salary or to pay higher disability insurance premiums, respectively.

Employees with a work handicap are entitled to facilities to keep or return them to work (e.g. transport, communication, workplace alterations which can be moved to another employer).

Conclusion

A large part of the costs of transforming disability into ability are reimbursed for employers, free-rider behaviour is punished, and the coverage of collective agreements that help is extended. Policy in the Netherlands is rights-based (anti-discrimination legislation) and incentive-based (encouraging voluntary actions) rather than obligations-based (quota). Employers who are effective in transforming disability into ability have a competitive advantage over other employers as they are entitled to various government subsidies (for training, coaching, workplace adjustments, etc.), face lower costs (less sickness pay, lower disability premiums) and enjoy better work morale. Thus, there are strong financial incentives for employers to help people on disability benefits back to work. However, the flip side of the coin is that employers will screen new job applicants and existing employees more intensively on health risks. Protection thus seems to cover existing employees rather than those disabled seeking work. Such protection may, in fact, be counterproductive as firms become more hesitant in taking on persons with a work handicap. Enforcement of (re)integration actions announced in collective agreements seems difficult to monitor and enforce, also as they are often imprecisely worded. Although employers and tripartite bargaining have in the past also been responsible for letting older, less productive employees join the ranks of the disabled, they may be crucial for the (re)integration of persons with a work handicap.

In the near future the new Dutch government may also implement the proposals of the Donner Committee and the Social Economic Council. They amount to a debundling of disability policy and integration policy, which requires a clear distinction between the entitlement to disability benefit and rehabilitation with the aid of empowerment and participation packages. Of course, a reliable and non-contestable definition of disability is difficult to implement and administer and will lead to more litigation. Those handicapped that will never be able to work should receive a disability benefit, perhaps at a higher rate than presently (75% rather than 70% of last earnings), and all others who are partially disabled receive a (re)integration/empowerment income. The concept of mutual obligations implies that those who do not participate in (re)integration and refuse job offers that pay at least 70% of the wage they earned before, will fall back to welfare benefit. The advice is a compromise and also recommends dropping the premium differentiation for the employers. This would be a pity, since this would destroy incentives to try to get partially disabled employees back to work again. Raising the benefits of the structurally disabled before the number of people on disability benefit has substantially declined, may be dangerous as the higher benefit will attract new claimants unless medical and other tests are perfect.

Notes

1   I am extremely grateful for the help and advice I have had from Michel Rovers and his colleagues at the Ministry of Social Affairs and Employment in preparing this intervention.
2   Many commentators suggest that the Netherlands have one million disabled people. However, last year 992,996 benefits were given to 979,400 people, but 134,351 of those were given to disabled people who have never worked (in Belgium, for instance, they would have to rely on welfare). Also, 56,177 benefits were given to self-employed. In addition, 26,300 benefits are not paid, because their recipients earn too much. Hence, 776,186 benefits are paid to previously employed people. Less than a million, but still very many.
3   There is some evidence, however, that some disability is disguised as pre-pension in France, unemployment in Belgium and welfare in Great Britain.

Special Theme:

Barriers to Participation: A Session Organized by the European Disability Forum / EDF

Transforming Disability into Ability.
Session Report on Barriers to Participation

Stefan Trömel

Overall Comments to the Report

The OECD report presents useful and comprehensive information.

The report rightly highlights that the available data do not allow to draw any strong conclusions about the effectiveness of policies to promote employment among disabled people. The number of influential factors and the fact that they change over time, do not allow a cause-effect analysis.

The most delicate part of the report is its section on conclusions, where I will need to disagree with some of the conclusions and recommendations.

The section of the report that deals with the role of employers is too short and should probably not have been part of it.

The report deals with the interaction between passive and active measures and a section on the role of employers is probably out of the scope of the report. The section addresses the issue of the role of employers not very deeply and it might have been better, in my view, not to address it at all. Also, the fact that almost no employers attended the conference confirms this point.

Another comment made in the report also needs to be challenged. The report states that the employment rates of disabled people in countries with anti-discrimination legislation are lower than in countries with quota systems. I would not challenge the fact, but one has to be careful when drawing conclusions.

Anti-discrimination policies have a major impact on the social inclusion of disabled people. The impact on employment levels is not immediate, but indirect through its impact on education, information society and public transport. To improve the employment levels of disabled people, anti-discrimination legislation needs to be complemented by other policy measures, like financial incentives to employers, awareness raising campaigns and others. Also, quota systems, although not accepted in all countries, have a positive impact on the levels of employment of disabled people.

The report also proposes a mutual obligations approach among all stakeholders. From a disability point of view, one cannot argue against this. It is obvious that rights also imply responsibilities. Combating a paternalistic approach implies accepting this.

However, the question is: Are we already in a position where the barriers that disabled people face in society to exercise their rights and responsibilities have been eliminated? I think we can agree that the answer is no. It is therefore much too soon to speak about sanctioning disabled people who do not comply with supposed obligations. Moreover, there is a big threat of misuse of this approach.

The most relevant proposal included in the OECD report is the one that refers to the unbundling of benefits. It is daily practice that a disabled person, who manages to enter the labour market, will lose his/her benefits, even those that compensate the extra costs linked to his/her disability. Moreover, to recover these benefits when exiting the labour market, is also often difficult and slow. These are real disincentives for disabled people seeking employment.

The contribution by Ms Mabbett addresses the issues of definition of disability and rightly states that relevant definitions of disability would be different for different purposes.

I also agree with Ms Mabbett's comments challenging the need for a medically-based analysis to determine disability, as well as challenging the need for a single definition.

There must be more flexibility in the benefit system, accounting for the increasing number of flexible work arrangements like part-time arrangements, temporary work agencies and others.

There is nothing against early intervention, but let's be careful in the way it is implemented. Each case is different and often some time is needed for the person who has become disabled, to get used to this new situation, before the person should be obliged to undertake work training programmes. Also, more efforts need to be made to maintain the link of the person who has become disabled with his/her employer.

The report correctly states that disability benefit systems often function as early retirement programmes. Disabled people, of working age and who want and can work, should not be classified with those that cannot work. If done, no efforts will be made to bring disabled people into the labour market.

Session on Barriers to Employment of Disabled People

Introductory Speeches

The so-called special session was organised by the European Disability Forum and seeked to provide a complementary angle to the OECD seminar and report.

Three speakers introduced the session, representing a French employer, a UK local authority and the Swedish umbrella organisation of disability organisations.

Agnès Roche de la Porte des Vaux, from Adecco France, presented the work of her company in the promotion of employment of disabled people.

One of the most challenging points made in her presentation was to state that quota systems (as existing in France) have a negative impact on the attitudinal barriers, as quota systems focus on disability and not on ability.

In fact, she questioned whether positive discrimination contributes to overcoming attitudinal barriers. She suggested to establish a real non-discrimination policy which is based on the competences of disabled people and a protection against all form of discrimination.

I would respond by saying that we have to be careful in exchanging concrete results (like those obtained by a quota system) with a promise of a new thinking in society, which will take its time to produce concrete results in terms of employment. It seems that this transition or exchange needs to be handled very carefully.

The attitudinal barriers among disabled people themselves were also highlighted by this speaker. Surprisingly, nothing was mentioned about the attitudinal barriers among employers.

Mikael Klein, from the Swedish national disability organisation HSO, challenged whether the labour market is prepared to welcome disabled people. In Sweden, a country with high levels of employment, a significant part of the disabled people is not in the labour market, but provided with early retirement pensions.

There is a need to change the way the labour market operates, to ensure that society benefits from all the abilities of the working population.

It is the responsibility of all to contribute to the employment of disabled people, but the main responsibility continues to remain with public authorities.

Inclusion does not mean fitting disabled people into a society (labour market), but redesigning society to make it really open for all.

David Morris, Disability Advisor of the Greater London Authority (GLA), started his presentation by giving some personal examples of the attitudes that still exist in society towards disabled people.

He then presented the work of the GLA and gave some interesting statistics, comparing the employment rates of white male non-disabled people (88%) with those of disabled women from ethnic minorities (30%).

Disability equality is high on the agenda of the GLA, in particular in 2003, the European Year of Disabled People, and a survey has been undertaken to analyse how disabled people are excluded from mainstream life.

General Discussion

The potential of the so-called third sector was highlighted. It is a fact that a significant percentage of new jobs is being created in this sector. However, it is important to state clearly, that disabled people have to be present in all sectors. It is not about having a first labour market for non-disabled people and a second labour market for disabled people.

The importance of individual assessments was also stated. This approach is becoming more and more a key issue in labour market policies and must also be considered a key issue in labour market policies targeted at disabled people.

The role of disability NGOs in this process has to be not only one of criticism, but also one of making concrete proposals on how the situation can be improved.

As a recent European Commission report highlighted, policies need to focus both on the supply and the demand side. The attitudinal barriers (prejudice, stigma, low expectations) and the inaccessible environment continue to be the main reasons for the low employment level of disabled people. Policies need to address these issues, while at the same contributing to an increase in the work competences of disabled people.

The need to empower disabled people also has to be a central element of any policy in this field.

There is also an important role for public authorities, who can use public procurement and other measures to increase the business case for employing disabled people.

Closing Session

From a disability NGO point of view, I tried to summarise the session and the conference overall as follows:

The report has to be welcomed, because it has raised attention on a very important issue.

The starting point of the report, which is not to equal "disabled" with "unable to work" is very important.

It is important to be clear about what should be the guiding principle of the interaction between passive and active labour market policies. From my point of view, the guiding principle should be that of full participation, equal opportunities and full empowerment. Often, economic savings will also be achieved in the mid and long term, but economic savings should never be the guiding principle of these policies.

The focus has to be on the elimination of all the barriers that disabled people continue to face: Attitudinal barriers, barriers in transport and education.

Disability benefits, linked to the extra costs related to a disability, and unemployment benefits and other minimum income benefits should be separate.

To promote employment, anti-discrimination policies need to be complemented by positive action measures.

The extreme diversity of disabled people requires comprehensive employment plans, which include a variety of measures, based on an individual assessment.

Finally, in this as in all other areas, policy-makers need to consult with representative organisations of disabled people before implementing new policies.

Any Further Issues

As proposed by the representatives of the OECD, EDF would like to suggest to be closely involved in all future OECD work in the field of disability.

The lack of reliable data imposes some limitations on any research that is only based on statistics.

It seems to be wise in studies like these, to compare the conclusions deriving from statistical research with surveys among a selected number of disabled people. This would enrich the conclusions of the studies.

The importance of reliable statistics can not be underestimated. Often, the lack of statistics provides a good excuse for inaction. If you can't measure the problem, why should it be tackled.

In 2002, the EU Labour Force Survey included an *ad hoc* module on disability, which for the first time will provide comparable statistics on employment rates throughout the EU. Unfortunately, this module will not be kept beyond 2002.

It will be important to continue having statistics on the employment levels of disabled people.

The Change in Mentality Needed for Society to Promote Employment Opportunities for People with Disabilities

Luis Cayo Pérez Bueno

- Employment is one of the most effective factors of socialisation and normal participation in the life of the community. For people with disabilities, the importance of access to the labour market is even more important than for those who are not disabled since employment brings with it the advantages of social inclusion. Not having a job makes it very difficult to live an independent life and make one's own decisions. Jobless and disabled people find themselves in a situation of dependence, caught between their families and the authorities, and in permanent danger of marginalisation and social exclusion.
- The employment situation of disabled people in Europe is by no means satisfactory, showing clearly that as a group they run a definite risk of exclusion. Disabled people have less access to employment than those without disabilities (lower participation rates) and have much higher rates of unemployment. The skill and salary levels of the still very few disabled people with jobs are well below the average for those without disabilities.
- Integrating disabled people in the labour market requires decisive and energetic action on the part of the authorities, social actors and society in general and also, especially, the disabled themselves who have to be those mainly responsible for their own integration.
- Given this situation, which unfairly excludes nearly 10% of the population from the society of which they ought legitimately to be part – with equal responsibilities and obligations – it is important to take

357

concrete measures to bring this population group into closer contact with the labour market so that they too may contribute to the wealth of the country and the development of the community to which they belong.

- It is up to society as a whole to overcome and reject for good the prejudices that exist with regard to disabilities. Disabled people *too* are members of society, with their particularities, and what is important is that they should be compensated when their disabilities give rise to a disadvantage, inequality or lack of opportunity.

- Employers must be fully aware of the work capacity of the disabled and provide them with job opportunities. They should also be encouraged to take as an example those companies that have already successfully tested such labour market access measures. Disabled people must be seen as human beings, with abilities and skills, and not as limited individuals.

- Unequal treatment or, more specifically, discrimination against disabled people entering or already in the labour market must be forbidden and punished by law, given that such acts are in breach of the rights to which every citizen is entitled. All European Union countries need urgently to bring their legislation into line with Council Directive 2000/78/EC of 27 November 2000 establishing a general framework for equal treatment in employment and occupation, which has still to be implemented in some countries, so that the disabled and the organisations that represent them have effective defence mechanisms and can guard against discrimination in the area of employment and training.

- Disabled people and the organisations that represent them must be told to devote special attention to training provided by the public authorities so that they secure good skills and are equipped to enter the labour market in the same way as other citizens.

- With regard to disabled people who cannot work or who have limited social capabilities, the authorities must guarantee their social protection or sheltered employment arrangements suited to their circumstances.

- The celebration, in 2003, of The European Year of People with Disabilities is a great opportunity to adopt amibitious measures to promote the entry of disabled people into the labour market.

- Employers' associations and unions, which play a fundamental role in regulating the labour market via collective bargaining, have to undertake seriously to oversee the completion of labour market and social legislation aimed at improving access to employment for the disabled.

- Sheltered employment is a perfectly valid form of labour market access and social integration, which fulfills the employment needs of many disabled people with special difficulties.
- The social situation of disabled women, whose labour market participation rates are much lower than those of disabled men, while their unemployment rates are higher, requires specific measures to ensure that, as a group, they are the target of active employment policies that need to be developed for the future.
- Also, the active employment policies developed in the coming years need to place the emphasis on promoting access to employment for the disabled suffering most seriously from labour market exclusion, including the mentally handicapped, the very seriously disabled, the mentally ill, people with cerebral palsy, etc.
- Used intelligently, new technologies are naturally conducive to the social integration of disabled people. It is vital to ensure that new technologies that are inaccessible or designed on the basis of exclusion criteria do not become a chasm that would further exclude disabled people from employment and the vital and concrete possibilities such technologies offer.

Mental Barriers in General Labour Market Policy

Mikael Klein

The topic of this conference *Transforming Disability into Ability*, puts the focus on an exciting challenge. From a labour market point of view, the challenge consists in creating opportunities for persons with disabilities, to change from being objects (targets for social welfare) to become subjects (citizens empowered by their own support).

Two years ago, the Swedish parliament adopted a national action plan for disability policy, expressing the same ambition. This national plan is meant to influence all policy fields for the next decade, and is entitled "From Patient to Citizen", which by its name catches the same idea as the topic of this conference.

However I would like to change focus for a moment, and instead apply the question on the labour market itself. We could start by asking ourselves about the conditions of working life today.

In Sweden we have a long political tradition of aiming for a high level of employment. Enforcing the possibility for every citizen to have a job and thereby secure his/her own support, has been a priority for all. Looking at the conditions of today, we may say that unemployment rates of 4.3% are quite low. Anyhow, a large number of the workforce of almost 6 million people does not participate in the job market.

For example, we almost have half a million people receiving early retirement pensions. They are not in the labour market and do not have any impact on the unemployment rates.

In the last couple of years, we have had a rapidly increasing number of people suffering from long-term illnesses, which has led to dramatically

361

increasing costs for governmental finances. A large part of those being on long-term sick leave suffer from illnesses related to stress, mainly caused by their work situation.

At the same time, we still have groups of people that are not fully integrated into the labour market, for example immigrants and persons with disabilities. As in other parts of Europe, Sweden faces the problem of an ageing population that, in a near future, will create an urgent lack of labour force.

Summing up today's state of the Swedish labour market, we have a situation where different groups are excluded from the labour market, an increasing number of the working population is getting ill because of their work situation, and at the same time there is a lack of people entering the labour market. From the Swedish disability movement's point of view, we draw the conclusion that we actually have a "disabled" working life. Or at least, there is a labour market unable to be economical with its labour force.

With the challenge of transforming disability to ability, we can apply the following question not only to persons with disabilities, but to the labour market as a whole: How can we transform the labour market from its currently low ability of providing a working life enabling the healthy administration of the working force, including the ability to benefit from every single citizen's working abilities?

Such a challenge demands essential changes in various fields of the working life. Our traditional understanding of working hours, working places and work organisation has to be redefined. If the labour market shall be able to safeguard the working capacity of every citizen, it has to focus on the varying conditions for individuals to carry out work. In that sense, we need a working life much more adaptable to different conditions within the manpower than today. Roughly speaking, we have had the same structure of working life since the start of industrialisation. Even today, the main idea is to adapt the manpower to the conditions of the labour market to a much wider extent than the other way round.

Approaching the issue in such a different manner raises many questions: Is this approach really realistic or is it like reaching out for Utopia? Who should carry the responsibility for such a development? And above all, does every citizen really have a work capacity that could be of use to society?

The latter of these three questions is perhaps the most interesting, at least from an ideological point of view. The question puts our own view of people in the focus of attention.

Do we really believe that every person in our society, to some extent can carry out a job that is useful for others?

If we are talking about today's labour market, the definite answer to that question must of course be "No". Today, there are many people who cannot manage a job, for various reasons. It is hard to imagine how that could be possible for all, even with great support efforts for those in need.

However, within the Swedish disability movement it is understood that each and every person actually has a capacity (and also the wish) to contribute to the benefit of society, if provided with a chance to do so as well as with the appropriate conditions.

If we want every citizen of our society to participate in an equal citizenship, we must guarantee him/her equal rights. But not less important, every citizen must be prepared to contribute to society, too. Many people with disabilities are presently denied both their rights and duties that come with complete citizenship. These incongruences in the long run are untenable for the prosperity and stability of our society. Amongst the obligations for every citizen, there is the duty to work. This means that society is obligated to create conditions for every citizen to be able to actually participate in working life.

The United Nations Declaration of Human Rights besides other fundamental rights includes the right to work. To fulfil the obligations of the declaration, we cannot continue to create separate solutions in the labour market for people with disabilities. Neither can we do so in other fields of our society. A much better way to proceed would be by trying to adapt the labour market itself to all our citizens. That way, we can be sure of a much more sustainable development of our working life and of society at large.

Well then, whose responsibility is it to ensure a sustainable development of the labour market? An easy answer to that would be that the responsibility lies with the employers. Of course they have an important role in the process as they determine the conditions of each workplace.

But as we all carry similar cultural values and have similar views of the conditions of working life and the working capacity of people, we all have to be involved in such a change in thinking. How often do we, for example, think of people with disabilities mainly as an asset to the workforce?

The main responsibility, however, lies on the part of the state. Through legislation and by the power of its authorities, the state has the possibility of starting a process of change. Our cultural values and how we regard people with disabilities, have an impact on how policies are designed. We should not be naive and believe otherwise. Our common opinions, our prejudices etc., are shared by both politicians and civil servants working in the field. Our traditions and cultural values give us many benefits, but also create mental barriers, both in disability policies and in labour market policies.

In the wider political context, for example when the objectives of national or international labour market policies are under discussion, one very seldom finds representatives of rare experiences involved in the process. The discussion mainly includes different experts of the particular political field but lacks the variety of experiences needed to arrive at good results.

I would like to give you a highly topical example of this. Presently, there is a debate in Sweden about the increasing ill-health of working life, and the government is fumbling for solutions that will straighten up the growing deficit of the national finances. It has put pressure on the stakeholders of the labour market to find ways to prevent a further aggravation of the problem. Unfortunately, there has been no success with regard to that matter yet.

The disability movement was not invited to participate in the discussion, and is probably not regarded as having suggestions for feasible solutions.

And maybe we do not have the necessary solutions? We certainly do not have any hidden trump card, but the point is that our experience is not even asked for.

The issue of ill-health in working life has been a growing problem for Swedish government during the past three or four years. The disability movement's experience of dealing with the issues of ill-health and working life for at least 60 years now, was probably considered as too short a time to be worth asking for ...

*

* *

We all have good intentions of solving different problems, but we easily focus on matters differing from the mainstream. In labour market issues, we try to find solutions for those who do not fit in. Instead, we should try to find ways of broadening the labour market, making it possible for more people to actually fit in. If we could find ways to benefit from every citizens individual ability, we would get access to new experiences that we lack today.

Amongst them, the unique experiences of people with disabilities. So, is this possible or is it like reaching for Utopia?

I think there is no objective answer to that question; we all must find our own answer to that. Instead, I would like to raise a counter question:

Can our society in the long run afford to abandon the diversity of knowledge and experience represented by our fellow citizens, be it in working life or in the field of policy-making?

Moving towards Equality for Disabled Londoners

David Morris

First of all let me start with a little context. I am one of those in-your-face card-carrying severely disabled people. I use personal assistance and need it in a 24-hours sort of way. Other than that I am relatively ordinary. Car, flat, relationship, job, football team, bad habits. Oh and I don't wear shoes. They get in the way.

My career path has led me towards championing disability rights at the Greater London Authority, via consumer rights, advocacy and not for profit management. I have happened to use my skills in this area not because I have an impairment, but because of the experience I have had as a disabled person. It could, however, have led me in a number of directions had I had the opportunity. Agile business should want me on board. So often it doesn't though. When you hear the words "you have done so well to be short-listed from such a strong field" at the beginning of the interview, you just know it isn't going to be your day!

In 1981 I was contemplating why I was having such difficulty in getting a job and somewhere to live over a beer having just graduated and, probably emboldened by all the publicity around "the disabled", somebody decided to engage me in conversation with my favourite chat up line of all time: "I've got a friend like you. He is a vegetable!" Two weeks ago probably emboldened by all the publicity around the European Year, while I was contemplating firefighting procedures, over a beer, somebody decided to ask whether they could borrow the ashtray on my table and then returned to the party sitting on the table behind me and loudly announced: "I've never talked to a cripple before. It wasn't as scary as I thought!"

It is on these occasions when I realise that for some people I still continue to exist on another planet. The fact is when this attitude is linked into power, the amusing anecdote becomes a dangerous experience. When we move beyond the arts and acces and being special and brave; when we ask questions and protest; when we want to be in control of our lives, when we start to affect other people's "normality" the veneer starts to crack. The fact is that the experience of living as a disabled person in 2003 is still too often the experience of exclusion; the experience of humiliation; the experience of prejudice; the experience of discrimination. Disablism is alive and well and just as pernicious and damaging as racism and sexism and homophobia.

There are of course a number of psychological and attitudinal barriers to our full and effective participation as equal citizens. My experience tells me, however, the most important of these has been the consistent failure to link the discrimination faced by disabled people in the workplace fully to the Equalities agenda. In many ways we are still treated as "special" and different. We are still expected not to work, we are still expected not to achieve, we are still expected not to have aspirations. Increasingly this is not the case from a policy and legislative prospective. However it continues to be from a psychological perspective. Fifteen years ago I was told that it would not be appropriate for me as a disabled person to work with members of the public in my job in a government department. Ignorant and irrational behaviour by the human resources department which now would be accepted as being discriminatory and illegal under the Disability Discrimination Act. Two months ago I was told that I could not come into my office because I would be a fire risk during the fire fighters strike. To me this was similar psychological failure to accept the essence of my equality. Prejudice and ignorance welded into an organizational culture leads to institutionalized discrimination.

It is not until we are able to change our perspective on disability that I believe we will effectively influence the disadvantage of being a disabled person. Only when we clearly recognise that the experience of disabled people is of a society that continues often to disable us rather than accept our difference will we move beyond creating our world in a refracted and false reflection of normality. When we are effectively able to talk about sexism, racism, disablism as common and interlinking phenomena; when disability naturally is as synonymous with ability, as ability is to being black or a woman.

368

The Greater London Authority – What Is It and What Does It Do?

- The Greater London Authority (GLA) was created as a new form of strategic citywide government, consisting of an elected Mayor and a separately elected Assembly in 2000.
- The GLA stands apart from the London boroughs, looking at the needs of London as a whole and representing the city on a national and an international level.
- The Mayor is elected by the people of London every four years. The next election will be in 2004. The current Mayor is Ken Livingstone, who was elected in May 2000. The Mayor represents London and Londoners, in the UK and internationally. He takes a strategic look at what is happening in London, drawing up policies for the social and economic development of the city.
- The Mayor's powers and responsibilities are set out in the Greater London Authority Act 1999. This Act also covers the London Assembly and the Greater London Authority (GLA).
- The Mayor sets the budget for the Metropolitan Police Service (under the oversight of the Metropolitan Police Authority), Transport for London, the London Development Agency, the London Fire Brigade (under the oversight of The London Fire and Emergency Planning Authority) and the GLA.
- He is responsible for setting policies on transport, buildings and land use, economic development and regeneration, culture and the environment. He has a duty to promote the health of Londoners. He must ensure that all of the policies work together and that they benefit all Londoners.
- The London Assembly acts as a check and balance on the Mayor. Elected by the people of London, the Assembly consists of 25 members. Fourteen of the members are elected to represent particular areas of London. The other 11 are elected by a system of proportional representation and are known as Londonwide members. They examine the Mayor's activities, questioning him about his decisions and scrutinising his policies. They are also able to investigate other issues of importance to Londoners.

The Mayor's Equality Vision

To create a fair city, promoting social inclusion and tackling deprivation and discrimination.

We will be an equalities champion and leader in:
- Promoting equality.
- Challenging and eradicating discrimination.
- Providing responsive and accessible services for Londoners.
- Ensuring our workforce reflects the diverse population of London.

The Social Model of Disability – A Tool for Understanding Disability Equality

The GLA rejects the medical model of disability and accepts
- that disability is a social phenomenon,
- that while many individuals have physical or sensory impairments or learning difficulties or are living with mental health needs, it is the way society responds to these which creates disability and not the impairment,
- that disablism is a form of oppression in the same way as is for example racism, sexism and homophobia.

The medical model of disability encourages explanations for the discrimination and disadvantage experienced by disabled people in terms of the features of an individual's body. The social model, however, encourages explanations in terms of characteristics of social organisation. The social model of disability makes the important distinction between "impairment" and "disability" and is the response of the disabled people's civil rights movement to the oppression of disabled people. Disability is caused by "barriers" or elements of social organisation that take no or little account of people who have impairments. It follows that if disabled people are to be able to join in mainstream society, which is their human right, the way society is organised must be changed. Removing the barriers that exclude (disable) people who have impairments will bring about this change.

Disabled Londoners – Some Facts

EMPLOYMENT

- Disabled Londoners are twice as likely to be unemployed than non-disabled people. 11% of disabled Londoners are unemployed compared with 6% of non-disabled Londoners. Young disabled people (26%) and black disabled people (19%) are more likely to be unemployed.
- Disabled workers living in London are much more likely to be doing routine and elementary jobs. Only 38% of disabled workers were employed in managerial, professional and technical occupations compared with 53% of non-disabled workers.
- Disabled workers earn considerably less than non-disabled workers. The average hourly wage for disabled Londoners was £10.25. This is 20% lower than the average for non-disabled Londoners.
- In London, 28% of disabled people want to work but do not have a job, compared to 11% of non-disabled people.
- 88% of white male non-disabled people of working age were employed, compared with 30% of ethnic minority disabled women.

EDUCATION

- Disabled people are less likely to have access to education. Only 39% of disabled 16-24 year-olds participate in some form of education compared with 50% of young non-disabled Londoners.
- Disabled people are generally less well qualified than non-disabled people. Only 18% of disabled people have higher-level qualifications compared with 34% of non-disabled people.[1]
- 11% of disabled people have degree level qualifications compared with 22% of non-disabled people.[2]
- 39% of disabled people have no educational qualifications compared with 19% of non-disabled people.

Notes

1   Disabled people and the labour market: an analysis of the Labour Force Survey 2001/2002 GLA (2003).
2   London Household Survey.

The Employment of People with Disabilities in France

Agnès Roche de la Porte des Vaux

I should like first of all to give you some thoughts on the impact of French legislation on workers recognised as being disabled and then, secondly, share with you my experiences as a mediator on the labour market.

Does Positive Discrimination Help to Overcome Psychological Barriers?

The Act of 10 July 1987 made it compulsory for firms in France with 20 or more employees to recruit disabled persons (6% quota). This is referred to as "positive discrimination" in favour of the disabled.

To discriminate is, in actual fact, to acknowledge the differences in nature of the persons concerned. In the case of disabilities, to discriminate is to consider that the disability in question is part of the make-up of the person: to be disabled is to be not like other people – not as regards the difficulty of living in society, but as regards what is the very essence of a human being, i.e. his or her status as a citizen.

Discrimination, even when positive, is in contradiction with equality of opportunity. By making a distinction at the outset, the damage is done. It even has a more perverse effect – on the person himself – who will come to the conclusion that he can "demand" a job by virtue of being disabled. Whence the line used by certain disabled people to the effect that "you have to employ me because you have jobs that are reserved", bringing to mind a picture of job "reserves" or questioning the meaning of the adjective "reserved": a routine, undemanding little job that will not bother anybody.

The right to work is not a variable right which depends on the characteristics of the individual. To give a person the idea that his disability can give him an occupational identity is to mislead him and make it difficult for him to access the world of work.

The scar becomes the emblem: "my disability obliges you to recruit me", with the result that the disabled person is able to dispense with the obligations that any employee has to fulfil.

Then again, in an economic environment in which a lot of people are excluded from the labour market, this sort of "favour" cuts the disabled off from the job-seeking community.

The substantial increase in specialised legislation in France has contributed to this exclusion. Occupational redeployment establishments have not always benefited from the advances in the ordinary network and are often no longer in tune with the economic community, whence the need at present to develop the considerable momentum required to free those concerned from the context of being disabled.

And yet, by putting the spotlight on disabled persons, French legislation has put in place systems that have served very largely to take the mystery out of disablement, to change collective representation, to raise funds to offset the shortcomings and to oblige firms to adopt active policies.

Even if France is still to a large extent rooted in the obligation to employ disabled workers, the Acts of 12 July 1990 protecting people against discrimination because of their state of health or their disability, and of 16 November 2001 on measures to combat any form of discrimination should compel us to outlaw the term positive discrimination. In fact we could certainly go further. These justified distinctions, which resulted in the introduction of active policies and differential treatment, should be seen as temporary breaches of the principle of equality and enable us now to formulate a real policy of non-discrimination based on contractual commitment, enhanced skills and protection against all forms of discrimination.

Adecco: Access to Employment for Disabled Persons via Temporary Work

For 17 years the Adecco Group has been endeavouring to promote labour market entry for people with disabilities. It made a strategic choice not to set up specialised agencies for the disabled, but to develop support, training and skill-building resources. In its 1,000 branches in France, its staff are able to receive, assess and delegate disabled persons and also heighten its clients' awareness as to how to receive disabled people. To this end the Group has set up a national "Disability and Skills" centre which manages, trains and gives backing to 20 regional representatives.

Temporary work is an excellent way of conveying the message about disabled people's skills; nothing can replace experience in a context which is not too binding for the firm. The entry criterion is the skill requested by our client: if we send the client somebody whose skills match those asked for, it is easy for us afterwards to have him acknowledge that the person's disability was not an obstacle and to have a different opinon about disabled people.

At present, the psychological barriers are very often felt by the disabled person, who does not dare to go into a temporary work agency or who has a wrong impression of the world of work. As a result, such people have difficulty adapting to the increasingly volatile and demanding world of business. Even more damning, however, than these psychological barriers are the skill-level barriers. In France, 75% of people recognised as being disabled workers are level V or below (CAP/BEP). There are also a number of disabled people whose training is incompatible with their actual abilities: for example, a computer technician who is deaf and therefore cannot use the telephone.

I also believe that disabled people and the relevant associations should emphasise the success stories (citing examples to be followed is a very good way of conveying messages) and not always point the finger at firms that have done a lot to change mentalities in their own particular environment.

Undoubtedly, a lot remains to be done, but we are determined to use our convictions and professionalism to help the disabled and our client firms.

What About the Future?

If disabled people's access to working life is to be improved, it is vital that the integration issue be raised at every stage of life in society.

At present, the fact that the environment is not suited to people's actual capabilities prevents them from exercising their rights as citizens. Young disabled people do not have access to ordinary establishments, yet it is at school that the seeds of socialisation are sown and attitudes towards others are formed.

The issue of initial training in fact persists in training systems throughout life. A number of people acquire disabilities which prevent them from pursuing their professional activities, meaning that redeployment mechanisms need to be strengthened, adapted, customised and incorporated in ordinary training establishments, and also need to be in contact with firms so as to find out about their requirements in terms of occupational skills and their constraints, and also to bring their expertise to bear on work organisation questions and occupational risk prevention.

By providing them with the necessary information and tools, these mechanisms will enable disabled people to gain control of their professional futures. Being themselves convinced about the capacities that they can develop in the framework of a job, they will really be in charge of their professional lives.

If we want to improve the employment of the disabled, a vigorous policy of incentives will be needed to change collective representation in depth and transpose that change to the world of work. Also, considerable resources will be needed to implement really efficient, customised back-up and training schemes on the labour market.

Provided these efforts are made, many of the present difficulties will be ironed out and disabilities will cease to be an unsurmountable obstacle to work.

Notes on Contributors

Andrews, Emily S. is a Lead Economist at the World Bank. She specializes in social protection issues in transition economies, including old-age and disability pensions, labour market developments, and social assistance. Her work has taken her to over a dozen countries in Europe and Asia. Earlier in her career, Ms. Andrews worked for the U.S. government, academia, and the private sector. Immediately prior to joining the Bank, she was Senior Economist at Mathematica Policy Research, Inc. and, before that, Research Director for the Employee Benefits Research Institute. Her government work included positions at the Department of Labor and the Social Security Administration. She received her PhD in Economics from the University of Pennsylvania.

Apfel, Kenneth S. holds the Sid Richardson Chair at the LBJ School of Public Affairs at the University of Texas at Austin. From 1997-2001, he served as Commissioner of the Social Security Administration. Before 1997, he served in senior capacities at the Office of Management and Budget in the Executive Office of the President and at the U.S. Department of Health and Human Services. From 1980 to 1993, Apfel worked on Capitol Hill for Senator Bill Bradley and for the U.S. Senate Budget Committee. From 1978 to 1980, he held a Presidential Management Internship at the U.S. Department of Labor.

Ásgeirsdóttir, Berglind an Icelandic national, is one of the four Deputy Secretaries-General of the Organisation for Economic Co-operation and Development (OECD) based in Paris. Within OECD, she is, among other things, responsible for overseeing work on the environment, education, health, labour and social policy as well as for the multidisciplinary projects on Health and on Sustainable Development which involves most OECD Directorates.

Before taking her current appointment in September 2002, Ms. Ásgeirsdóttir was Secretary-General in the Ministry of Social Affairs in Iceland most recently since 1999 and between 1988 to 1996. In this capacity, Ms. Ásgeirsdóttir was responsible for the leadership of the Ministry of Social Affairs in its responsibilities in the area of employment, state/municipalities relations, social services, housing, gender equality, child welfare, migration and refugee issues. Ms. Ásgeirsdóttir was Secretary-General of the Nordic Council in Copenhagen from 1996 to 1999, which is the forum for inter-parliamentary co-operation.

Askenazy, Philippe Researcher at CNRS and CEPREMAP (Paris, France), and Assistant Professor at the Ecole Nationale d'Administration. Published works in, e.g. *Economic and Industrial Democracy* or *Journal of Economic Theory*, dealing with the consequences of innovative workplace organization and information and communication technology on working conditions and firm performance; growth in open economy; and dynamical optimisation. Thirty-one years old, Philippe Askenazy is the youngest economist to have received a Great Prize from the Académie des Sciences Morales et Politiques.

Barnes, Colin is a disability activist, writer and researcher with an international reputation in the field of disability studies and disability research. He is a member of several organisations controlled and run by disabled people and research director for the British Council of Disabled People (BCODP). He teaches disability studies and is the founder and Director of the Centre for Disability Studies, an independent publisher: The Disability Press, and the electronic Disability Archive UK. He is an executive editor, reviews editor and regular contributor to the international journal *Disability and Society* – formerly Disability, Handicap and Society. His most recent publications include *Disabled People in Britain and Discrimination* (1991, reprinted in 1994 and 2000); *Disabled People and Social Policy* (1998) with Mike Oliver; and *Exploring Disability: A Sociological Introduction* with Geof Mercer and Tom Shakespeare.

Bengtsson, Steen is Senior Researcher at the Social Research Institute in Copenhagen and Associate Professor at the University of Roskilde, Denmark. In the 1980s he conducted research on disability pensions inspiring the reform of the 1990s building on decentralisation and active orientation. From 1991-92 he was on leave to function as social policy consultant with the Danish Council of Organisations of Disabled People. He has also done research on living conditions for people with disabilities. In later years his research has mostly been concerned with the quality of social services and the relation between citizens and authorities in this connection, and recently he has also returned to his work on disability pensions.

Burkhauser, Richard V. is the Sarah Gibson Blanding Professor of Policy Analysis and Chair of the Department of Policy Analysis and Management at Cornell University. He is a member of the Technical Committee on Assumptions Panel for the Social Security Advisory Board and a former member of the TTWWIA Advisory Board to SSA. He is the co-editor of the forthcoming book: *The Decline in Employment of Working Age People with Disabilities: A Policy Puzzle*. He has published widely on the behavioural and distributional consequences of disability policy.

Castellano, Carlo is Chairman and Managing Director of Esaote S.p.A., one of the world's leading producers of medical diagnostic systems. Formely Associate Professor at the University of Genoa, he is Vice-President of the Health Committee BIAC; member of the Economic Affairs Committee Cocir, the Eurpean Coordination Committee of the Radiological and Electromedical Industries; member of INFN, the Italian National Institute for Nuclear Research as well as holds a number of other positions in international bodies and societies.

Endean, Rebecca is a Senior Economic Adviser in the Working Age and Children Strategy Directorate of the Department of Work and Pensions.

She heads a division which is responsible for analysis and evaluation of programmes to help disabled and incapacitated people engage with the labour market and find work and state benefits for disabled people. Work is currently being undertaken on the evaluation of the New Deal for Disabled People and the recently announced pilots aimed at providing an integrated package of help for incapacitated people. She has previously worked within government on a range of social and labour market policy areas.

Furrie, Adele D. is President of Adele Furrie Consulting Inc., a private company that provides research and analytical services to governmental and non-governmental organizations. The company's foundation is the extensive experience that Ms. Furrie gained from her national work in disability, human rights and Aboriginal issues at Statistics Canada as well as her international work through consultancies with the United Nations Statistical Division. Since forming her company in 1995, Ms. Furrie has worked with government officials and researchers in Canada, New Zealand and the United States to provide information that informs social and economic policy development to address disability issues.

380

Golinowska, Stanislawa is Professor of Economics at the Jagiellonian University in Cracow. Since 2002 Director of the Institute of Public Health at the Jagiellonian University, former Director of the governmental research Institute for Labour and Social Studies (IPiSS) at the Ministry of Labour and Social Policy. Since 1996 member of the Rada Strategii Spoceczno-Gospodarczej (Council of Economic and Social Strategy) as an advisor for the Polish government.

As a co-founder and vice-chairperson of the Foundation Council from 1992 she closely co-operates with CASE (Centre for Social and Economic Research), an independent Polish think tank organisation oriented towards countries in transition. Author of numerous articles and books on social aspects of economics and social policy reforms in Poland and other Central and Eastern European Countries.

Grizzard, W. Roy was nominated by President Bush to be the first Assistant Secretary for Disability Employment Policy and was confirmed by the Senate on July 26, 2002. Dr. Grizzard is responsible for advising the Secretary of Labor on issues related to the employment of people with disabilities. He works with all agencies within the U.S. Department of Labor to provide leadership in the Department's efforts to increase employment opportunities for adults and youth with disabilities.

Prior to joining the Department of Labor, Dr. Grizzard served for six years as Commissioner for the Virginia Department for the Blind and Vision Impaired. This state agency provides comprehensive services to Virginia's citizens who are blind, visually impaired and deaf blind. Prior to his appointment as Commissioner, Dr. Grizzard was a teacher and administrator in Henrico County Schools.

Haines, Hartmut, studies in laws, economics, psychology; experience in industrial financing. Since 1971 working with the German Federal Ministry of Labour and Social Affairs (since 2002: Health and Social Security), since 1982 as senior ministerial expert in the field of rehabilitation, integration, and participation of disabled persons. Preparation of German legislation and of political reports; organization of rehabilitation research and the database REHADAT; international activities, e.g. in the ILO, Council of Europe, European Union, and OECD; counselling in this field, e.g. during the German unification process, in Western, Central and Eastern Europe, and overseas; publications in the field.

381

Hocquet, Jean-Yves is Deputy Director General of the Department for Social Welfare at the French Ministry of Social Affairs, Labour and Welfare. Before that he was Regional Delegate for Saint Gobin Development (1996-2001), Deputy Director for Professional Training and Deputy Director for Labour Relationships at the French Ministry of Labour (1991-1996), and Deputy Director of the French National Agency for the Improvement of Working Conditions (1988-1991). He studied Political Sciences, Law and Economical Sciences.

Hoskins, Irene has served as Senior Technical Officer in the Ageing and Life Course programme of WHO since 1998. Prior to joining WHO, she served as Senior Programme Specialist and International Representative of AARP (American Association of Retired Persons) to the United Nations and its specialised agencies. Her career spans over 20 years of professional activities devoted to international ageing issues, including policy development,

publications, management of research projects and advocacy. She was educated in Germany (University of Heidelberg), Switzerland (University of
Geneva) and the United States (George Washington University).

Hvinden, Bjørn is Professor of Sociology at the Norwegian University of
Science and Technology and Scientific Advisor to the Welfare Research Programme of the Research Council of Norway. He has written and lectured
about disability, activation and employment policies, comparative welfare,
self-organisation among marginal groups and the situation of Romany people in the Nordic countries. He is currently leading a Nordic project on Active
Citizenship and Marginality in a European Context. He is the author of
Divided against Itself. Integration in Welfare Bureaucracy (1994), and has co-
edited and co-authored *Nordic Social Policy* (1999), *Nordic Welfare States in
the European Context* (2001) and *Disability Policies in Europe* (2001).

de Jong, Philip R. is partner in APE, a research and consultancy bureau focusing on the public sector, and De Kruyff Professor of Economics of Social
Security at the University of Amsterdam. Before his involvement in APE he
worked at the Department of Economics of the University of Leiden (from
1977 until 1998), and was De Kruyff Professor of Economics of Social Security at Erasmus University Rotterdam (1992-1999). De Jong has published
extensively (in English and in Dutch) on the micro-economic and public
policy aspects of social welfare programmes. He regularly serves as a consultant to Dutch and foreign governments and international organisations
(World Bank, OECD, ILO).

Kalisch, David is an economist, with an interest in labour markets, social
policy and public policy. He has been an Executive Director in the Department of Family and Community Services, first looking after Economic and
Social Participation policies and programmes (including managing income
support and employment services for people with a disability) and then to
co-ordinate the Welfare Reform agenda. He has just moved to the position
of Executive Director, Family and Children. In 1997-98, he worked at the

OECD in the social policy division and was then with the Australian Permanent Delegation to the OECD in Paris between 1998 and 1999. He was Chief of Staff to a former Australian Minister for Social Security in 1996-97.

Klein, Mikael has the position of policy officer, responsible for labour market issues at the Swedish Disability Federation, an umbrella organisation for the main part of disability associations in Sweden. During 2002 a joint policy programme for the disability associations has been elaborated, targeting working life and labour market policy. His professional background is in various assignments within the Disability Movement of Sweden, mainly the youth organisations.

Kosic, Vladimir is the Head of Regional NGOs for disabled people since 2000. He has taught English literature and language until 1998. Quadriplegic since 1964 after a diving accident. In 1975 (Naples) he founded the FRI (Radical Front of Invalids), in 1977 (Caserta) the LpH (League of Handicapped People Problems), in 1978 (Rome) the League for the Right to Work of Handicapped People. Since 1985 leading roles in regional NGOs. Recently, one of the main organizers of the International Conference on Health and Disability, Trieste (17-20 April, 2002), held by WHO, the Italian Ministry of Health, and the Regional Government of Friuli-Venezia Giulia.

383

Mabbett, Deborah is an academic who has worked on a number of social policy research projects for the UK and New Zealand governments, the European Commission and the World Bank. Most recently she was project manager for the EC's "Definitions of Disability" project (www.brunel.ac.uk/depts/govn/research/disability.htm). She has a PhD in Economics from Oxford. Her publications include *Trade, Employment and Welfare* (Oxford University Press, 1995), and academic papers on multi-level governance, social insurance, free movement in the European Union and the comparative analysis of welfare states.

Marin, Bernd is Executive Director of the European Centre for Social Welfare Policy and Research, formerly Professor of Comparative Political and Social Research at the European University Institute (EUI) in Florence. He is expert and policy advisor on pension reforms, and international rapporteur to United Nations ministerial conferences on social affairs and ageing 1993-2002. His recent publications include *Facts and Figures on Disability Welfare* (2003, with C. Prinz); the Introduction to *European Disability Pension Policies* (2003, ed. C. Prinz); *Innovative Employment Initiatives* (2000, with D. Meulders and D. Snower); *Pensionsreformen* (1999, with C. Prinz); *Managing AIDS* (1997, with P. Kenis).

Morris, David works as Senior Coordinator Disability for the Greater London Authority (GLA). He is responsible for coordinating and developing disability equality initiatives, particularly a disability equality scheme designed to ensure that the GLA is proactive in developing a disability rights based agenda. He has worked in the disability rights movement in the UK over a number of years and has specific experience and expertise of advocacy, employment, independent living and personal assistance.

Nydegger Lory, Bruno since 1998 Scientific Collaborator at the Federal Office for Social Affairs, Research and Development Unit, with the main topic of "disability". From 1994-1998 he did research and evaluation in the field of drug policy at the Addiction Research Institute in Zurich, Switzerland.

Palme, Joakim is Director of the Institute for Futures Studies in Stockholm and an associate of the Swedish Institute for Social Research at Stockholm University. His research focuses on the development of welfare state institutions, and the causes and consequences of this development. He has published on pension rights and pension reform, the public-private mix in social protection, as well as on health and social insurance. Recently, he chaired the *Welfare Commission,* a large survey of the state of welfare in Sweden. He is currently involved in research on recent welfare state transformations in a comparative perspective.

Pearson, Mark is Head of the Social Policy Division at the OECD, responsible for work on policy advice to governments on how best to integrate income transfers with social and employment services in order to help individuals to fulfil their potential and to support a dynamic economy. Previously, he was head of a unit which worked on employment-oriented social policy at the OECD, where he oversaw work on reform of the tax and benefit system; work incentives and policies to make work pay; social indicators; social expenditure statistics; social assistance systems; family-friendly policies; sustainable development and links between social protection, inequality and economic growth. Prior to this job, he worked at the Fiscal Affairs division of the OECD on tax policy analysis and statistics. Before moving to Paris, he was employed by the Institute for Fiscal Studies in London, looking *inter alia* at the taxation of multinational enterprises, the move by transition economies to market-based tax systems, European tax harmonisation and environmental taxes. He has been a consultant for the World Bank, the IMF and the European Commission. He was editor of the journal *Fiscal Studies* and is on a number of editorial boards, including that of OECD *Economic Studies* and the *European Journal of Social Security*.

Pérez Bueno, Luis Cayo is Director of the Spanish National Council of Disabled Representatives, CERMI. He holds a Degree in Law and has specialised in Juridical Philosophy. He has professional experience in the social field of disability since 1994 and held several positions in SERVIMEDIA, the ONCE Foundation and ONCE. A publisher, writer, poet and translator, he has published a large number of works and translations, not only of literary creation but also concerning disability aspects.

van der Ploeg, Rick is Professor of Economic Policy at the Robert Schuman Centre, European University Institute, Florence and Research Fellow of CESIfo, Munich. Former State Secretary for Education, Culture and Science (1998-2002) and Chief Financial Spokesperson in Parliament for the Dutch Labour Party (1994-1998). Also, previously Professor of Economics at Tilburg University (1985-1991) and the University of Amsterdam (1991-1998). Before that at the University of Cambridge (1977-1983) and the London School of Economics (1983-1988). His research interests are in the twilight zones between international macroeconomics, public finance, the welfare state, the environment, and political economy.

Prinz, Christopher is the main author of the OECD report *Transforming Disability into Ability*. Degrees in statistics and demography; 1989-1994 Research Scholar in the Population Project at the International Institute for Applied Systems Analysis in Laxenburg, Austria; 1995-2000 Head of the Social Policy Modelling Unit at the European Centre for Social Welfare Policy and Research in Vienna, Austria; since April 2000 Administrator at the Social Policy Division, since 2004 Policy Analyst at the Employment Analysis and Policy Division of the OECD in Paris, France. He planned and directed several international comparative research projects in the area of demography (population ageing, family change) and social policy (pension reform, family policy, disability policy) and is author/editor of several books on these subjects.

Queisser, Monika is Principal Administrator in the Social Policy Division at the OECD. She works on retirement systems, disability policies, income distribution and other social policy issues. Prior to joining the OECD, she worked in the Financial Sector Development Department of the World Bank, in the pensions and insurance group. She has worked with governments in Latin America, Eastern Europe, Asia, and Africa and has published several articles and studies on pension reform issues.

Roche de la Porte des Vaux, Agnès 1999-2003 Responsable Nationale Pôle Handicap et Compétences – ADECCO; 1992-1999 Directrice adjointe d'un organisme de placement pour travailleurs handicapés – Ohé Prométhée Finistère; 1985-1992 Responsable d'un organisme de formation – Atelier Pédagogique Personnalisé.

Rydh, Jan is Chairman of various Governmental Committees, e.g. from 1999-2002 of the official Inquiry into The Swedish Insurance Scheme. Before that, he was Governor of the Swedish Province of Västmanland (1991-1999) and President of The Swedish Savings Banks Association (1979-1991).

Samoy, Erik since 2000 Director of the research department of the Flemish Fund for People with disabilities. PhD in sociology and PhD on Employment Policies for People with Disabilities in Belgium at the University of

Leuven where he worked for 25 years as a researcher in the field of social care and disability at the Department of Sociology and at the Higher Institute of Labour Studies.

Saraceno, Chiara is full Professor of Sociology of the Family at the Faculty of Political Sciences of the University of Turin, Italy, where she also teaches comparative social systems. From 1991-1998 she was Head of the Department of Social Sciences, presently she is head of the Inter-department Center for Women's Studies. From 1999-2001 she was Chair of the Italian Povery Commission at the Office of the Prime Minister and from 1995-2001 Consultant to the Minister of Social Affairs on issues concerning poverty, social exclusion and family policies. Her current research interests include social policies and poverty; comparative family patterns and policies; patterns of local welfare regimes; gender inequalities and differences.

387

Sarfati, Hedva is a political scientist and analyst of comparative employment, social protection and labour relations policies and practice. She is a consultant for the Geneva-based International Social Security Association (ISSA), for which she directed an international research project on the labour market and social protection reforms linkages in the OECD and CEEC countries, the results of which were published in 2002. During her career at the International Labour Office (ILO), she was Director of the Industrial Relations and Labour Administration Department; Chief of the Salaried Employees and Professional Workers Branch; Chief Editor of the ILO quarterly *Social and Labour Bulletin*.

Her two latest books are *Labour Market and Social Protection Reforms in International Perspective: Parallel or Converging Tracks?*, with Giuliano Bonoli (2002); *Flexibilité et création d'emploi: un défi pour le dialogue social en Europe* (1999).

Scherer, Peter is the Counsellor to the Director of the Employment, Labour and Social Affairs Directorate at the OECD, Paris. After studying at the Monash University, the Australian National University and Cornell University in the U.S., he lectured at Sydney University and was a research fellow at the Australian National University. He then worked in various Australian Government Departments, eventually becoming Acting Director of the Bureau of Labour Market Research. When that Bureau was abolished in 1986, he came to the OECD, initially heading the Division responsible for the annual OECD Employment Outlook. From 1981 to June 2002 he was Head of the Social Policies Division. He has published in the fields of labour economics, industrial relations, comparative social expenditures and social policy trends.

Schmidt, Christoph M. Since October 2002 President of the RWI (Rheinisch-Westfälisches Institut für Wirtschaftsforschung). From 1995 until 2002 he was Professor of Econometrics and Labour Economics at the University of Heidelberg. Schmidt was awarded a Princeton University Fellowship, 1987-1990, the Alfred P. Sloan Doctoral Dissertation Fellowship, 1990-1991, and was a Fellow of the Deutsche Forschungsgemeinschaft (DFG) 1992-1995. Since 1992 he has been a Research Affiliate of the Centre for Economic Policy Research (CEPR), London, since 1996 a CEPR Research Fellow, and since 1998 he is also a Research Fellow at the Institute for the Study of Labour (IZA), Bonn. From 1996 to 2002 he was Editor of the *Journal of Population Economics*.

Snower, Dennis J. is Professor of Economics at Birkbeck College, University of London; Director of the Welfare State Programme at IZA; and Fellow of the CEPR, London. He originated the "insider-outsider" theory of employment and unemployment with Assar Lindbeck, the theory of "high-low search" with Steve Alpern, and the "chain reaction" theory of unemployment with Marika Karanassou. He was a seminal contributor to the macroeconomics of imperfect competition, and has published extensively on labour economics, macroeconomic theory and policy, and the design of welfare systems.

He is the architect of the Benefit Transfer Programme for the unemployed, versions of which have been adopted in various OECD countries. He was a core member of the UK Treasury Academic Panel on Labour Markets and advises the governments of several continental European countries on employment policy.

Stapleton, David PhD is the Director of the Cornell Center for Policy Research, in Washington, DC. For the past 12 years, his work has focused on U.S. programs for people with disabilities and their impacts on employment and economic independence. He is Co-Principle Investigator for Cornell's Research, Rehabilitation and Training Center on Policy Research for Employment of People with Disabilities, and edited, with Richard Burkhauser, *The Decline in Employment of People with Disabilities, A Policy Puzzle* (2003).

Strümpel, Charlotte has been a researcher at the European Centre for Welfare Policy and Research since 1993 and Programme Coordinator of the Programme Area "Ageing, Care Policies and Social Services" since 2000. Her research interests and publications include vocational integration of people with a disability, integrating health and social services in care of the elderly, volunteering as well as political participation of older people. Most recently she was the European coordinator for the project "QUIP – Quality in Practice: Stakeholders' Views on Supported Employment" (www.quip.at) and Austrian project coordinator of the "Definitions of Disability" project that was led by Brunel University (www.brunel.ac.uk/ depts/govn/ research/ disability.htm).

Taipale, Vappu has been the Director General of the National Research and Development Centre for Welfare and Health (STAKES) since 1992. She was Professor in Child Psychiatry at the University of Kuopio from 1980 to 1982, Minister of Health from 1982 to 1983 and Minister of Social Affairs from 1983 to 1984. She has acted as advisor and chairperson to a number of Finnish state committees on social and health affairs. 1998-2002 Expert to the EU on Ageing and chairperson of the Fifth Framework Programme External Advisory Group on Key Action, "The Ageing Population". Membership of the Council of the United Nations University (2001-2006).

Trömel, Stefan is Director of the European Disability Forum. Before that, he worked for ten years with the Spanish Fundacion ONCE where he was in charge of the promotion and development of disabled people.

Wagener, Raymond PhD in Mathematics. Head of the Statistical, Actuarial and Social Programming Department of the Inspection générale de la sécurité sociale in Luxembourg. Teaches at the Master Programme in Social Protection Finance of the University of Maastricht, Netherlands.

Wilensky, Harold L. is Professor Emeritus of Political Science. He is a Fellow of the American Academy of Arts and Sciences and the author of 13 books, including *Rich Democracies. Political Economy, Public Policy, and Performance* (2002), *The Welfare State and Equality* (1975). His publications deal with four main problems: the interplay of knowledge and power, the role of the expert; the ascendance of the mass media in politics and culture; the fate of minority groups; the politics of taxing and spending and the welfare state. Before joining the University of California at Berkeley in 1962, he taught at the University of Michigan and the University of Chicago.

Transforming Disability into Ability
Policies to Promote Work and Income Security for Disabled People

How OECD countries can reconcile the twin, but potentially contradictory, goals of disability policy has yet to be resolved. One goal is to ensure that disabled citizens are not excluded from society: that they are encouraged and empowered to participate as fully as possible in economic and social life, and in particular to engage in gainful employment, and that they are not ousted from the labour market too easily and too early. The other goal is to ensure that those who are disabled or who become disabled have income security: that they are not denied the means to live decently because of disabilities which restrict their earning potential.

This book provides a systematic analysis of a wide array of labour market and social protection programmes aimed at people with disabilities. Analysing the relationship between policies and outcomes across twenty OECD countries, it gives the reader a better understanding of the dilemmas of disability policy and of successful policy elements or packages. The report concludes that a promising new disability policy approach should move closer to the philosophy of unemployment programmes by:

- emphasising activation;
- promoting tailored early intervention;
- removing disincentives to work;
- introducing a culture of mutual obligations; and
- involving employers.

It finds that many countries' policies already include some elements which are important components in such a new approach.

OECD Code: 812003021P1
ISBN 9264198873
Published 27/02/2003
220 pages, 65 tables, 43 charts

Price:
US$33 € 33 £25 ¥3800

Transformer le handicap en capacité
Promouvoir le travail et la sécurité des revenus des personnes handicapées
OECD

Paris: OECD, 2003. ISBN 9264298878, 236 pp., US$ 33 / € 33 / £ 21 / ¥ 3800

Behindertenpolitik zwischen Beschäftigung und Versorgung
Ein internationaler Vergleich
OECD

Frankfurt am Main: Campus, 2003. ISBN 3-593-37420-X, 408 S., € 34,90, www.campus.de

---

Facts and Figures on Disability Welfare
A Pictographic Portrait of an OECD Report
Bernd Marin / Christopher Prinz

Vienna: European Centre, 2003. ISBN 3-900376-98-0, pp. 104, € 15, www.euro.centre.org

European Disability Pension Policies
11 Country Trends 1970-2002
With an Introduction by Bernd Marin
Christopher Prinz (Ed.)

This book is the result of an extension of the European Centre's research on disability benefit policies which has been partly funded by the Swiss Federal Office of Social Insurance. It contains an introduction and theoretical overviews by Bernd Marin and Philip R. de Jong, respectively, as well as chapters on the following 11 European countries: Austria, Denmark, Finland, Germany, Italy, the Netherlands, Norway, Poland, Slovenia, Sweden, and Switzerland.

During the last twenty years, the longer-term sustainability of social insurance systems has become a major issue in all European countries. The debate is generally dominated by a focus on the rising costs of old-age pensions, driven by rapidly changing population age structures. In recent years, however, analysts and governments increasingly started to worry about the growth in the number of disability benefit recipients – a growth with significant variations in the composition of new recipients in terms of age, gender and health conditions.

After a long phase of expansion of disability benefit schemes via increasing benefits, broading coverage and easing access (in particular for elderly unemployed people), since the late 1980s and the beginning 1990s more and more countries have started to reform their systems – ranging from piecemeal changes (e.g. in Switzerland) to more far-reaching reorientation (e.g. in Germany) or even fundamental reconstruction (e.g. in the Netherlands). While policy measures differ widely, policy goals tend to converge. Some policy elements, such as the identification of and benefit provision for partial disability, seem particularly controversial.

The purpose of this book is to analyse and compare disability benefit policies in eleven European countries in the last two or three decades, and to examine the outcome of these policies. Often policies appear to have immediate short-term effects, while being much less effective in a longer perspective, thus asking for continual reform. For some of the newer challenges, such as the rapidly increasing number of benefit claims on psychological grounds, responses have yet to be found.

Christopher Prinz is Administrator at the OECD Social Policy Division in Paris.

Aldershot (UK): Ashgate, 2003. ISBN 0-7546-1972-9, pp. 430, £ 25, www.ashgate.com